The Confederate Ironclads

By Maurice Melton

Naval warfare during the War Between the States was a destructive, horrifying experience to many who were directly involved in its actions. But there were none more horrified or dismayed than those who witnessed the death and destruction inflicted by the never-before-seen Confederate ironclad *C.S.S. Virginia* —formerly the *Merrimac*—upon its wooden adversaries. Here indeed was Satan himself, disguised as an armor-plated, fire-breathing, seemingly indestructible floating weapon that could destroy unmolested.

The Confederate Ironclads is the story not only of that first ironclad, the *Virginia,* but of the entire Confederate iron fleet. This will prove to be the definitive work on these "iron maidens." Included in this fascinating history are the stories of the ships themselves (why and how they were built); of their officers and men; of the battles in which they fought; and of the Northern ships—both ironclad and wooden—which bravely, but sometimes futilely, set out to challenge them.

Here in one volume is an undertaking of monumental proportions, for the author has re-created the exploits of e v e r y Confederate armored ship ever put afloat. Maurice Melton has taken the four years of the Civil War and has brought all the panorama and sweep of naval

(Continued on

a must for bookshe

The Confederate Ironclads

The Confederate Ironclads

By Maurice Melton

South Brunswick
New York • Thomas Yoseloff • London

©1968 by A. S. Barnes and Co., Inc.
Library of Congress Catalogue Card Number: 67-17387

Thomas Yoseloff, Publisher
Cranbury, New Jersey 08512

Thomas Yoseloff Ltd
18 Charing Cross Road
London W. C. 2, England

21225

6483
Printed in the United States of America

To the memory of the officers
and men who served in the Confederate Navy

Contents

Chronology

1861

April

19 President Lincoln proclaims a blockade of the Confederate coast from Texas to South Carolina.
20 The U.S. Navy fires and abandons Gosport Navy Yard, Norfolk, Va. It is occupied the next morning by Virginia State troops.
27 The blockade is extended to include the coasts of Virginia and North Carolina.

May

10 Secretary Mallory asks the Committee on Naval Affairs to authorize the construction of ironclad ships of war.
13 Great Britain issues a proclamation of neutrality.
17 Lt. James H. North, C.S.N., is sent to France to purchase ironclads of the *Glorie* class.
20 $2,000,000 is authorized for the purchase of six ironclads from England and France.

29 Union troops occupy Newport News, Va.
The Confederate capital is moved to Richmond.

30 The *Merrimack*, scuttled and burned by the Federals, is raised from the bottom of Norfolk harbor and pulled into drydock.

June

10 France issues a proclamation of neutrality.

23 Chief Naval Constructor John L. Porter and Chief Engineer William P. Williamson arrive in Richmond to show Porter's model ironclad to Sec. Mallory and Lt. John M. Brooke.

July

27 The first Confederate Navy funds reach Europe.

August

24 The Confederate Congress appropriates $160,000 for the construction of two ironclads at Memphis.

September

28 Construction is started on the ironclad *Mississippi* above New Orleans.

October

12 The ironclad privateer *Manassas* is confiscated by the Confederate Navy at New Orleans.

13 The *Manassas* leads Capt. George N. Hollins' flotilla against the Union blockading squadron in the Head of Passes below New Orleans.

15 Construction is started on the ironclad *Louisiana* above New Orleans.

The blockade runner *Fingal* sails for Savannah with a cargo of war materials.

November

2 The *Fingal* arrives in Bermuda.
7 The *Fingal* leaves Bermuda.
8 Mason and Slidell are taken from the British mail packet *Trent* by the U.S.S. *San Jacinto*.
12 The *Fingal* slips into *Savannah*. Blockaded there, she will be converted to the ironclad *Atlanta*.

December

26 Mason and Slidell are released.

1862

January

14 Sec. Mallory asks Comm. James D. Bulloch, C.S.N., to attempt to get ironclads constructed in England.

February

17 The crew of the *Virginia* (late the steam frigate *Merrimack*) boards the vessel for the first time.
24 Captain Franklin Buchanan is assigned to command the James River Squadron.

The ironclad *Virginia* is commissioned.
25 The U.S.S. *Monitor* is commissioned.

March

6 The *Monitor* leaves New York for Hampton Roads.
7 The trial run of the *Virginia,* scheduled for this day, is postponed due to bad weather.
8 The *Virginia,* on her trial run, engages in combat with the Union blockading squadron in Hampton Roads, destroying two large ships of war and a gunboat.
9 The *Virginia* fights to a draw with the *Monitor* in Hampton Roads.
17 In Richmond, Col. Blanton Duncan, C.S.A., makes an appeal for funds to begin construction of another ironclad (the *Richmond*) at Norfolk.
21 Capt. Arthur Sinclair, C.S.N., is ordered to New Orleans to take command of the *Mississippi.*
24 Capt. Sidney Smith Lee relieves Capt. French Forrest of command of Gosport Navy Yard.

April

4 The *Virginia* is taken out of drydock after repairs.
8 Capt. Josiah Tattnall, relieving wounded Capt. Buchanan of command of the *Virginia,* issues battle orders for a second combat with the *Monitor.*
   Island No. 10 on the Mississippi falls, opening the way to Memphis.
10 President Davis submits to the House of Representatives a request from Mallory, asking for six ironclads to be constructed in Europe by a private party, and underwritten by the Confederate Government.
11 The *Virginia* steams out into Hampton Roads. The *Monitor* and other Union naval vessels remain at anchor at Fort Monroe.

Secretary of War George Randolph orders the *Louisiana* up to Memphis.

12 The *Virginia* again ventures out into Hampton Roads. The *Jamestown* captures two transports under the *Monitor's* guns.

14 Lt. North informs Mallory that he's opened negotiations for an ironclad in Great Britain.

16 David Farragut's invasion fleet arrives at Ship Island off New Orleans.

Mallory's bill for six privateer European ironclads is passed by a secret session of the House Committee on Naval Affairs.

J. C. Martin & Co. receives a contract for an ironclad in North Carolina.

18 Farragut's fleet opens a mortar bombardment on Confederate forts below New Orleans.

19 Comm. John K. Mitchell is given command of the Confederate flotilla at New Orleans.

The ironclad *Mississippi* is launched.

23 The *Manassas*, anticipating a Union attack, takes up a station at the forts below New Orleans.

24 Farragut attacks. The *Manassas* is disabled and scuttled, and defenses are penetrated.

25 New Orleans surrenders. The *Mississippi* is burned, the *Louisiana* blown up.

Lt. Charles McBlair, escaping the Federals above Memphis in the incomplete ironclad *Arkansas*, learns of the fall of New Orleans. He takes the *Arkansas* up the Yazoo River.

May

6 The ironclad *Richmond* is launched at Norfolk and towed to Richmond.

8 Six Federal ships bombard Sewell's Point off Norfolk. The *Virginia* steams out to fight, but the Federals retreat.

9 The Confederates abandon Norfolk.

11 The *Virginia* is blown up to prevent her capture.

21 Lt. North signs a contract with J. & G. Thompson for an ironclad.

26 Lt. Issac N. Brown is assigned to take command of the ironclad *Arkansas* on the Yazoo River.

28 Brown arrives at Greenwood, Mississippi.

29 Work is started to complete the *Arkansas*.

June

5 The *Arkansas'* sister ship *Tennessee* is burned at Memphis to prevent her capture.

20 The *Arkansas* is floated downriver to Liverpool Landing.

July

4 The *Arkansas* is moved down to Yazoo City.

13 The *Arkansas* moves to Satartia Bar, 60 miles from the combined Federal fleets above Vicksburg.

15 The *Arkansas* runs through the entire Federal force and reaches Vicksburg.

21 Comm. Bulloch contracts with Laird's shipyard, Birkenhead, for two ironclads.

22 The Union ironclad *Essex* and ram *Queen of the West* attempt to destroy the *Arkansas* under the Vicksburg bluffs.

30 The ironclad *Atlanta*, built from the blockade runner *Fingal*, makes her first appearance at Savannah.

August

6 The *Arkansas,* ordered to support Breckenridge's attack on Baton Rouge, is destroyed when her engines fail under fire.

September

17 J. C. Martin & Co. receive a contract for an ironclad to be built at Tarboro, North Carolina.

November

1 The ironclad *Cotton* is chased from Berwick's Bay by Union gunboats working in conjunction with Gen. Wietzel's expedition from New Orleans.
3 The gunboats fight the *Cotton* on the Teche River. The *Cotton* retreats when her ammunition is exhausted.
5 The *Cotton* and the gunboats engage at long range.
6 The gunboats open a slow fire from long range. The *Cotton* fails to reply.

December

2 Bulloch first voices his fears that the British Government will not allow his ironclads to sail.
28 Bravay & Co. (of Paris) begin negotiations for the purchase of Bulloch's ironclads, supposedly for Egypt.

1863

January

14 Union forces make a combined land-water attack on the *Cotton* and Confederate defenses on the banks of the Teche River.

15 The *Cotton* is burned.
30 The ironclads *Chicora* and *Palmetto State* attack and disburse the Federal blockading fleet off Charleston.

February

16 Comm. Wm. McBlair, commanding the *Atlanta*, dies.
18 Comm. Arthur Sinclair assumes command of the *Atlanta*.

March

3 The interior skin of North's ironclad is finally finished.

April

3 North's ironclad's teak backing is half completed.

May

2 Comm. Wm. A. Webb assumes command of the *Atlanta*.
6 Mallory informs Bulloch of the South European Act for the construction of ironclads, and appoints him superintendent over all construction.

June

1 The original delivery date for North's ironclad.

July

10 Lt. Washington Gwathmey is assigned to command the ironclad *Georgia* at Savannah.

16 Bulloch signs a contract for two ironclads to be built in France.

17 The ironclad *Atlanta* engages the monitors *Weehawken* and *Nahant* outside Savannah. The Confederate is captured.

October

17 J. C. Martin's Tarboro ram is burned when threatened by raiding Federal cavalry.

27 Great Britain seizes Bulloch's two Laird rams.

1864

January

15 Comm. J. W. Cooke is ordered to the command of the ironclad *Albemarle* building on the Roanoke River.

February

18 Bulloch notifies Mallory that his French ironclads have been forbidden to sail.

20 Adm. F. Buchanan makes his first inspection of the ironclad *Tennessee* building at Selma, Ala.

24 Mallory consents to the sale of North's ironclad.

March

7 The first load of the *Albemarle's* armor plate arrives at Halifax, N.C.

10 The ironclad *Columbia* is launched at Charleston, S.C.

April

1 The *Albemarle* is towed to Hamilton, N.C.
17 The *Albemarle* leaves Hamilton for Plymouth.
19 The *Albemarle* engages Union gunboats off Plymouth, sinking one and driving off another. During the day she shells Plymouth into submission.
22 The ironclad *Neuse* grounds on the Neuse River.

May

5 The *Albemarle*, *Cotton Planter*, and *Bombshell* engage nine Union gunboats in Albemarle Sound. The *Bombshell* is captured.
6 The ironclad *Raleigh* steams out of Wilmington to attack blockaders. On reentering the harbor, she grounds and is destroyed.
18 The *Tennessee* is floated over Dog River Bar and brought into Mobile Bay.
20 Preliminary terms of sale of the Laird rams to the British Navy are settled.
22 Buchanan raises his pennant on the *Tennessee*.
24 The *Albemarle* appears for the last time, dragging for torpedoes in the Roanoke River.

June

4 The ironclad *Nashville* arrives at Mobile.
21 The James River Squadron tries to draw the Federal Navy into combat. A long-range artillery duel results.

August

4 The last of the Federal monitors, the *Tecumseh*, arrives off Mobile to take part in Farragut's assault.

5 Farragut strikes Buchanan's squadron in Mobile Bay. The *Tecumseh* is sunk but the *Tennessee* and a gunboat are captured while another Confederate gunboat is destroyed.

13 On the James River, the *Richmond, Fredricksburg*, and *Virginia* open fire at long range against several gunboats and a monitor. Neither side is damaged.

September

19 Federal troops capture Confederate Fort Harrison on the James.

October

22 The James River Squadron's ironclads are fired on by a masked battery near Fort Harrison. A small engagement follows, during which the Federals are repeatedly driven from their guns.

27 Union Lt. Wm. Cushing torpedoes and sinks the *Albemarle* at the Plymouth wharf.

November

26 Lt. J. W. Bennet, C.S.N., receives command of the *Nashville* at Mobile.

December

7 The James River Squadron shells Union Fort Brady.

16 Details of acquiring the *Stonewall*—one of the French-built ironclads—for the Confederacy are settled.

17 Samuel Barron, flag-officer of Confederate naval forces in Europe, issues orders for the *Stonewall's* cruise.

20 As Sherman's army closes in on the port of Savannah, Gen. Hardee's Confederates escape under cover of a bombardment by the ironclad *Savannah*.

21 The *Savannah* engages Union gunners in captured Fort Jackson. The ship is destroyed that night.

1865

January

7 The *Stonewall* sails from Copenhagen.

8 The *Stonewall* makes port at Elsinore.

11 Officers and crew for the *Stonewall* arrive at Gravesend, England.

15 Fort Fisher, N.C. falls.

23 An attempted surprise attack on the Union blockaders by the James River Squadron is foiled.

24 The *Stonewall* makes rendezvous with her tender at Belle Isle.

28 The *Stonewall* and her tender leave Belle Isle, heading south.

February

2 The *Stonewall* ports at Ferrol, Spain.

18 Admiral Raphael Semmes takes command of the James River Squadron. Charleston falls.

March

21 The *Stonewall* attempts to provoke a battle with the Union cruisers *Niagara* and *Sacramento* off Ferrol.

23 The *Stonewall* again attempts to provoke a battle.

24 The *Stonewall* sails from Ferrol.

26 The *Stonewall* ports at Lisbon.

27 The *Nashville* arrives on the Blakely River, below Mobile, and runs aground on the Apalachee.
The *Niagara* and *Sacramento* make port at Lisbon.
28 The *Stonewall* leaves Lisbon.
30-31 The *Nashville* engages with Federals attacking Mobile's outer defenses.

April

1 The *Nashville* steams to Mobile for repairs.
A battle is fought at Five Forks, Va.
The *Stonewall* sails from Teneriffe, Canary Islands.
2 The *Fredricksburg*, *Richmond*, and *Virginia* are burned as Richmond is evacuated.
3-6 The *Nashville* engages continuously with Federals, harassing them with slow fire at night.
4 The ironclad *Missouri* arrives at Alexandria, La.
8 The ironclads *Nashville* and *Huntsville* engage Union troops for the last time.
9 Lee surrenders the Army of Northern Virginia.
12 Mobile falls. The *Huntsville* and *Tuscaloosa* are scuttled. The *Nashville* and several blockade runners seek refuge in the Tombigbee River.
26 Johnston surrenders to Sherman in North Carolina.

May

6 The *Stonewall* ports at Nassau.
10 Confederate naval forces on the Tombigbee River surrender. Jefferson Davis is captured near Irwinsville, Ga.
11 The *Stonewall* makes port at Havana.
19 The *Stonewall* surrenders.

June

3 The *Missouri* surrenders.

The Confederate Ironclads

1

The James River Squadron

Gray smoke and the smell of burned wood hung like a blanket over Gosport Navy Yard. Chunks of charred wood bobbed drunkenly amid a scum of soot and ash which covered Norfolk harbor. An area that had, a day earlier, stood crowded with buildings and teemed with life now lay reduced to a few acres of fire-blackened bricks and charred timbers, still giving off tendrils of filthy smoke.

Officers and men of the Provisional Army and Navy of Virginia poked and prodded through the rubble in the early morning hours of April 20, 1861, searching for any materials of war that might be salvaged from the desolate remains of the largest naval yard south of New York. The Federal Navy — for months frightened by rumors of ensuing hostilities with Virginia, confused by conflicting orders from Washington, and shackled with an aged and befuddled commander — had taken flight. Captain Hiram Paulding and a few marines had managed to take out several ships and a small fortune in naval stores. What they couldn't take, they burned. The entire north face of the yard — lofts and buildings containing gun carriages, rope and wire rigging, full suits of sails for frigates and sloops, hammocks and bags in abundance, and "immense quantities" of canvas, cordage, pitch, and other naval stores — had gone up in flames. Ship houses A and B, the line of battleship *New York* on the A-house stocks, had gone up, along with the barracks. The larger part of 2,890 stand of small arms — carbines, rifled muskets, navy pistols, and Colt revolvers — were carried out in the sloop of war *Cumberland*.

Their attempts at the destruction of the yard and all war materials had not been completely successful, however. The foundry, boiler house, powder magazine, ordnance building, provisions store, the 600-patient naval hospital with all its dependencies — surgeon's residence, keeper's house, cemetery, stables, and grounds "covered with a growth of shade trees" — customhouse, and the marine hospital (for merchant marine) at Washington Point had been spared.[1] Four thousand shells and those small arms not taken out aboard the *Cumberland* had been thrown into the water and would be recovered. Over a thousand heavy guns — from 11-inch to 32-pounders — lay scattered over the yard and in the water: several brass howitzers were fished up early. Two thousand barrels of powder and a large number of shells and fixed ammunition were found in the powder magazine. And the priceless granite drydock had been spared. Commander John Rodgers and Captain H. G. Wright, with 40 men from the crew of the *Pawnee*,[2] had mined it with 26 barrels of powder, "a quantity sufficient to have destroyed the dock and every building at the south end of the yard." The barrels had been connected by a train to which a slow match was applied. Apparently the train failed to ignite, and when Lt. Charles F. M. Spotswood of the Virginia Navy was informed of the presence of the powder, he had the dock flooded. Most important, however, a fleet of ships had been fired, then scuttled so fast that most were saved from total destruction. The historic old frigate *United States*, too decrepit for repairs, had not been touched. The ship of the line *Pennsylvania,* the frigate *Columbia,* and the brig *Dolphin* were all beyond repair, burned to their floor heads. Their lower timbers and keels remained, showing above the water's surface at low tide. The frigate *Raritan* was burned badly and sunk in the deep water channel, and the steam frigate *Merrimack* had her upper works burned off. The sloop of war *Germantown* was sunk, burned to her bulwarks on her port side. The old line of battleships *Delaware* and *Columbus* and the sloop of war *Plymouth* were all scuttled, undamaged by fire.[3] Of the ten, nine would fade into obscurity. But much more was to be heard of the *Merrimack.*

On May 23, the sovereign state of Virginia voted to ally herself with her sister states in the Confederacy. Officers and men of Virginia's provisional armed services were transferred to Confederate service, the Southern capital was moved to Richmond, and Gosport Navy Yard at Norfolk came under the control of the Confederate Navy Department. Commodore French Forrest assumed command of the yard.

Immediately after the move to Richmond, a special committee convened on the subject of naval affairs. Secretary of the Navy Stephen Mallory submitted a report urgently advocating the construction and use of the revolutionary new ironclad warship.

I regard the possession of an iron-armored ship as a matter of the first necessity. Such a vessel at this time could traverse the entire coast of the United States, prevent all blockades, and encounter, with a fair prospect of success, their entire navy.

If to cope with them upon the sea we follow their example and build wooden ships, we shall have to construct several at one time; for one or two ships would fall an easy prey to her comparitively numerous steam frigates. But inequality of numbers may be compensated by invulnerability; and thus not only does economy but naval success dictate the wisdom and expediency of fighting with iron against wood, without regard to first cost.

Naval engagements between wooden frigates, as they are now built and armed, will prove to be the forlorn hopes of the sea, simply contests in which the question, not of victory, but of who shall go to the bottom first, is to be solved.

Should the committee deem it expedient to begin at once the construction of such a ship, not a moment should be lost.[4]

With the committee's approval Secretary Mallory sent Lieutenant James H. North to London to negotiate contracts with French and British firms for the construction and purchase of iron-armored ships. Two million dollars was earmarked for the purchase of six ironclads from the two European powers.[5]

In Washington, D.C., Union Secretary of the Navy Gideon Welles was to address a special session of Congress on the same subject.

. . . it is for Congress to decide whether, on a favorable report, they will order one or more iron-clad steamers, or floating batteries, to be constructed, with a view to perfect protection from the effects of present ordnance at short range, and make an appropriation for that purpose.[6]

On May 30, Commodore Forerst sent the following telegram: "We have the *Merrimac* up and just pulling her into dry dock."[7] Seemingly routine, the message marked the end of naval warfare as it was then known.

An inspection of the *Merrimack's* hulk revealed a final gift from the departed United States Navy — 2,200 ten-pound cartridges, all undamaged, in water-tight tanks.[8]

Since the outbreak of hostilities, an inventive young lieutenant, a veteran of the U.S. Navy and winner of a gold medal for science from the king of Prussia, had plagued Secretary Mallory with plans and schemes for building an iron-armored warship. He was John Mercer Brooke. Now openly advocating the construction and use of such ships, Secretary Mallory, on June 10, sent a communication to Brooke directing him "to aid the department in designing an ironclad war vessel, and framing the necessary specifications." The lieutenant complied, presenting the Secretary with plans for a ship employing an iron casemate surrounding and protecting the gun deck, the casemate sides inclined at an angle to ricochet striking enemy shot.

John L. Porter, a Norfolk naval constructor, and William P. Williamson, ex-senior Chief Engineer, U.S.N., were called to Mallory's Richmond office on June 23 to study and pass judgment on Brooke's plan. Porter introduced a design of his own, an inclined iron-armored casemate like Brooke's, but mounted on a hull like a flatboat rather than that of a sea-going ship.[9] Years before, he had submitted this plan to the U.S. Navy Department, but no one had been interested in experiments with ironclad vessels at the time and his drawings had been returned with thanks.[10] Within a year iron-armored gunboats of a similar design, built by James B. Eads in St. Louis, would operate under the Union flag on the Mississippi.

Brooke's design was chosen as the better of the two. The lieutenant and Chief Engineer Williamson visited the Tredegar Iron Works in search of suitable engines and, finding none, journeyed to Norfolk with Porter to inspect the remains of the *Merrimack*. They reported to Mallory on the feasibility of converting the old frigate, stating that:

It would appear that this is our only chance to get a suitable vessel in a short time. The bottom of the hull, boilers, and heavy and costly parts of the engine being but little injured reduces the cost of construction to about one-third the amount which would be required to construct such a vessel anew.

We can not, without further examination, make an accurate estimate of the cost of the proposed work, . . . the most of which will be for labor, the materials being nearly all in the navy yard, except the iron plating to cover the shield.[11]

Henry Ashton Ramsey, formerly first assistant engineer aboard the *Merrimack*, protested the use of the old frigate's machinery, proclaiming the engines unreliable and the boilers totally unsafe.

The cost of raising and docking the *Merrimack* came to $6,000. The total cost of converting the old frigate to an ironclad was estimated at $172,523.[12]

Brooke now busied himself with the testing of iron plates. Firing the heaviest guns in Federal service at the time, he found that a plate of 4-inch armor, inclined at an angle of 45°, would withstand shot and shell at any range.[13] Unfortunately, there wasn't a rolling mill in the South that could turn out plates of 4-inch thickness. Two 2-inch plates would have to suffice. The order was placed at the Tredegar works in Richmond.

Mr. Porter, meanwhile, surveyed the slime-and-seaweed covered *Merrimack* and began reworking the remains. Her hull was cut down to the berth deck and braced and strengthened with massive beams: she would need plenty of strength to withstand the burden of her armor. Holes were plugged and the engines cleared of mud, rust, and seaweed.

The ironclad's rather unique design called for a wooden frame, 170 feet in length and 7 feet high, to be erected amidship. This frame was to support a 24-inch thickness of oak and pitch-pine planking to which the armor would be bolted.[14] When afloat, the ends of the ship would be submerged, only the casemate showing above water.

By January, 1862, the ironclad was beginning to take form. Her hull had been caulked and plugged, her engines overhauled, and her woodwork almost completed. Lieutenant Catsby ap R. Jones, who had superintended the placing of the original battery of Dahlgrens aboard the *Merrimack* at her completion in 1856,[15] gathered a sufficient battery for the new ironclad and had the guns set up for test firing near the naval hospital. There were ten guns, smoothbores and rifles, the latter of a make devised by Lt. Brooke and bearing his name.

Providing a crew for the new ironclad posed a problem. Many of the officers of the "Old Navy" had come south with the secession, but the seamen — almost all from the north — had stayed in the U.S. service, leaving the Confederacy with a serious shortage. A few experienced sailors from the seafaring families around Norfolk had already been assigned to the ironclad, but their number was far from the several hundred needed.

To procure a crew, Lieutenant John Taylor Wood, grandson of ex-President Zachery Taylor, set out for the camp of General John Magruder. Naval officers at Norfolk had heard that Magruder had several New Orleans' regiments among his command. Perhaps some seamen could be found there.

Although short of men himself, Magruder agreed to let Wood call for volunteers. Officers paraded their men and Wood made his plea. About 200 answered the call, of which Wood picked 80 with sea experience. These were sent aboard the old frigate *United States*, now referred to as the receiving ship *Confederate States*, or sometimes just *States*, at Norfolk while Wood journeyed to visit other army camps. Selecting a few here and a few there, the lieutenant had soon collected the near 300 needed to efficiently man the ironclad.[16] The only problem was that few, if any, of the men had ever handled a naval gun before. But they would soon learn.

Most of the ironclad's officers had already been assigned. Almost all were from the Old Navy, well versed in the art of naval warfare. They were as follows:

Executive officer, Catsby ap R. Jones; Lts., Charles C. Simms, R. D. Minor, Hunter Davidson, John Taylor Wood, John R. Eggleston, Walter Butt; Midshipmen, Robert C. Foute, H. H. Marmaduke, H. B. Littlepage, W. J. Craig, J. C. Long, L. M. Rootes; Paymaster, James Semple; Surgeon, Dinwiddie B. Phillips; Assistant Surgeon, Algernon S. Garnett; Acting Chief Engineer, H. A. Ramsey; Assistant Engineers, John W. Tynan, Loudon Campbell, Benjamin Herring, C. A. Jack, R. Wright; Boatswain, Charles H. Hasker; Gunner, C. B. Oliver; Carpenter, Hugh Lindsey; Clerk, Arthur Sinclair; Captain of Marines, Reuben Thom.

To be added to these before the ironclad went into her first action were:

Volunteer Aide, Lt. Douglas Forrest, C.S.A.; Signal Officer, Sgt. Tabb; Commander, detachment of United Norfolk Artillery, Captain Kevill.[17]

Through January and February, work on the ironclad, now nearing completion, progressed rapidly. Secretary Mallory kept up a flow of communications to Commodore Forrest on subjects pertaining to the ship. She was renamed the C.S.S. *Virginia*.

On February 24, the day of the *Virginia's* commissioning, Captain Franklin Buchanan received orders to take command of the James River Squadron. Buchanan, first superintendent of the United States Naval Academy at Annapolis and Commandant of the Washington Naval Yard at the outbreak of hostilities, had resigned his commission when it looked as though his native Maryland would secede. When that state's secession movement fell through he tried to withdraw his resignation. Welles refused to have him reinstated and the old captain went south.[18] His new squadron consisted of five tug boats and coastal steamers armed with relatively light guns, and the, as yet, untried *Virginia*. Secretary Mallory directed him to "Hoist your flag on the *Virginia*, or any other vessel of your squadron." Buchanan, of course, chose the new ironclad.

A later directive from Mallory to the new flag officer revealed the great hopes and expectations the Secretary had in his novel iron ship:

Could you pass Old Point and make a dashing cruise on the Potomac as far as Washington, its effect upon the public mind would be important to the cause. The condition of our country, and the painful reverses we have just suffered demand our utmost exertions, and convinced as I am that the opportunity and the means of striking a decided blow for our Navy are now for the first time presented, I congratulate you upon it, and know that your judgment and gallantry will meet all just expectations. Action—prompt and successful action—would now be of serious importance to our cause.[19]

As the date set for the *Virginia* to come out of drydock drew near, officers at Gosport became concerned with security measures. Fearing that a Union spy or sympathizer would send up a signal rocket when the *Virginia* came out of dock, Forrest arranged with General Huger to have every

Confederate battery in the area fire a rocket if the signal went up, deceiving the Federals into thinking the Rebels were communicating among themselves.

It was far too late for secrecy and counter-espionage measures, however. Commander G. J. Van Brunt of the *Minnesota* wrote to Commodore Goldsborough on the subject of the *Virginia*: "We are told she came out of dock on Monday last and is everything they expected to make her; in other words, a complete success. We are all ready, and the sooner she gives us the opportunity to test her strength the better."[20]

The Federal Navy had amassed a formidable force around Hampton Roads to contain the *Virginia*. Guarded by the big batteries at Newport News lay the frigate *Congress*, a 50-gun ship, and the sloop *Cumberland*, a 30-gun ship. To the east, near Fortress Monroe, lay the remainder of the fleet: the *St. Lawrence*—50 guns; *Minnesota*—40 guns; *Roanoke**—40 guns; and the gunboats *Dragon, Mystic, Whitehall, Oregon, Zouave,* and *Cambridge.* The Union shore was lined with heavy batteries, behind which were camped regiments of infantry.

Against this armada, the Confederates put the James River Squadron, originally consisting of the cockle-shells *Jamestown*—two guns; *Raleigh*—one gun; *Beaufort*—one gun; *Teaser*—one gun; and the larger *Patrick Henry*— twelve guns. The first four of these were tiny tugs converted to gunboats. An example is the *Beaufort:*

---

* The *Roanoke*, a sister-ship to the *Merrimack* and witness to the world's first combats by and between ironclad vessels of war, was, herself, soon to be converted to an ironclad. She was cut down to her berth deck, overlaid with a deck of iron, and given three two-gun turrets. In this form she rejoined the North Atlantic Blockading Squadron, where she proved to be an uncomfortable and unsuccessful ship, due to the weight of her armor, which caused her to roll excessively and decreased her speed.

A small river tug about forty feet long and carrying one small gun on her forecastle; her complement consisted of two officers and eight men—she was crowded.[21]

The *Virginia* bore no resemblance to these tiny make-shifts. At her completion she was 275 feet in length and 38 feet abeam. Her ends were both awash, with only her case-mate protruding seven feet above the water. At her bow she carried a 1500 lb. cast-iron ram, capable of puncturing the side of any wooden ship. In her casemate she mounted ten guns. Her broadside consisted of a 6-inch rifle and three 9-inch smoothbores. At bow and stern she carried a 7-inch rifle, pivot-mounted to fire straight on or from her quarters. Two thicknesses of two-inch iron had been laid on her casemate, the first layer running horizontally, the second placed vertically. No shot, said Brooke, would be able to penetrate this.

The *Virginia* came out of drydock and, on February 17, received her crew. Drills and duties began immediately to let the men familiarize themselves with the new ship. With-in ten days the ironclad was ready for action but for one thing — gunpowder. She needed 18,000 lbs. to service her guns and had only 1,000 lbs. aboard. Commodore Forrest sent out orders to the gunboats of the James River Squad-ron, directing them to send all surplus powder to the *Vir-ginia*. General Huger received a short note, asking for all the powder he could spare from his artillery batteries around Norfolk.[22]

In the last days of February, Secretary Mallory suggested to Captain Buchanan a daring move: a raid up the Atlantic coast and an attack on New York. Buchanan, however, knew what Mallory did not: While the *Virginia* might serve admirably for river and harbor defense or for smashing a blockade on inland waters, she could never leave the tran-

quil surface of Hampton Roads. With her gun ports un-
sealed and but a few feet above the water line, she would, in
all likelihood, soon founder in the open sea.

On March 2, Commander Van Brunt wrote Flag officer
Goldsborough:

We have nothing new here, all is quiet. The *Merrimac* is still
invisible to us, but reports say she is ready to come out. I sin-
cerely wish she would; I am quite tired of hearing of her.

That same day Captain Buchanan wrote to Commander
John R. Tucker aboard the *Patrick Henry*:

It is my intention, if no accident occurs to this ship to prevent
it, to appear before the enemy off Newport News at daylight on
Friday morning next [March 7]. You will, with the *Jamestown*
and *Teaser,* be prepared to join us. My object is first to destroy
the frigates *Congress* and *Cumberland* if possible and turn my
attention to the destruction of the battery on shore, and the gunboats. You will, in the absence of signals, use your best exertions to injure or destroy the enemy. Much is expected of this
ship and those who cooperate with her by her Countrymen,
and I expect and hope that our acts will prove our desire to do
our duty, to reflect credit upon the Country and the Navy . . .
No. 1 signal hoisted under my pennant indicates 'Sink before
you surrender.'[23]

On March 6, a Norfolk newspaper published an article
stating that the entire ironclad project was a failure and the
Virginia was worthless.[24] Bad weather set in that evening,
delaying for a day the *Virginia's* debut.

Soldiers and civilians, women and children crowded the
banks of the Elizabeth River and packed the shores of
Craney Island, waving caps and handkerchiefs and cheering

wildly. Tugs and small boats of every description dotted the water. Slowly, majestically, the C.S.S. *Virginia* moved up the river from Gosport Navy Yard. Attending her were the two tug-gunboats *Beaufort* and *Raleigh*. John Tucker had the rest of the squadron far up the James at Mulberry Island. A stiff breeze ruffled the waters and rolled fluffy white clouds across a bright blue sky. March 8, 1862, was a beautiful day.

A few maneuvers by the *Virginia* brought out some serious defects. Her speed was disappointingly slow; five knots was the best she could do. Also, it took a good length of time (a little over a half an hour) and a lot of space to turn her. She answered her helm poorly. Her large draft — 21 feet — confined her to deep water.

Aboard the ironclad, Captain Buchanan called Chief Engineer Ramsey to the pilot house. "Ramsey," he asked, "what would happen to your engines and boilers if there should be a collision?"

"They are braced tight," Ramsey answered. "Though the boilers stand 14 feet, they are so securely fastened that no collision could budge them."

"I am told," said Buchanan, "that the *Cumberland* has the new rifled guns, the only ones in their whole fleet we have cause to fear. The moment we are in the Roads I'm going to make right for her and ram her. How about your engines: Should they be tested by a trial trip?"

"She will have to travel yet some 10 miles down the river before we get to the Roads," Ramsey replied. "I think that will be sufficient trial trip."[25] Buchanan descended to the *Virginia's* gun deck and addressed the crew.

Men, the eyes of your country are upon you. You are fighting for your rights—your liberties—your wives and children. You must not be content with only doing your duty, but do more than your duty! Those ships must be taken, and you shall not complain that I do not take you close enough. Go to your guns.[26]

The *Virginia* halted briefly and discharged a boatload of mechanics to be put ashore on Craney Island. H. A. Ramsey, returning to his post, was offered a last bite to eat: "Your last chance," a steward said. "The galley fires must be out when the magazines are opened."[27] The ironclad's big propeller throbbed again and she slowly pushed toward Newport News. A breakwater on the bow rose above the river's surface and pushed the water away before it, preventing its climbing up the front of the casemate and pouring into the open bow gun port.

It was wash day in the Union fleet and the riggings hung thick with clothes. Sailors leaned on the rails, admiring the warmth of the day after a hard winter, or bent to sundry tasks assigned them. No one aboard the *Congress* or *Cumberland* noticed the *Virginia* and her two consorts, now in sight and moving closer. Nor did the fleet at Fort Monroe have any idea that the *Virginia* was coming out. They lay, swinging lazily at anchor, without a spark of fire in their furnaces or a pound of steam pressure in their boilers.

A few Federals, however, did notice the advancing ironclad. The gunboat *Zouave* had, about 11:00 A.M., sighted smudges of smoke on the Elizabeth River and had gone to investigate. She lay still now, watching the three Confederates come on; she signaled the *Congress* and *Cumberland*. No one noticed the signals, either aboard the frigates or in the shore bateries. Silently, ominously, the *Virginia, Beaufort,* and *Raleigh* pushed toward the unwary Federals.[28]

Around 12:40 the watch aboard the gunboat *Mount Vernon* approached the officer of the deck. "I believe that

thing's a-comin' down at last, sir," he said. The officer of
the deck took the watch's glass, studied the approaching
ram, and ordered a signal hoisted. It went unnoticed.[29]
Both gunboats eventually fired off a few rounds to gain
attention. The *Roanoke*, immobile with a broken propeller
shaft, took notice and fired off a few rounds of her own.
Blue jackets and officers aboard the *Congress* and *Cumberland* and soldiers ashore glanced in the direction of the
firing, then gaped in awe and disbelief at the *Virginia*, which
seemingly had appeared from nowhere.

From the ironclad and the two gunboats, the Confederates watched as the activity began. Whistles blew, guns
roared, signal flags ran up and down, and tugs chugged
here and there. The *Mount Vernon,* immobile with some of
her machinery ashore for repairs, signaled in vain for a
tow.[30] Aboard the two warships off Newport News, sailors
could be seen dropping small boats astern and getting booms
up. Tiny figures of men ran helter-skelter over the decks
and climbed up and down the rigging. Gunners manned
their pieces and ran them out. Chief Engineer Ramsey
described some of it:

As we rounded into view the white-winged sailing craft that
sprinkled the bay and long lines of tugs and small boats scurried
to the far shore like chickens on the approach of a hovering
hawk.[31]

The appearance of the *Virginia* caused a stir among sup-
porting combatants. Confederates at Sewell's Point opened
fire on the frigates *Minnesota, Roanoke,* and *St. Lawrence,*
which were being towed toward the area of combat. The
Federal battery at Fort Wool, on the Rip Raps, opened fire
on Sewell's Point.

As the *Virginia* and her consorts moved into range the

Cumberland opened fire. Her first shots were wide and high, and only kicked up water spouts on either side and behind the ironclad. The Rebels held their fire as they pushed on. The *Cumberland* was lying broadside-on to the *Virginia* and, as the range decreased, her shots began coming in torrents. The *Congress*, lying closer to the *Virginia* and at right angles to the *Cumberland*, was ominously silent. She couldn't, from that position, bring any of her guns to bear.

Closing the gap between his bow and the *Cumberland's* long oak side, Buchanan called for all the speed the *Virginia's* tired engines could muster. Through the ironclad's gunports, glimpses of the *Congress* could now be seen. She slid into view as the *Virginia* surged ahead, a quiet, stationary target patiently awaiting her executioner. As the ironclad drew abreast of the big frigate, the Federal's guns roared, belching forth rolling clouds of blue-white smoke that momentarily obscured her entire hull. Water spouts splattered around the *Virginia*, solid shot banged against her iron plates, and shells shattered from the concussion as they struck. The *Virginia's* armor had met and passed its first test under fire. Eager hands sighted the ironclad's broadside and the Confederates answered with a noisy salute of their own. Shells smashed easily through the Union frigate's oak walls and exploded deep in the ship's innards, crushing and smashing. An officer aboard the *Congress* decribed the scene:

One of her shells dismounted an eight-inch gun, and either killed or wounded every one of the gun's crew, while the slaughter at the other guns was fearful. There were comparatively few wounded, the fragments of the huge shells she threw killing outright as a general thing. Our clean and handsome gun deck was in an instant changed into a slaughter pen, with lopped off legs and arms, and bleeding, blackened bodies, scattered about by the shells; while blood and brains actually dripped from the beams. One poor fellow had his chest transfixed by a splinter of oak as thick as the wrist.[32]

Slowly, steadily, the squat *Virginia* narrowed the distance between herself and the immobile *Cumberland*. At the bow of her casemate, just under the pilothouse, Lt. Charles C. Simms readied the pivot gun, a wicked-looking 7-inch rifle. The gun was loaded, run out, and aimed. Simms took a final sighting, then snapped the lanyard. His aim was perfect. The shell exploded near the sloop's after-pivot gun, killing and wounding most of its crew.

The *Virginia* was unable to strike the *Cumberland* with much speed, but her tremendous weight lent power to her punch. She struck a heavy blow near the bow, her ram snapping planking and timbers, opening a hole big enough to admit "a horse and cart."[33] The force of the ramming sent the *Cumberland* heeling far over, then brought her snapping back upright, throwing men about on her deck. Lt. Simms found this an opportune time to deliver another shell. His long black rifle roared again, sending a projectile biting deep into the big sloop's innards. Buchanan, at this point, called on the *Cumberland* to surrender. Lt. George U. Morris, commanding in the absence of Captain Radford, returned: "Never! I'll sink alongside first."[34]

Buchanan ordered the engines reversed and the *Virginia* backed her way out of the *Cumberland*. Her heavy iron ram caught and ripped off, remaining in the wound and leaving the ironclad with a leak in her bow. Clearing the dying Federal, the *Virginia* rounded-to, giving Lt. Wood a chance to use his stern rifle for the first time. He put three well-placed shots into the *Congress* just as that ship slipped anchor, loosed her bow top sail and, attempting to escape, piled up hard and fast aground.[35]

With the *Cumberland* sinking and the *Congress* aground,

neither able to flee, the *Virginia* took time to carefully choose a position from which she could best pound them both. As the ironclad withdrew, the men of the *Congress* sent up a cheer, thinking that they had driven her off. They soon learned the truth, however, when the Confederate slowly rounded-to and opened fire on them.

From the position the *Virginia* had chosen, only the stern guns of the *Congress* could be brought into play. Of these, one was quickly dismounted and the other ceased firing when its muzzle was broken by a shot. Broken muzzles held no terror for the Confederates, however. A shot struck the muzzle of one of Lt. Hunter Davidson's guns, shortening the barrel considerably. The Confederates continued to fire the piece, setting the rough pine woodwork around the gun port afire with each discharge. One of Marine Captain Thom's guns, manned by Captain Kevill's United Norfolk Artillery, also had its muzzle shot away. Kevill, like Davidson, continued firing without let-up.

The *Cumberland* was dying. Her bow settled in the water, all her forward guns out of the fight. All ammunition was brought aft. Her wounded were also carried aft, laid on the deck where exploding shells and flying splinters wounded them again.

The deck was covered with dead and wounded, slippery with blood, the large gallery demolished and its scattered contents added to the general destruction, some guns run in as they had last been fired, many of them bespattered with blood. Rammers and sponges, broken and powder-blackened, lay in every direction.[36]

Reinforcements began arriving for both sides. From Mulberry Island, Commander John R. Tucker — whose last cruise with the U.S. Navy had been aboard the *Cumberland* — brought the *Patrick Henry, Teaser,* and *Jamestown* into the Roads. Drawing far less water than the *Virginia*, the smaller ships of the James River Squadron got in close to the grounded *Congress* and peppered her with shot. From Fortress Monroe, the rest of the Federal fleet belatedly arrived on the scene.

The *Minnesota*, coming into the arena of combat, touched bottom. Her commander, Van Brunt, attempted to force her over into deep water, but only succeeded in grounding her more. Her position, however, was one from which she could actively engage the enemy. She was broadside to the *Virginia* and in water so shallow that the ironclad couldn't get within less than a mile of her.

With a roar, the *Cumberland* went down. About 10 feet of her mast remained above water, still flying a defiant Federal flag. Heads bobbed briefly, fighting for life; but they were pulled down by the suction, not to return to the surface again.

A Union general, watching the contest from shore, best summed up the situation as it then stood when he telegraphed his superiors: "The *Virginia* has it all her own way on this side of Signal Point . . ."[37]

The *Congress* was a shambles. The *Jamestown*, *Patrick Henry*, and *Teaser* had left her and were now harassing the *Minnesota*, but she still suffered under the heavy shells of the *Virginia*. The number of bleeding and broken bodies lying around the guns had doubled, then tripled. The decks were slippery with blood: there had been no time to sand them down before the action began. Spars hung broken and tangled in the rigging and shell holes pock-marked the frigate's sides. Somewhere aboard her, still among the living, was Paymaster McKean Buchanan, Frank Buchanan's younger brother.

Unable to withstand the continuous battering of the *Virginia's* great guns, the *Congress* surrendered. The *Beaufort* and *Raleigh* ranged alongside to remove the crew and fire the ship.

Commander Joseph Smith having been killed, the duty of surrendering the *Congress* devolved upon Lt. Comm. Pendergrast. He stepped aboard the *Beaufort* and formally surrendered to Lt. William H. Parker the frigate's flag and, in lieu of his naval dress sword, an ordinary ship's cutlass. He then asked that he and his officers be allowed to return to the *Congress* to help transfer the wounded. Lt. Parker consented after receiving the Yankee's verbal parole and Pendergrast and his officers returned to their ship. They had hardly left the *Beaufort* when the gunboat *Zouave*, which had spent the engagement behind the *Congress* trying to pull her free, surged out into the open and fired upon the *Beaufort,* killing and wounding several Confederates and a few Federal prisoners. The shore batteries now turned their fire against the *Beaufort* and *Raleigh*, laying down a barrage too hot for the little gunboats to face. They drew off with few prisoners.

Captain Buchanan, observing this scene from the *Virginia's* casemate roof, announced to his officers: "That ship must be burned." Flag-Lieutenant Minor, standing near, volunteered to take a small boat and burn the frigate. Buchanan consented and the lieutenant and a boat's crew were soon on the water. They were within 50 yards of the *Congress* when a regiment of soldiers ashore directed a volley of musketry upon them. The boat hurredly put about, Minor and several others being wounded, and returned to the *Virginia*. Buchanan, on witnessing the wounding of his men, directed his gunners to resume fire on the *Congress* with hot shot. The order had just been uttered when a Minie ball struck him in the left thigh. He was carried below and command of the *Virginia* passed to Lt. Catsby Jones.

The *Virginia's* searing hot shot proved its worth. It transformed the *Congress* into a seething mass of flames. The Federal's crew, those that were able, took to the water to save themselves. Turning from the dying *Congress*, the *Virginia* sought a third victim, the *Minnesota*. But the one-mile range, coupled with the uncertain light of falling darkness, made accurate shooting impossible. Also, a falling tide threatened to leave the *Virginia* aground, as helpless as the *Congress* and *Minnesota*. Accordingly,, Lt. Jones broke off the engagement and turned toward Norfolk.

Night had fallen when the *Virginia* moored off Sewell's Point. The crew immediately set to work, loading wounded for transfer to Norfolk and repairing damage to the wooden gunboats and the ironclad's smokestack. Supper was served near midnight; it was the first meal the Rebels had had since 8:00 that morning.

After supper, the *Virginia's* crew gathered atop the casemate roof to watch the *Congress* burn. From the Confederate shore every line of the blazing frigate's rigging stood out like a black pencil mark on the yellow flames. The water around the flaming hulk sent black ripples through the reflections cast by the flames. Now and then a gun, heated by the fire, would discharge, sending a dull roar across the dark water.

A little after 1:00 A.M. the *Congress* blew up. Her powder tanks exploded in succession, each blast seeming to rival the other for height and grandeur. The sight of the gallant old sailing frigate in her death agonies was sad indeed for the naval officers and regular seamen in the crew. Not so with the army volunteers. A Georgia private, who had retained his sense of humor through the sad and awesome spectacle, wrote that the *Virginia* had "invented a new way of destroying the blockade. Instead of raising it, she sinks it. Or I believe she is good at both, for the one she burned was raised to a pretty considerably height when the magazine exploded."[38]

In the early morning of Sunday, March 9, the crewmen of the James River Squadron rose to again venture into battle with the blockading fleet. But their efforts to eradicate the Union squadron in Hampton Roads were already doomed to failure, the *Virginia's* advantage over wooden ships neutralized. The U.S.S. *Monitor* had arrived.

The *Monitor*, the United States' counter to the *Virginia*, arrived almost unnoticed amid the pathos and despair left in the wake of the *Virginia's* first visit. She was little more than half the length of the *Virginia*, but she possessed speed and agility to more than double that of the Rebel brute.

Daylight revealed the *Monitor* lying close under the *Minnesota*, giving all the appearances of a Pigmy beside a giant. The two ships lay amidst a pool of baggage and excess gear, which had been thrown overboard to lighten the *Minnesota* and float her free of the mud bar that still held her. Tugs had pulled at her all night, but without success.

At 8:00 A.M. observers aboard the *Monitor* spotted the *Virginia* coming out. The Confederate headed east. She passed the *Minnesota*, then turned west and approached by the same channel through which the Federal frigate had come the day before. Both ironclads would be fighting under a handicap: The Confederates, counting on meeting only wooden ships, had come out to battle carrying mostly shells, few solid shot. The *Monitor* advanced to combat under orders to fire only half-charges — the peace-time 15-pound powder loads — in her big guns.

The *Monitor* moved into the open and waited. Aboard, as naval observer, was Alban Stimers who, in happier years, had served as the *Merrimack's* chief engineer, with H. A.

Ramsey his assistant.[39] At 8:45 the *Monitor* shattered the morning quiet with a screaming shot past the Confederate's casemate.[40] The *Virginia* answered with a single shot of her own. "Her first shell made a circular dent in the iron plate of the turret, a scar 2½ inches deep, a perfect mold of a shell."[41] The *Virginia* kept her course for the *Minnesota*. the *Monitor* stepped boldly out to meet her and the battle was joined.

The *Monitor* brought her twin guns to bear and lashed out savagely with a pair of 11-inch bolts. The *Virginia* answered, first with a bow gun, then a broadside. The Confederate was able to bring four or five guns into play against the *Monitor's* two, but the Federal made up for it in weight of iron, thickness of armor, and the fact that she used solid shot. But even the *Virginia's* shells, shattering against the *Monitor's* armor with no hope of penetrating, gave the Federals a difficult time in the cramped turret: concussion loosened plating bolts on the inside, then sent them flying, bruising several men. One gunner, leaning against the turret wall, was sent sprawling when a shell struck outside.[42]

The *Monitor's* guns roared repeatedly. Her ponderous iron projectiles hammered mercilessly at the *Virginia's* casemate, ricocheting into space to drop with a hissing splash in the waters of the Roads. The *Minnesota* was much in the fight, her shot and shell adding to the ringing clatter on the *Virginia's* casemate. More than once her shells struck the *Monitor*.

The *Monitor's* gunners soon found the hoisting of the heavy iron port shutters to be too much of a chore. They adopted a system of turning the turret's back toward the *Virginia,* loading the guns, running them out, and setting the turret spinning, discharging the twin pieces "on the fly" as the gunners caught sight of the *Virginia* sweeping past the open ports. Confederate gunners, seeing the gun ports constantly open, began trying to put a shell through them, but found it impossible: the turret spun too fast.

Occasionally the *Virginia's* gunners turned from the *Monitor* to throw a few shells at the *Minnesota*. Several of these were quite effective. The gunboat *Dragon,* lying alongside, caught a shell in her boiler and blew up. One shell hit the frigate, smashing through the engineer's stateroom, the engineers' messroom, and the boatswain's room, where it exploded, blowing out four bulkheads, touching off two powder charges, and starting a small fire.[43] Hits on the *Minnesota*, however, were few and far between. The *Virginia's* pilots refused to bring the ironclad in closer than a mile to the frigate for fear of grounding her.

Early in the action the *Virginia's* flagstaff was shot away. Her colors flew from a boat hook the remainder of the fight.

With her keel in the mud for most of the fight, the *Virginia* eventually grounded. The *Monitor* circled slowly, battering at intervals with her 11-inch solid shot and taking the Rebels' 6- 7- and 9-inch shell in return while the *Virginia* strained to get free. Said Ramsey:

We lashed down the safety valves, heaped quick-burning combustibles into the already raging fires, and brought the boilers to a pressure that would have been unsafe under ordinary circumstances. The propeller churned the mud and water furiously, but the ship did not stir. We piled on oiled cotton waste, splints of wood, anything that would burn faster than coal. It seemed impossible that the boilers could stand the pressure we were crowding upon them. Just as we were beginning to dispair, there was a perceptible movement, and the *Merrimack* slowly dragged herself off the shoal by main strength.[44]

Around 11:00 Lt. Jones descended from the pilot house to the gun deck, where he found Lt. Eggleston's gun division standing "at ease." When questioned as to why his gun wasn't firing, Eggleston replied: "Why, our powder is very precious and after two hours' incessant firing I find I can do her about as much damage by snapping my thumb every two minutes and a half."[45]

Eggleston's comment induced a change in Confederate strategy. Rather than continue the futile attempts to pound a hole in the *Monitor's* tough armor or put a chance shell through a port, Lt. Jones resorted to ramming. Even though the cast-iron prong had been left in the *Cumberland's* wound the preceding day, Jones hoped to deliver a blow severe enough to generally unbalance things aboard the Federal ironclad and give a boarding party time enough to get aboard and secure control.

For nearly an hour the *Virginia* maneuvered, attempting to gain a favorable position on the *Monitor*. Time and again Jones ordered "full speed ahead" when he saw the *Monitor* before him, only to have the Federal dart away. Finally, the *Monitor* crossed the *Virginia's* bow and stopped. Jones called for speed and the *Virginia* lumbered forward, gathering momentum. Boarders tensed in anticipation of the task ahead as the big Rebel bore down on her smaller counterpart. At the last instant the *Monitor* cut her wheel and moved. The *Virginia* struck a glancing blow, her hull sliding part way up on the *Monitor's* iron deck. The *Monitor* slid along the *Virginia's* port side, her turret revolving to again bring her guns to bear on the Confederate. From point-blank range she unleashed two of her terrible bolts. They struck side by side, about midway up the casemate near the aft. Iron plates snapped under the violent double blow. Woodwork bowed inward and everyone in the area of impact was dashed to the deck, bleeding from nose and ears.[46]

Angry Confederates returned to their guns with renewed vigor. Already satisfied that the *Monitor's* turret was invulnerable, gunners began searching the Federal for weak spots. They needed go no farther than the pilot house. One shell exploded against it with gratifying effect. The force of the explosion cracked one of the 9-inch iron logs comprising the house and lifted its roof a few inches. A good amount of powder was blown through the forward viewing slot, striking the *Monitor's* captain, John L. Worden, full in the face.

Blinded, and ignorant of the extent of the damage caused by the exploding shell, Worden ordered the *Monitor* into shallow water. The *Minnesota,* under the impression that the *Monitor* was leaving her to fend for herself, prepared to fight to her death. The tide was falling, however, and pilots told Lt. Jones that, if the *Virginia* didn't withdraw immediately, she would be unable to reach Norfolk until noon the next day.[47] Accordingly, the *Virginia* slowly turned toward Sewell's Point.

Aboard the *Monitor,* damage was assessed, more ammunition was hoisted to the guns (she had started the engagement with 168 shot and charges in the turret), and she steamed back into deep water in a fruitless attempt to draw the *Virginia* back into battle. She threw a final shot at the retreating Confederates, of which they took no notice.

In two days of fighting the *Virginia* had exacted a terrible toll on the Federal Navy: two hundred fifty men had been killed and wounded; two ships of the line, the *Congress* and *Cumberland,* had been destroyed, along with the gunboats *Dragon* and *Whitehead* and an army transport; another transport was captured, as was the *Reindeer,* sole supplier of fresh water to the blockading squadron and the forts; the *Minnesota* was leaking heavily through a large shell-hole in the after quarter at the water line, one of her gun carriages was destroyed, her spar deck shot up, and one-third of her mainmast knocked away.

The timid *St. Lawrence* received only one shell during both engagements. It struck 4 inches above the water line, passed through the wardroom pantry and into the assistant surgeon's stateroom, where it struck an iron bar and bounded back into the wardroom. The *Monitor* was struck nine times in the turret, twice in the pilot house, eight times in the side, and three times on the deck.

On arriving at Gosport, the *Virginia* sent her crew ashore and was hauled into drydock. In two days' fighting she had collected 97 shot indentations. Six plates on her outer layer of iron had been broken and two gun muzzles and an anchor were shot away, along with all railings, boats, boat davits, and flagstaffs. Her smokestack and steam pipes were completely riddled.

Still with a vision of attacking New York, Secretary Mallory ordered the *Virginia* readied for sea duty. Buchanan answered that this would be impossible: she had no buoyance and would sink like a stone in open sea. Mallory said no more.

From a bed in the Norfolk Naval hospital Captain Buchanan dictated a full report of the events of March 8 and 9, praising highly the crew of the *Virginia* and the entire James River Squadron. Lt. Wood, ordered to convey the report to Secretary Mallory, found the people of the Confederacy wild with enthusiasm over the *Virginia's* first smashing victory. At every railroad stop between Norfolk and Richmond his car was beset with cheering crowds who begged to hear first-hand an account of the two great naval battles.

Arriving in Richmond after a long and exhausting ride, Wood reported to the office of the Secretary of the Navy. He emerged a short time later in the company of Mallory and was escorted to the Confederate White House where he was introduced to Secretary of State Judah P. Benjamin, future Secretary of War James A. Seddon, Inspector General Samuel Cooper, and others of the Confederate hierarchy. The government heads listened, fascinated, as Wood related his accounts of the *Virginia's* exploits. President Davis questioned him closely concerning the ironclad's speed, draft, maneuverability, armor, and other points, then asked about another contest with the *Monitor*. Wood replied, quite frankly, that another battle between the two ironclads would be a tossup; the *Virginia* stood just as good a chance of being sunk or captured as she did of destroying or capturing the *Monitor*.

During the evening a trophy was brought in, the flag of the *Congress*. Unfurled for the group to see, it was discovered, with horror, to be covered with blood stains. Quickly, quietly, the big banner was folded and taken to the Navy Department building. It remained there for the rest of the war and, presumably, was burned with that building during the evacuation of Richmond.[48]

The indecisive outcome of the *Virginia's* combat with the *Monitor,* coupled with the terrifying destructiveness of her first day's sweep, left the Union element at Hampton Roads with mixed feelings. Assistant Secretary Gustavus V. Fox, Welles' chief advisor, telegraphing Washington immediately after the *Virginia-Monitor* clash, said of the Southern warrior:

Nearly all here are of the opinion that she is disabled. I was the nearest person to her, outside the *Monitor,* and I am of the opinion that she is not seriously injured. She retreated under steam without assistance. The *Monitor* is all ready for her tomorrow but I think the *Merrimac* may be obliged to lay up for a few days. She is an ugly customer and it is too good luck to believe we are yet clear of her. Our hopes are upon the *Monitor* and this day's work shows that the *Merrimac* must attend to her alone.[49]

Northern philanthropists sent down private steamers to aid in the *Virginia's* destruction. The *Vanderbilt*, its equippage financed by that railroad magnate, was the first to arrive. When Flag Officer Goldsborough ordered the private steamers *Illinois* and *Arago* to run the *Virginia* down the next time she appeared, their crews refused to be a party to such insane antics. Goldsborough had them removed and replaced by navy regulars.[50]

On Sunday, March 23, the men of the James River Squadron massed in the naval yard, forming in a hollow square. Officers took the center and read to them a resolution of thanks from the Confederate Congress. On August 21, Captain Buchanan was promoted to the rank of admiral "for gallant and meritorious conduct in attacking the enemy's fleet in Hampton Roads and destroying the frigate *Congress*, sloop of war *Cumberland*, and three small steamers, while in command of the Confederate squadron in the waters of Virginia on the 8th day of March, 1862."[51]

A small command shake-up followed in the wake of the Hampton Roads combats. The Confederate high government judged Lt. Catsby Jones too young to carry the responsibility of commanding the all-important *Virginia*. They replaced him with Captain Josiah Tattnall, distinguished veteran of the Old Navy and personal friend of Buchanan's. Lt. Jones returned to his old post as first lieutenant. On March 24, French Forrest was given the post of Chief of Bureau of Orders and Detail. Captain Sidney Smith Lee assumed command of Gosport Navy Yard.

Captain Tattnall, on arriving at Gosport, found his new command still in drydock, where she would remain for a good while. Her broken plates had long since been replaced; she was now being strengthened for another clash with the *Monitor*.

Despite the danger of losing the *Virginia* in another scrap with the *Monitor,* the people of the South expressed a deep desire to see their ironclad crush her Northern rival and sweep aside the blockade that had shut Norfolk in.

The public sentiment worried Tattnall. Buchanan had managed to catch the Union Navy napping, entrap two frail warships and, safe behind his iron shield, destroy them at will. The victory had created in the minds of the Southern people the image of the *Virginia* as an invincible machine, capable of destroying with little difficulty any warship sent against her. Tattnall was expected to uphold this image by engaging in combat with a now totally alert fleet that was supplemented with an iron guardian superior to his craft in nearly every way; and he was supposed to come home with another smashing victory. An unsuccessful battle with the *Monitor* could well mean the loss of a reputation that had taken years to create.

In an effort to add to her lethality and invulnerability, several modifications were made in the *Virginia* while she lay in drydock. A 2-inch thickness of iron, extending four feet below the water line, was added to her hull. A heavier ram was fitted, secured more firmly than the first. Several tons of ballast were added to her fantail, iron port shutters (which proved themselves workable only on occasion) were added, and her magazine was stacked with steel-point shot. These "improvements" increased her draft to 23 feet and reduced her speed to a maximum of four knots.[52]

On April 4, the *Virginia* came out of drydock. Tattnall, evidently piqued by the public outcry, began preparing a battle plan. "There must be," he said, "a combat with the *Monitor.*"

On April 8, battle orders were issued, revealing the flag officer's scheme of action. A large fleet of Federal Army transports had taken anchorage in Hampton Creek near Fort Monroe; the *Monitor* and the blockading fleet were anchored nearby. The *Virginia* was to strike the transports, drawing the *Monitor* out to defend them. When the iron-clads clashed, the *Beaufort, Raleigh,* and two other small tugs, all carrying assault parties, were to draw alongside the Federal and board her. Tattnall pointed to the *Monitor's* ventilators, smokestacks, pilot house, and turret base as weak spots. A wedge, driven at the joint of the turret and deck, would jam the turret so it couldn't revolve. A wet cloth or tarpaulin thrown over the pilot house would effectively blind the helmsman. Another tarpaulin covering the smokestacks would fill the ironclad with smoke, forcing her crew out on the deck. Oil-soaked rags and gunpowder thrown down the stacks would add to the general confusion.

On April 11 the *Virginia* appeared at the mouth of the Elizabeth River. The *Monitor* and the fleet raised steam quickly, but remained at their moorings. The transports took flight at the first sight of the Confederates' smoke, seeking safety in the open sea.

The *Virginia* pushed boldly into the Roads and settled down to slow cruising, inviting combat. None came. The *Monitor*, under orders not to risk an unnecessary engage-ment, remained at her moorings, watching her antagonist. A battery on the Rip Raps opened a slow and ineffective fire. Its shots flew wide and the Confederates paid no mind. Finally, convinced that the *Monitor* would not fight, Tatt-nall ordered the *Virginia* back to Norfolk.

The following day found the Confederates back in the Roads. The *Monitor* once again raised her steam but made no move to come out and engage. The *Virginia* resumed her slow cruising until Tattnall noticed three small trans-ports, lying almost within range of the *Monitor's* great guns. Signals flew from the flag-ship's staff and the little *James-town* cut away from the Confederate squadron, heading for the transports. She captured them with no difficulty, took them in tow, and headed back, steaming near the British corvette *Rinaldo,* just arrived in the Roads to observe any combat between the ironclads. The *Monitor* made no move to aid the captured trio, but watched the affair calmly from her moorings. As the *Jamestown* passed under the *Rinaldo's* stern, English seamen crowded the rail, cheering. Her Majesty's officers lifted their hats in salute, beaming their approval of the cockle-shell Confederate's daring deed.[53]

On the morning of May 8, six ships of the Federal blockading squadron, including the *Monitor* and a new ironclad, the *Nagatuck,* appeared off Sewell's Point and commenced an artillery duel with the Confederate batteries there. As the sounds of firing reached Norfolk the *Virginia* raised steam, upped her anchor, and stood for the point ready to engage. But as she neared the scene of action the Federals broke off the engagement, turned and steamed for Fort Monroe. The *Virginia* followed, falling far behind the faster Federals, and soon had the Roads to herself. The Rip Raps battery opened fire, their gunnery unimproved. The ironclad moved toward the battery and shells flew far over her head. After several hours of slow cruising, Tattnall ordered: "Mr. Jones, fire a gun to windward, and take the ship back to its buoy."[54]

Early the next morning it was noticed that the flag wasn't flying over the Sewell's Point batteries. Catsby Jones was dispatched to Craney Island to investigate. He returned with distressing news: General Joseph Johnston had withdrawn all troops from the area to defend Richmond against McClellan's drive. Norfolk was practically undefended. Tattnall pondered this, then sent Jones to Norfolk to confer with Captain Lee.

Arriving at Gosport, Jones was appalled to find it, for the second time in a little over a year, abandoned and in flames. Pushing into the city, he found the streets mobbed with streams of soldiers, artillery, and baggage wagons, all moving out. Masses of civilians mixed and mingled with the military, clogging traffic and creating confusion. Strangely, Norfolk's civilian populace seemed to wear a festive air. Women brought their children out to watch the army leave: it was like a picnic.[55]

Lt. Jones threaded through the crowds, asking where he might find General Huger or Captain Lee. Someone finally told him that all the officers were gone. The Yankees had already landed they said, and the mayor was preparing to surrender the city.

It was 7:00 P.M. before Jones returned to the *Virginia* to tell Tattnall of the evacuation of Norfolk. The abandonment of the city left the ironclad little hope of survival. But the pilots offered an avenue of escape: if the ship could be lightened to draw only 18 feet of water, they could take her up the James to City Point. A hurried conference among the officers resulted in a decision to lighten ship and make the attempt. The crew was assembled on deck, informed of the emergency, and set to the task of lightening the ship. They threw overboard ballast, provisions, luggage — anything not immediately necessary for the operation of the ship. Tattnall, suffering from an illness, left the operation to Lt. Jones and retired for the night.[56] About 1:30 P.M. he was aroused by an officer. The ship had been lightened to the point that she rode with a depth of 20 feet, and the pilots had just stated that it was useless to go on, as they couldn't get the ironclad up the river after all.

Chief Pilot Parrish was soon on the carpet, the old captain demanding an explanation. Parrish stated that, with an easterly wind, the James River would carry a ship drawing 18 feet. But, for the past few days the wind had been from the west and the James was running too shallow.

The *Virginia* was in serious trouble. She rode with several feet of one- to two-inch armor plate exposed above the water line, inviting fatal penetration by enemy shot. She could not hope to survive a battle in this condition — this was definite.

Considering his position, Captain Tattnall concluded that the best course of action would be to attempt to save the crew by destroying the *Virginia*. Accordingly, the ironclad was driven aground near Craney Island. Her crew landed with small arms and provisions and set off through the night in the direction of Suffolk while Lt. Jones remained behind to set the fatal fire.

From Hampton Roads and the northern shore Federal soldiers and sailors watched the *Virginia* burn. Her casemate glowed dull red as its oak and pine foundation disintegrated under the crackling flames. Her guns discharged occasionally, each sending its dull, lonely boom across the darkened waters in a vain call of distress. She burned for two hours, ending her death agonies at 5:00 A.M. with an explosion that shook houses for miles around.

2

The Loss of New Orleans

Mr. Lincoln's coastal blockade, instituted on April 19, 1861, had not become effective at the mouth of the Mississippi by early May. In fact, many ships entering New Orleans and the Gulf area at that time were not even aware that there was a war on. Hastily armed gunboats and privateers took to lurking just off the mainland, watching for any ships, ignorant of the war, that flew the United States flag. Tugs and assorted craft like the *Ivy*, *Calhoun*, and *Music* — made warlike by the addition of a gun or two — did a roaring business for the Confederacy by accosting steamers making port from South America, Africa, and other foreign lands. The Confederate Government encouraged such privateers with easily obtained letters of marque and with large bounties — 20 per cent of a prize's value — on each capture.[1]

John A. Stevenson, secretary of the New Orleans Pilots' Benevolent Association[2] and prominent man in the Crescent City's boating business, thought the privateering trade a risk good enough to warrant his interest. Perhaps he foresaw the big Union warships of many guns that would soon be

59

cruising the Gulf area and probing into the mouth of the Mississippi, for the privateer he intended to captain was to be ironclad.

May 12 found Stevenson, with several men who had entered into the privateering venture with him, at the Merchant's Exchange, subscription books before them, soliciting the sum of $100,000 to finance their ironclad. Their pirating company apparently impressed local speculators as a sound business investment or it appealed to the patriotism of many people, for Stevenson and Company collected $50,000 the first day.[3]

The vessel selected for conversion to an ironclad privateer was the *Enoch Train*. Built for service as an icebreaker in Bedford, Massachusetts in 1855, she had been brought to New Orleans for tugboat service in 1859.[4] She was a single deck, two-masted vessel, 128 feet in length, 28 feet abeam, with a 12½-foot draft and a displacement of 385 tons. Her engines were two-cylinder, each cylinder 36 inches in diameter with a 30-inch stroke, pushing two screw propellers.[5]

The *Enoch Train's* conversion, undertaken by the John Hughes & Co. shipyard in Algiers,[6] was begun by cutting her down to her deck. To allow her to ram without crushing her own bow, she was lengthened, the bow braced, then filled in solid to a thickness of 20 feet. A wood backing — curved like a half an egg — was added, entirely encasing her deck. The thickness of this backing is debatable. Some sources list it as 17 inches. Lt. Alexander F. Warley, who later commanded her, gives it as no more than 5 inches. At any rate, it was considerably less than the thickness of backing found on the majority of ironclads. The armor was thin, too. One solitary inch of worn and indifferent railroad iron covered the privateer.

Stevenson hoped to keep the building of his ironclad privateer secret. Surprisingly, New Orleans newspapers cooperated, making no mention of her. On July 11, however, the story broke in a Washington paper. Other Northern newspapers picked it up and, for weeks after, ran rife with rumors and exaggerations of the iron monster under construction in New Orleans. When completed, they told their readers, she would drop down the Mississippi and attack the blockader *Brooklyn*, just arrived off the Mississippi's mouth. She would ram the Federal, attach herself with grapnels, then bore holes in the blockader until she sank, all the while spewing forth scalding water to keep the Yankee gun crews down. David Porter, commanding the *Brooklyn*, viewed the alarm as so much nonsense. He wrote Flag Officer William Mervine that "there is no danger to be apprehended from the boat with the iron horn."[7]

The ironclad was launched in mid-August. Her armament consisted of a single, small 32-pounder carronade, mounted in the bow and firing through a rise or bubble in her turtle back. The gun port was equipped with a shutter, hinged at the top to be pushed open as the gun was run out and dropped closed by its own weight as the gun came in for reloading. Entry and exit was gained by means of two hatches, one forward and one aft of her twin smokestacks.[8] Conversion of the *Enoch Train* to an ironclad had lengthened her by 15 feet, widened her 5 feet, and increased her draft by 4 feet.[9] She was rechristened the *Manassas*.

The second of New Orleans' ironclads proved to be the prototype for the hull structure of almost all succeeding iron-armored craft built in the South. Nelson Tift of Albany, Georgia, devised a system of construction that was both novel and, in an agricultural nation nearly destitute of shipwrights and skilled laborers, quite practical: his ship would be built with all surfaces flat. Where a curve or bend was needed, he straightened it out and compensated with a sharp angle. The absence of delicately curved ribs and fitted planking eliminated the need for non-available ship-wrights and ships' carpenters, enabling the craft to be built by ordinary house carpenters.

Asa Tift, after Union troops confiscated his ship-repair yard in Key West, Florida, joined his brother Nelson in Georgia. They built a small wooden model of Nelson's ship and entrained for Richmond to see Secretary Mallory. En route, they stopped at Savannah and Charleston, showing their model to various prominent people, including Flag Officer Josiah Tattnall. Most of the military authorities with whom they discussed the ship voiced the opinion that an ironclad built along this plan should be able to clear the entire Confederate coast of the blockade and destroy Union warships wherever she found them.

On August 26, the Tifts, in a communication to Mallory, proposed "to give to the government the use of the invention and to superintend and direct, as your agents, the construction and completion of one or more vessels, without pecuniary compensation from the Government for our service, or any other reward than that which every citizen must feel who can, in any way, contribute to the defense of our country."[10] On September 1, Mallory entered in his diary: "I have concluded to build a large warship at N. Orleans upon Nelson Tift's plan, & will push it." The next day he got off a telegram to Commodore George N. Hollins, who commanded the mosquito fleet at New Orleans, directing him to enquire as to the cost and time needed for the manufacture of three high-pressure engines, three propellers of eleven-foot diameter, and ten boilers. Hollins showed the telegram to John Roy, an ordnance wizard who had set up shop at the New Orleans customs house, then sent out a circular asking for bids.[11] Mallory, meanwhile, called in John L. Porter to make the necessary drawings for construction. Porter did his work from the wooden model the Tifts had brought.[12]

Nelson Tift took the time to visit Gosport Navy Yard, where he observed Lt. John Brooke's experiments with armor plate. He then rejoined brother Asa in Richmond; they received instructions from Secretary Mallory on September 5, and departed for Albany to put family affairs in order before continuing to New Orleans. Asa left the family matters to Nelson and visited Savannah, looking for engines for the big ironclad, and for two ironclad gunboats which the brothers had tentatively agreed to build. He visited two of the city's principal shipyards, left his specifications, and continued on to Charleston. There he found every shipyard and machine shop in the city overloaded with war contracts, unable to promise any marine engines. Returning to Savannah on September 12, he was offered contracts for the two gunboat engines, but could find no one willing to take on the job of building the three giant engines needed for the big ironclad. After passing this information on to Mallory via letter, Asa joined Nelson in Albany and they boarded a train for New Orelans, arriving there on September 18.[13] The ironclad they were to construct, to be called the *Mississippi*, was to be 260 feet in length, 58 feet abeam, and was to draw 14 feet of water. Her armament was to consist of 16 guns with a gallery above for sharpshooters. She would displace 4,000 tons and be capable of steaming 14 knots.

On September 18, as the Tifts reached New Orleans, the Secretary of the Navy signed a contract with E. C. Murray, a Kentuckian with 20 years' shipbuilding experience (who claimed that he, not John Brooke, had furnished plans for the *Virginia*),[14] to construct a third ironclad, the *Louisana*, in the Crescent City. Terms of the contract stated that the *Louisiana* would be finished, commissioned, and in the Confederate naval service by January 25, 1862. Her total cost would be $196,000, payments to be made in six installments of $24,500 each, and a final payment of $49,000 on delivery. A bonus-penalty clause was included: for each day before January 25 that the *Louisana* was completed, Murray was to receive $98. For each day over the deadline, he would be penalized $98. If construction ran over the allotted time due to delay in the delivery of materials, the penalty would not be invoked. Any price rise above $60 per ton for iron would be covered by the Navy Department.[15]

The *Louisiana* was to be slightly larger than the *Mississippi* (by the latter's original plan), with a length of 264 feet and a beam of 62 feet.

Many miles below New Orleans a neck of land juts into the Gulf of Mexico, ending in three fingers pointing southeast, south, and southwest. The Mississippi runs like an artery through the neck, then splits off into three main passes through the fingers — Pass A Loutre, South Pass, and Southwest Pass. The point at which the three passes part is known simply as Head of Passes.

When the Union blockade first reached New Orleans, the Federal Navy stationed its ships off the passes, giving chase to any sail that showed itself in the area. When Raphael Semmes slipped past the *Brooklyn* in the cruiser *Sumter*, however, the blockading squadron placed several ships in the Head of Passes, where they had only to guard the main channel rather than the three outlets.

On July 31, 1861, George N. Hollins, a sixty-two-year-old Marylander, who had fought the Algerian pirates with Stephen Decatur, assumed command of the Confederate fleet at New Orleans with the rank of Commodore.[16] His command consisted of the *McRae, Ivy, Tuscarora, Calhoun,*

Watson, and *Jackson*. The *McRae*, largest of the squadron and flagship, was an old steamer much like the ship which now raided under the name of *Sumter*. Before the war she had traded on the New Orleans-to-Havana route. The others were tugs and river steamers, their only identification as warships being the small guns they carried, usually one mounted forward and one aft.

Hollins had watched the blockading strength grow at the Mississippi's mouth and now, in early October, proposed an attack on the Federals. Before the battle the ironclad privateer *Manassas* was commandeered to add some authority to the fleet. James Morris Morgan, a midshipman on the *McRae*, tells how it was done:

On arriving alongside of the ram we found her crew lined up on the turtleback, swearing that they would kill the first man who attempted to board her. There was a ladder reaching to the water from the top of her armor to the water line. Lieutenant Warley, pistol in hand, ordered me to keep the men in the boat until he gave the order for them to join him. Running up the ladder, his face set in grim detirmination, he caused a sudden panic among the heroic crew of longshoremen who incontinently took to their heels and like so many prairie dogs disappeared down their hole of a hatchway with Mr. Warley after them. He drove them back on deck and then drove them ashore, some of them jumping overboard and swimming for it. With the addition of two fire rafts our fleet was now completed and we proceded to the forts, where we anchored awaiting an opportunity to attack the enemy.[17]

The *Ivy,* a small tug mounting a brand new English Whitworth rifle, left the area of Forts Jackson and St. Philip (on the Mississippi approximately 75 miles below New Orleans) on October 8. She had been making daily scouts in the vicinity of the Head of Passes for some time and

Hollins knew from her reports that the blockading force there consisted of the *Richmond*, flagship, 26 guns; the *Vincennes* and *Preble*, sailing sloops, 22 guns each; and the *Water Witch*, steamer 5 guns. John Pope commanded the squadron.

The *Ivy*, arriving at the Head of Passes, commenced a preliminary engagement, shelling the Federals from a great distance. Pope's comments on the skirmish indicate the quality of the Whitworth gun:

It is evident that we are entirely at the mercy of the enemy. We are liable to be driven from here any moment, and, situated as we are, our position is untenable. I may be captured at any time by a pitiful little steamer mounting only one gun. The distance at which she was firing I should estimate at 4 miles, with heavy rifled cannon, throwing her shot and shell far beyond us. This may be an experiment to ascertain the range of our guns, which they now have, and of course will quickly avail themselves of the knowledge.[18]

On the morning of October 9, the *Calhoun*, *Jackson*, and *Tuscarora* left the forts. The *Manassas* was to have gone with them, but she stayed behind to repair a leak in a valve or condenser. She left on Oct. 10, a crowd on the levee cheering her on.[19]

Pre-battle orders directed the *Calhoun* to keep clear of the fray. With her walking-beam engines, she was considered too vulnerable to engage. The *Jackson*, a high-pressure paddle-wheeler, was ordered to stay as far behind as possible until the action started: she made so much noise that Hollins feared she would warn the Federals of the attack.[20]

Hollins' plan of battle called for the *Manassas* to lead the squadron into the Head of Passes in the pre-dawn darkness, make the initial attack, then signal the squadron in by firing a rocket. Accordingly, in the early hours of October 13, the *Manassas* pushed cautiously into the Head of Passes. Charles Austin, the first officer, piloted the ram. He knew this stretch of river well, but could see little of it out of the 4-inch opening in the hatch through which he peered.[21] Ahead of him, hidden in the darkness, the *Vincennes* lay near the western bank. To the east lay the *Richmond*, *Preble*, and *Water Witch*. The *Richmond* was taking coal from the schooner *Joseph H. Toone*. Also nearby was the prize schooner *Frolic*.

At 3:40 A.M. the master of the *Frolic* sighted the *Manassas* and shouted a warning to the Richmond: *"Richmond ahoy! There's a boat coming down the river on your port bow!"* No one aboard the *Richmond* heard: the noise of coaling operations drowned the shout.[22]

At about the same time, a midshipman aboard the *Preble* spotted the ironclad and went below to warn Commodore French. French had been on deck most of the night and had been sleeping in his clothes. As he followed the midshipman on deck he glanced out a gun port and saw "an indescribable object not 20 yards distant."[23]

Aboard the *Manassas*, First Officer Austin was taken by surprise when the *Richmond* loomed out of the fog in front of him. He cried to Engineer William E. Hardy, "Let her out, Hardy, let her out now!" Hardy piled tar, tallow, and sulphur into the furnace — anything to get a hotter fire and more steam.[24]

The *Manassas* struck with a jolt, crushing in the planking of the coal schooner and driving her into the *Richmond's* side. The Federal flagship hoisted a red danger light and beat "to quarters." A hawser from the schooner slid across the *Manassas'* turtle top, slicing off her smokestacks even with the deck. The ironclad drifted off and Austin spotted another ship. "Now let her out, Hardy," he called again, "and give it to her!" The engineer called back that the shock of ramming had broken a condenser, rendering one of her engines useless. The *Manassas* circled away.[25]

A midshipman scrambled up on top to fire the signal rocket. In his excitement he lit it, then held on. It roared, burned his hand, then zoomed down an open hatch into the ram's interior. Crewmen, thinking it a shell, stumbled over each other in their haste to get cover.[26]

Guns had begun to roar aboard the *Richmond*. Soon concentrated broadsides from all four ships screamed threaugh the area. None of the Federals knew where their attacker was. They fired blindly, hoping the noise would drive the iron beast away.

One of the *Manassas'* stacks had fallen over the vent, blocking it and driving the smoke inside. Engineer Hardy, realizing that the men would either suffocate or be driven out onto the exposed roof, grabbed an axe and headed for the top. As he brushed past Warley, the Lieutenant tried to stop him, but couldn't hold him. Austin, realizing that Hardy probably couldn't keep his footing on the roof while swinging an axe, followed him out. He held Hardy while the engineer cut several guys and dropped the smokestack overboard.[27]

The tiny tugs *Watson* and *Tuscarora* now steamed down, towing five blazing fire rafts. They set the rafts adrift to float down on the Federals, then hastily retreated. All five burning barges drifted aground near the east bank.

Heading upriver, the *Manassas* met the *Ivy*, under Captain Joseph Fry. Fry offered assistance in the form of a tow, which Warley declined. But a few minutes later the ironclad found herself aground and in need of help. The *Ivy* passed a cable and started pulling, but the cable broke. Another cable was passed and secured. It, too, broke. The *Ivy* pulled off to look for help. Instead, she found the

Tuscarora, also aground. It occurred to Fry that the Federals, if they moved upriver, could shell the grounded vessels into submission, so he headed down to stand them off.[28]

The blockaders, however, had no thoughts of launching a counter-offensive. Instead, they hauled off and headed for the open Gulf. The *Water Witch* and *Preble* crossed the bar with ease. The *Richmond* and *Vincennes* weren't so fortunate. They grounded hard, the *Vincennes* stern-on to any attack the Confederates might make, the *Richmond* in a position to make good use of her deadly broadside. But the Confederate attack faltered. Unsure of the situation and fearing to give his position away with signal lights, Hollins settled down to wait for dawn.

Commander Robert Handy, of the *Vincennes,* dispatched a note to John Pope aboard the *Richmond*:

We are aground. We have only two guns that will bear in the direction of the enemy. Shall I remain on board with my crippled ship and worn-out men? . . . would it not be better to leave the ship? Shall I burn her when I leave?

Pope's reply was negative:

It will be your duty to defend your ship to the last moment, and not to fire her, except it be to prevent her from falling into the hands of the enemy. I do not think the enemy will be down tonight, but in case they do, fight them to the last. You have boats enough to save all your men. I do not approve of your leaving your ship until every effort to defend her from falling into their hands is made.[29]

In an effort to get his ship afloat, Handy ordered thrown overboard fourteen 32-pounders, all his 32-pound shot, and 27 stand of grape. His efforts were in vain.[30]

As the sun rose the remainder of Hollins' flotilla steamed

downriver. They captured the crippled coal schooner and a cutter from the *Richmond* and took possession of a pile of lumber that the Federals had accumulated ashore. With this in hand, the Confederates opened a bombardment at long range. The blockaders replied, neither side scoring a damaging hit. Commander Handy had removed two bulkheads and pushed a brace of 8-inch guns into the *Vincennes'* stern to fire on the Rebels.[31] Pope threw whole broadsides upriver.

The *Richmond* ran up signal flags, signaling "get underway" to several ships outside the bar. Seaman Nathaniel P. Allen, stationed on the *Vincennes'* poop deck to assist in signaling, sighted the signal. He later reported: "I . . . saw a flag — blue, white, blue — and I knew it to be the No. 1 signal because I have studied the numbers on the paper inside the signal chest." He turned to the first lieutenant and reported: "The *Richmond* is signalizing," and stated that it was the No. 1 signal. The lieutenant looked at the signal book and reported to Handy: "It means to abandon ship." Handy sent most of his men to the *Water Witch*, then he and his officers boarded the *Richmond*.[12] He reported on board, the United States colors wrapped around his middle, with "In obedience to your signal, sir, I have abandoned my ship, leaving a slow match, connected with the magazine, burning." One of the *Richmond's* officers observed and recorded the resultant scene.

I shall never forget the expression on poor Captain Pope's face as he listened to this astonishing report. He was anything but a profane man in his daily habit, and I am sure the Recording Angel dropped a tear over the swear words with which our commander emphasized his reply.[33]

But when the *Vincennes* failed to explode, Pope sent

Handy back to his ship. A quartergunner on the *Vincennes* had lit the fuse and then, thinking better of it, had cut off the burning end and pitched it into the water before leaving.[34]

At 10:00 A.M. Commodore Hollins' squadron broke off the action and headed for New Orleans. Confederate shot and shell had smashed several small boats aboard the *Richmond,* but none had punctured the boilers or destroyed the engines. Captain Pope later found a bolt from the *Ivy's* Whitworth gun in his bureau drawer.[35] The Confederates sustained no damage.

The Richmond *Dispatch* published a communique sent by Hollins from Fort Jackson at 2:30 that afternoon:

Last night I attacked the blockaders with my little fleet. I succeeded, after a very short struggle, in driving them all aground on the South West bar, except the sloop-of-war *Preble,* which I sunk. I have captured a prize from them, and after I got them fast on the sand I peppered them well. There were no casualties on our side. It was a complete success.[36]

His reporting the sinking of the *Preble* came from Joseph Fry, who had thought that to be the vessel that the *Manassas* had rammed instead of the *Richmond*, and had not seen her outside the bar.

The Head of Passes foray decided nothing, but it gave the general morale of the city of New Orleans a tremendous lift. Hollins became somewhat of a local hero. Bands serenaded his headquarters at the St. Charles Hotel that night, and military units paused to offer their salutes as they marched by. Citizens later presented him with a beautiful set of colors.[37]

Those few privateersmen who had elected to stay with the *Manassas* for the battle were inducted in the Confederate Navy, along with their ship. Hardy was awarded the rank of 3rd assistant engineer and Austin was now master, not in line of promotion.[38] On December 13, Hollins officially received authority to purchase the confiscated *Manassas* for the Confederate States Navy.[39] He paid $100,000 for the ram, the amount that Stevenson's privateer company had raised to convert the vessel.[40]

On arriving at New Orleans, the Tifts contacted John Hughes at Algiers, across the river. He offered them space in his yard and the use of a sawmill, in common with himself, for $60 per day, and hands at $1.75 per day, and carpenters for $3 per day. Harrem & Co. at Algiers offered to build the *Mississippi's* hull for $147,000, but refused to be bound by a time limit. Hyde & Mackey offered the same terms for $125,000. When refused, the latter company offered ground in their yard at $60 per month, but without a sawmill. The Tifts failed to find any of these terms acceptable. In addition, all the shipyards were on the west side of the river, which necessitated the transportation of timber, iron, machinery, guns, and all other materials from the eastern side, thus creating undesirable delay and extra expense.

Wealthy New Orleans landowner Laurent Millandon soon came to the Tift's rescue: He offered river-front land on the eastern side, just north of the New Orleans corporate limit in Jefferson City. His tract consisted of approximately an acre between a paved street and the levee, and three acres between the levee and the river. He offered it, free of charge, to the Confederate Government for their use until February 1.

The Tifts immediately accepted, and began constructing a shipyard. With Millandon's permission they cut the levee, connecting all the land. An office was rented for $10 per month, a 12-horsepower sawmill was purchased for $3,200, and 200 sticks of timber were bought at 8 to 18 cents per running foot.[41] Most of the *Mississippi's* timber came from Ponchatoula, Louisiana and Summit, Mississippi, although the brothers traveled all over the southern Mississippi Valley in search of wood. Some of it came from as many as 700 miles away.

Leeds & Co., the largest iron works in New Orleans, was approached to build her machinery, but they were so swamped with previous government contracts that the best they could promise was delivery in four months. They asked $65,000 for the work. Jackson & Co. of the Patterson Ironworks promised it in three months for $45,000, plus a $5,000 bonus if they actually finished it in that time. The Tifts accepted this, and wrote Mallory on the particulars of her machinery. She would receive 11 double-return flue boilers, they told him, each 32 feet in length and 42 inches in diameter, with mat drums 24 inches in diameter, and a steam driver 30 inches in diameter and 41 feet in length, with all components complete. She would be powered by three engines, each with a cylinder 36 inches in diameter and a 2-foot stroking length. Two doctor engines were included to run pumps and blowers, one set for ventilators and one for pumping boiler bilges and supplying air for the furnaces. On September 27, the brothers purchased 150 tons of pig iron necessary for her machinery and other castings.

The Tifts found that they would be held to doing their business on a cash only basis: late payment of bills in the New Orleans area had dropped the Navy Department's credit rating to the cellar. In late February, Louisiana Governor Thomas O. Moore telegraphed Secretary of the Treasury Christopher C. Memminger:

The Navy Department here owes nearly a million. Its credit is stopped. If you wish I will place $2,000,000 on account of the war tax to the credit of the Government, so that the debts can be paid and the works continued.

Memminger declined with thanks, stating that "All the Navy requisitions on the Treasury have been passed, and the Treasury has sufficient notes to pay them."

The brothers went so far as to lecture Mallory on economics:

The economy and facility with which we can build and fit this vessel will depend in a great degree upon our always being prepared with money to purchase what may be necessary at the right time and pay all our contracts promptly.

There is no surer way to pecuniary ruin for governments or individuals than the discredit and consequent high price which are the sure results of a lack of punctuality with deferred payments.

We regret to learn that the credit of the Government is now suffering here from this cause.

Paymaster Felix Senac was soon supplied with a $75,000 Treasury draft, but he had great difficulty in cashing it.[42]

On September 27, Joseph Pierce,* acting naval constructor, arrived from Richmond to supervise the construction of the *Mississippi's* hull. He brought with him 17 ship's carpenter's. Three more, together with all the tools sent from Richmond, arrived the next day. Construction started on October 14.

Meanwhile, E. C. Murray had arrived in New Orleans and was working feverishly to get construction started on his *Louisiana*. Before leaving Richmond, he had contracted for lumber with a Mr. McRae in Florida. The blockade cut

---

* Pierce had been briefly connected with the *Virginia*, setting up the targets John Brooke had used for testing the Norfolk ironclad's armor plate.

off the coastal trade between New Orleans and Florida, however, and he was forced to buy the 1,700,000 feet of lumber needed for the craft from W. W. Cary at Lake Pontchartrain and from the New Orleans & Jackson Railroad. He purchased the steamer *Ingomar* for her engines and contracted with Robert Kirk's ironworks to pull them and place them aboard the *Louisiana*.

Murray set up his yard just south of the Tifts, the two sites separated only by a wooden fence. He stole some time on the brothers, arriving well after them, but laying the *Louisiana's* keel on October 15, the day after the first planks went down for the *Mississippi's* frameless hull.[43]

In late September, Commodore Hollins sent to the Tifts a civilian named Borough — an assistant to First Assistant Engineer John H. Loper at the navy yard — for the purpose of making the drawings and specifications necessary for the *Mississippi's* construction, and to superintend the construction and placement of her machinery. The brothers, at Borough's request, recommended him for the post of first assistant engineer in the navy, but soon withdrew their recommendation when it became apparent that he had no idea of what he was doing. On October 5 he was fired, being replaced by E. M. Ivens of the Tredegar Iron Yorks.[44]

It was soon called to the Tifts' attention that the steam machinery they had contracted for might not be sufficient to push a ship of the *Mississippi's* size at the projected 14 knots. They conferred with Confederate engineers, workmen at Leeds, and Mr. S. Saunders, chief engineer for the Southern Steamship Co. All agreed that the boiler capacity provided for in the original plans was far from enough to provide the desired horsepower. Ivens computed an expanded boiler plan, sent it to Chief Engineer James H. Warner at the Columbus (Ga.) naval works, received his approval, and presented it to Patterson's. The final plan called for 16 boilers of the original dimensions (30 feet by 42 inches), set in two rows amidship. The addition lengthened the ship by 20 feet, bringing her to 280 feet overall. The Tifts wrote Mallory that ". . . the efficiency of the vessel will be greatly increased by her greater steaming power, and she can carry two more heavy guns." The completion date was moved up to January 31.[45]

The angle of her casemate was also changed. Original plans had called for it to be inclined at an angle of 36°. Further calculations convinced them that a slope of only 30° would suffice.

On November 6, the entire shipyard force of New Orleans went on strike for a dollar raise in wages. Murray persuaded some of his force to remain by promising to pay whatever increase was asked if it went into effect, while at Millandon's, all but the 20 Richmond ship's carpenters walked off the job. The next day 40 strikers appeared at Millandon's and forced the Richmond men to quit work, then marched to Murray's to threaten the workers on the *Louisiana*.

Major General Mansfield Lovell, military commander of the New Orleans area, had, meanwhile, ordered the arrest of several of the strike's ringleaders. Most of New Orleans was out of sympathy with the strikers, wishing to see the ironclads finished. Hollins' little flotilla was soon to be taken from New Orleans to go into combat upriver, and the citizens wanted some protection on the water. New Orleans' shipbuilders were almost unanimous in their decision not to give the raise, to hold off until the strikers were starved into going back to work. But the Tifts and Murray wanted their ships finished. After six days without work, Asa sent constructor Pierce to a workers' meeting at John Hughes yard. In the names of both Murray and the Tifts, he offered the dollar increase and work on the ironclads resumed.[46] But other delays threatened the completion of the vessels. Local militia company commanders had a penchant for stealing the shipyard workers to attend company drills. Murray put the problem before the Committee of Public Safety — a local vigilance committee composed of the leaders in New Orleans society — who quickly got exemptions for shipyard workers from Governor Moore. The local company commanders presisted, however, resorting to arrest to get the workers to drill. After the *Virginia's* historic combats, the *Louisiana's* future commander — Charles F. McIntosh — visited the yard and added a five-day delay by demanding that the ironclad's gunports be cut oval rather than square.[47]

More than 200 men returned to work on the *Mississippi* after the strike. The Tift brothers, in a note to Secretary Mallory dated November 21, left a picture of the ironclad under construction.

We are progressing very well with our structure; today we will complete the fourth streak of timber all around, the next week we will have the sides up to 8 feet. We fasten, calk, paint, and finish perfectly as we advance.[48]

On December 26 they began laying the gun deck. The Tift brothers began looking for armament and Hollins suggested that guns cast in New Orleans might be procured more cheaply and quickly than those cast in Richmond which would have to be transported. When tested, however, they proved unable to stand even ordinary examination firing. In addition to infeiror casting and sub-standard gun metal, the rifles cast there were rifled too short and the grooves cut too deep, so that the projectiles failed to take the rifled spin. The result was poor accuracy, and the deep grooves allowed so much windage that the rifle's range was considerably less than that of a smooth bore.[49] Consequently, the ironclad's guns were ordered from Tredegar's. Her ordnance plan called for four 7-inch Brooke rifles for bow and stern chasers, her broadsides to be composed of large-caliber shell guns. John Roy was called in to make her chassis and carriages.

To date $375,000 had been expended on the *Mississippi*. The bothers had also, by this time, begun work on the two smaller ironclads, to cost approximately $150,000 each. John Hughes & Co. had, meantime, landed a contract for a large ironclad, its cost estimated at $1,000,000.[50]

Construction lagged on the *Louisiana*, delayed for want of lumber and iron. Murray's work crews sat idle for over two weeks, waiting for iron to arrive to start the armoring. He had contracted, soon after his arrival from Richmond, with W. Folger & Co. to supply rolled armor plate through the Cumberland Iron Works. The presence of Federal gunboats on the Tennessee rivers, however, prevented the execution of the contract. Attempts to procure iron at Baton Rouge failed, and he finally purchased 500 tons of railroad T-iron, at $65 per ton, from the Vicksburg & Shreveport Railroad. A dispute then arose over the ownership of the iron and, when Commander John K. Mitchell (then commanding the New Orleans naval station) and General Lovell failed to take a hand in the matter, Murray took the problem to the Committee on Public Safety. They had approached both Murray and the Tift brothers with offers to assist in any way possible, so Murray took advantage of the offer in settling the ownership question. They told him to take the iron, promising to back the action with their own influence "and 2,000 muskets," if necessary. When Kirk lagged in transferring the *Ingomar's* engines, the committee again stepped in, prodding him into action.[51]

Armament for the craft created a problem. Extensive

ordnance works had yet to be set up in the Confederacy, Tredegar's gun-casting facilities were already overloaded with orders, and the great supply of heavy guns captured at Norfolk had dwindled out — already claimed for coastal and river fortifications all over the Confederacy. Several guns — four 32-pounders, two banded rifles of medium caliber, and two new rifles of large caliber — had been sent to Memphis to arm the ironclads *Arkansas* and *Tennessee,* which were being built there, but the ships were not yet ready to be armed. Murray, therefore, requested that these guns be shipped to New Orleans for use aboard the *Louisiana.* They were brought down and had just been gotten aboard when several army officers came aboard and commandeered them. Murray complained to Hollins, who telegraphed Mallory, who wrote Secretary of War Randolph, who ordered them returned.[52] General Duncan, who had taken the guns for the forts, protested to Randolph, but to no avail.

From both Washington and Richmond, men and ships were being manipulated to set the stage for a clash at New Orleans. A fleet of Union ironclads and wooden rams left St. Louis, intent on descending the Mississippi and securing the adjacent land for the Union as far down as possible. In Washington and New York, plans were being discussed and ships being bought and built for a thrust up the Mississippi from the Gulf. David G. Farragut was assigned to command the Gulf expedition.

From Richmond, the War Department had assigned Mansfield Lovell to command the New Orleans district. On arrival in the Crescent City, Lovell found the district stripped of practically every soldier and piece of war material that had been produced in the area: it was all going north to Kentucky, Virginia, or Tennessee. His pleas to leave New

Orleans something with which to defend herself were met with demands for more men and supplies.

In February Secretary Mallory, against protests by Lovell and Commodore Hollins, ordered the New Orleans mosquito fleet north to New Madrid, Missouri, in a vain attempt to halt the southward push of the Federal ironclads.[53] Government directives continued to drain the delta area, sending men and equipment northward.

The major defenses of New Orleans consisted of two strong fortifications — Forts Jackson and St. Philip — situated on either side of the Mississippi below the city. Fort St. Philip was considered the stronger of the two. Built by the Spaniards, she was solidly constructed of brick and rock, then covered over with sod. Fifty-two guns were mounted there. Fort Jackson, a brick and mortar fortress mounting 75 guns, had been built by Union General John G. Barnard, author of *Seacoast Defenses*, who gave Farragut a few tips on reducing the work.[54] Both forts were under the command of General Johnson Kelly Duncan.

On his way to New Orleans in mid-September, General Lovell had paused in Centreville, Virginia, to confer with General Pierre G. T. Beauregard. The creole had voiced the opinion that, unless the river was effectively obstructed, a Federal fleet would be able to dash past the forts and rush the city. Lovell, on his arrival in New Orleans, inspected the lower river and decided that a large chain would make an effective obstruction. A group of speculators bought a heavy chain in Mobile at 5 cents per pound, reselling it to the New Orleans authorities at 15 cents per pound. On the last day of September the chain went across the river, stretching between the two forts and supported by the hulks of six sunken schooners.[55]

In early January, David Farragut left New York, bound

for New Orleans. On the 20th of that month Union Secretary of the Navy Welles wrote him at Hampton Roads:

Destroy the armed barriers which these deluded people have raised up against the power of the United States Government, and shoot down those who war against the Union, but cultivate with cordiality the first returning reason which is sure to follow your success.[56]

On February 2, Farragut sailed from Hampton Roads, heading south. On the 5th he touched at Port Royal; on the 11th he was at Key West, and he arrived at Ship Island, off the Mississippi's mouth, on the 20th.[57]

Meanwhile, on February 6, the ironclad *Louisiana* had been launched. A mass of people packed the levee and cheered as the big ironclad, flying Confederate and Louisiana flags, slid broadside into the river.

The *Mississippi*, by this time, had her woodwork completed and her boilers were being installed.[58] The Tifts wrote to Schofield & Markham, Atlanta, on the subject of iron plates. They were informed that the company couldn't supply them, as it would entail changing their rollers to turn out plates of the desired thickness. A letter from William P. Williamson at Norfolk stated that the Tredegar works were now equipped to roll three-inch plates, but a check with the Richmond foundry revealed them too busy to take on any more work. Secretary Mallory stated that the Navy Department was unable to supply armor and suggested that, if good armor plate were unobtainable, railroad iron should be substituted. Nelson Tift, unwilling to accept an inferior grade of armor, visited Atlanta. Monetary inducements persuaded Schofield & Markham to change their rollers to do the job, and the Tifts contracted to buy just under 1,000 tons at 6¼ cents per pound drilled for fastenings, or 6 cents per pound undrilled. Immediately after news of the contract became public, Col. Beggs of the Committee on Public Safety entrained for Atlanta to rush work on the armor. At the same time, another committee member left for Richmond to hurry Tredegars, who had agreed to provide the ironclad's central propeller shaft. Her braces, bolts, and iron fastening had already been purchased, found in sufficient quantity in New Orleans, Mobile, Chattanooga, Macon, and Atlanta.[59]

In later communications, Secretary Mallory urged the brothers to move with all possible speed to complete the *Mississippi*. "Work night and day to get your ship done, without regard to expense." In a telegram: "Strain every nerve to finish ship. Expend money to encourage mechanics if essential to speed completion." Again; "Cannot you hire night gangs for triple wages?"[60]

Toward the end of February, constructor Pierce began voicing doubts about the stability of the ground on which the *Mississippi* was being built. He felt that the rising river and heavy rains would flood and soften the ground on which the *Mississippi's* foundation had been laid. If the foundation settled, launching the ironclad would be rough work. Accordingly, he asked the Tifts to launch immediately. They made an examination of the grounds, found the foundation stable, and told Pierce there was no need to launch the vessel.

The *Mississippi* needed three propeller shafts. Her outside shafts, 40 feet long and 9 inches in diameter, were originally to be forged by Ward & Co. of Nashville. In a letter to Nelson Tift they agreed to put up the necessary air furnace and hammer and make the shafts for $1500 each. Brother Nelson telegraphed back, authorizing them to begin as soon as possible and offering a $500 bonus for early completion. A few weeks later Wards replied by let-

ter stating that they couldn't, after all, make the shafts. The
Tifts went to Clark & Co., New Orleans, who were retooling
to cast Armstrong guns for the government and were, consequently, putting up an air furnace and a large trip hammer. The brothers asked Clarke to build his furnace large
enough to take their shafts. He agreed, and began forging
them in March, as soon as the furnace was completed. Leeds
agreed to finish them on their lathe.

The center shaft, 50 feet in length and 9 inches in diameter, was to be prepared by the Tredegar works in Richmond. They pulled two shafts from the steamer *Glen Cove*
on the lower James, brought them up to Richmond, and
began work on them. From the very start work went slowly.
The shafts were old, pitted, and rusty, and had to be re-
conditioned. They had no trip hammer, so the usually
quick and simple process of forging the shafts together had
to be done by hand. Fifty men worked in the project, working days, nights, and Sundays. The Tifts requested that Mr.
McPherson, foreman at the Gosport machine shop, be sent
to mold the ironclad's propellers.[61] On January 18, Secretary Mallory informed the Tifts that the *Mississippi's* center
shaft was still at the foundry and would be shipped as soon
as possible. On February 22, the Tifts wrote Richmond,
bemoaning the work holdup caused by the delay in delivery. "It is unfortunate we have not the shaft, as we could
put up one of the engines at once." There followed, throughout March, communications from Mallory promising the
missing shaft.

March 15: "The Tredegar Works have disappointed us
terribly. The shaft is not ready, and although
promised from day to day, may not be ready
for a week. If you can supply its place do so
immediately."[62]

March 17: "The shaft will leave in two days . . ."

March 20: "Shaft leaves here in two days . . ."

March 22: "The shaft leaves on Monday morning, the 24th, complete; a beautiful piece of work."

On the evening of April 3 the center shaft arrived in New Orleans. It was sent to a machine shop, where its couplings and the first of McPherson's propellers were fitted.

Orders dated March 21, 1862, directed Commander Arthur Sinclair, a veteran of 39 years' service in the Old Navy, to proceed from Norfolk to New Orleans to take command of the *Mississippi*. On his arrival he found that he would take command only after the ship was launched. Until then, the brothers would take into consideration any suggestions that he could make, but they retained complete control over the ironclad and would allow no interference.[63]

On March 27, constructor Pierce sent the Tifts a note, again calling attention to the rising river, softening ground, and "the accumulation of the immense weight" of the *Mississippi*.

I deem it actually necessary to launch the ship . . . The interest of the Government demands it. The water is still rising, and I fear the ship will settle on her ways; and if this should be the case, we will have trouble to get her off. Again, if she was afloat I would put on the iron, which is not prudent to do now. The foundation is getting softer every day, and I can see no reason why she will not settle.

The Tifts remonstrated, stating that, if the *Mississippi* were launched, they would have much difficulty installing the propeller shafts, at least one of which was still at the Leeds foundry. Reporting to Mallory on the matter, the brothers stated that, from the first, they had doubted the stability of the ground, and had immediately constructed launchways, completely finishing the hull as they built so that, in the event of such an emergency as that forecasted by Pierce, the ship could be quickly launched. They ordered Pierce to keep everything in readiness to launch the ship at the first sign of weakening ground, but directed him to keep her on the ways for as long as possible, until the center shaft was installed and connected, at least, "so as to be able to control the ship by steam after she was launched." The news of the dispute reached the ears of the Committee on Public Safety. A sub-committee was formed to investigate the matter, and constructor Pierce, E. C. Murray, Comms. John K. Mitchell and Arthur Sinclair, and John Hughes were called to appear at an impromptu hearing and give their opinions on the subject. All advised against launching the vessel at that date. Asa Tift, on April 7, was called before the committee to give his views. Unconvinced by the opinions of everyone of any authority to speak on the subject, the sub-committee censured the brothers strongly. Their reputation in New Orleans was badly damaged by the incident.[64]

In early April, with the Union army and navy massing off the Mississippi's mouth, Secretary of War George W. Randolph raised a storm by ordering the *Louisiana* up the river to join the few Confederate gunboats in staving off the Union fleets above Memphis. General Lovell fired off a telegram to the War Department:

With forty vessels in the lower river, please protest in my name against sending the *Louisiana* up the river.

Four days later he telegraphed Randolph that 27 vessels were in sight of the forts and that "the enemy is preparing for a formidable attack."[65]

Louisiana Governor Thomas O. Moore telegraphed President Davis on the subject of the *Louisiana's* removal:

Commodore Whittle has orders from Secretary Navy to send the *Louisiana* to Tennessee. Duncan and Higgins both telegraph she is absolutely a necessity at the forts for the safety of New Orleans, and that it is suicidal to send her elsewhere. With the enemy's plan of attack, our safety may depend upon her timely arrival there. I earnestly beg her destination may be changed, and protest against her being sent up the river. Excitement among the people great on the subject.

The President replied:

The wooden vessels are below; the iron gunboats are above. The forts should destroy the former if they attempt to ascend.

The *Louisiana* may be indispensible to check the descent of the iron boats. The purpose is to defend the city and valley: the only question is as to the best mode of effecting the object. Military men must decide, and today their discretionary power has been enlarged.[66]

On April 18, Commander David Porter's "bummers," schooners mounting 13-inch mortars, opened fire on Fort Jackson. They anchored behind a neck of wooded land, hidden from the Confederates, and rained their big shells on the fort by directions from lookouts in their mastheads.

As the bummers opened their fire, attempts were being made, almost a hundred miles upriver, to launch the *Mississippi*. Steamers strained to pull her into the water, but no amount of tugging would budge her. The next day purchases and levers were added, and the tugs tied on with 14-inch hawsers. As soon as pressure was applied to the levers the big ship began to move, sliding into the river before the tugs had time to take up the slack in their hawsers. A foreman told the Tifts that he and two workmen had inspected the launch ways the night after the first attempted launch and had found that a locust pin had been driven through a way and into the ironclad's hull, holding the ship to her ways while the tugs tried to get her off. They had drilled it out, they said, allowing the ship to slide free the next day. The Tifts took it to be an attempted sabotage, the work of Union spies and agents. Pierce, however, scoffed at the story, stating that he had inspected the way that night and had found no such thing.

After the *Mississippi's* launching Captain William C. Whittle, Sr., now commanding the New Orleans Navy Yard, ordered the *Louisiana* sent down to the forts. Commander John K. Mitchell had been moved to flag officer, replacing Commodore Hollins as commander of the depleted Confederate fleet. The old warrior, ordered to defend the upper Mississippi, had made such a nuisance of himself with his pleas to return with the fleet to defend New Orleans that he had been called to Richmond, where he would spend the rest of the war sitting on a board to examine midshipmen.

Commander Mitchell's fleet had been whittled to the *McRae, Manassas,* and *Louisiana.* He chose the *Louisiana,* under Commander Charles F. McIntosh, as his flagship.

The *Louisiana,* as she prepared to depart for the forts, was still unfinished. The steering propellers, situated under her quarters, had not been installed; most of her guns were unmounted, and her internal finishings were incomplete.

On the move downstream her paddle wheels, situated amidships — one before the other — were tested. The results were not encouraging. The wheel houses hadn't been caulked: water came gushing through cracks in the house and cascaded down open hatches that hadn't been provided with combings, flooding the magazines and shell rooms. Worse, the ironclad's engines, never intended to propel such a heavy weight of wood and iron, couldn't supply enough power for the big ship to stem the Mississippi's current when she was turned against it.

When the new ironclad anchored at Fort St. Philip, other oversights in construction were revealed. Once her anchors were let go they were hard to weigh — no one had thought to install capstans and they could only be raised with deck tackle. One, too heavy to raise, had to be slipped and lost.[67] The chains of her stern anchor created a threat to her rudders and would foul the propellers. Both rudders and propellers were unprotected, inviting disability by enemy ramming or shot. She could not, at the moment, even serve as a floating battery — those guns that were mounted had been fixed in such a way as to prevent their firing.

Carpenters and mechanics had been at work on the ironclad on her entire cruise down the river. As soon as she anchored, her skeleton crew joined in the work. A gang was borrowed from the *McRae* and the task of dismounting and remounting the heavy guns, amid a swarm of carpenters and mechanics and on a deck littered with beams and planks, was begun.

Lieutenant John Wilkinson, one of the *Louisiana's* officers, took the opportunity to journey downriver under a flag of truce to see an old friend, De Camp, now commanding a sloop of war in Farragut's fleet. The lieutenant returned convinced that the Federals could take the forts and New Orleans any time they wished.[68]

Early the next morning General Duncan arranged a brief meeting with Commander Mitchell. The general asked that the *Louisiana* be taken below the obstructions and moored on the Fort St. Philip side of the river, "where her fire could dislodge the mortar boats from behind the point of woods and give sufficient respite to Fort Jackson to repair *in extenso.*" Mitchell explained that the ironclad's motive power would not be complete and sufficient to propel her reliably for several days. He told Duncan that the *Louisiana* could not be looked for to act "as an aggressive steamer" and be brought into action on the offensive.[69] Mitchell asked for some men to bolster his flagship's thin crew and Duncan sent aboard Captain T. H. Hutton's company of the Crescent Artillery, a detachment of Lt. Dixon's artillery, and a company of Captain Ryan's sharpshooters.[70]

By the time the army artillerists arrived the ironclad's guns had been remounted. Gun drills began and another fault became apparent: the gun ports had been cut too small. They allowed only 5° elevation, giving the guns a maximum range of 2,000 yards. The *Louisiana's* battery consisted of:

Bow: two 9-inch smoothbores, one 7-inch rifle.
Starboard: three 32-pounder rifles, two 8-inch smoothbores.
Port: four 32-pounder rifles, one 9-inch smoothbore.
Stern: two 8-inch smoothbores, one 7-inch rifle.

The *Louisiana* was no comfort ship. Crew's quarters proved to be inadequate and uncomfortable. Officers' quarters were non-existent. They slept under tents pitched on the *Louisiana's* casemate roof or aboard the ironclad's two tenders, *Landis* and *W. Burton*.

Later in the day, General Duncan dispatched a message to Commander Mitchell, again asking him to go below and engage the Federal mortar fleet. Mitchell answered immediately, declining to move his ship, but stating that "the very moment I can venture to face our enemy with any reasonable chance of success, be assured, General, I will do it, and trust that the result will show you that I am now pursuing the right course."[71] Duncan returned:

It is of vital importance that the present fire of the enemy should be withdrawn from us, which you alone can do. This can be done in the manner suggested this morning, under cover of our guns, while your work on the boat can be carried on in safety and security. Our position is a critical one, dependent entirely on the powers of endurance of our casemates, many of which have been completely shattered and are crumbling away by repeated shocks; and therefore I respectfully but earnestly again urge my suggestion of this morning on your notice. Our magazines are also in danger.[72]

On receiving this, Mitchell called a conference with Commander McIntosh, Executive Officer George S. Shryock, and Lieutenants Thomas B. Huger of the *McRae* and A. F. Warley of the *Manassas*. All expressed the opinion that it would be unwise to send the *Louisiana* into combat before completion.

In the midst of this Mitchell received a nearly insubordinate communication from Captain John Stevenson, now commanding the army's collection of armed riverboats known as the River Defense Fleet. General Lovell had told the Captain he would take his orders from the navy, and Stevenson immediately rebelled, writing to Mitchell:

Every officer and man on the river-defense expedition joined it with the condition that it was to be independent of the Navy, and that it would not be governed by the regulations of the Navy, or be commanded by naval officers. In the face of the enemy I will not say more. I will cooperate with you and do nothing without your approbation, and will endeavor to carry out your wishes to the best of my ability, but in my own way as to the details and the handling of my boats. But I expect the vessels under my charge to remain a separate command. All orders for their movements addressed to me will be promptly executed, if practicable, and I undertake to be responsible for their efficiency when required. I suppose this is all that is intended by the order of Major-General Lovell or that will be expected of me by you.[73]

Mitchell asked Stevenson to keep several of his rams on guard below the chain that night. Stevenson refused, explaining that he had no confidence in his commanders.[74]

Late that night the gunboats *Pinola* and *Itasca* quietly made their way upriver with the intention of opening a gap in the chain obstruction. An explosive charge intended to blow out a large section of the links failed and Confederate sentries ashore discovered the Federals and opened fire. In backing off, one of the gunboats fouled the chain, carrying away a good part of it and leaving a gap large enough for Farragut's warships to get through.[75]

On April 23, the *Manassas*, along with her tender, the *Phoenix*, arrived and anchored near the forts. The *McRae* soon took up a position nearby.

Mitchell sent a reply to Duncan's note of the previous day, reporting his decision not to engage the enemy. He added:

I know the importance to the safety of Forts Jackson and St. Philip and the city of New Orleans of having this vessel in proper condition before seeking an encounter with the enemy. If he seeks one or attempts the passage of the forts before this vessel is ready, I shall meet him, however unprepared I may be. We have an additional force of mechanics from the city this morning, and I hope that by tomorrow night the motive power of the *Louisiana* will be ready, and that in the meantime her battery will be in place and other preparations will be completed, so as to enable her to act against the enemy. When ready, you will be immediately advised.[76]

Mitchell then departed in a small boat for a personal reconnaissance downriver, in preparation for an attack on the "bummers."

General Johnson Duncan, sensing the nearness of a major attack, would not wait for "tomorrow night." He telegraphed General Lovell, asking him to put pressure on Mitchell through Captain Whittle. Lovell, soon after his arrival in New Orleans in 1861, had asked President Davis and the Secretary of War for overall command of both the army and navy at New Orleans, and had been refused. He probably wished mightily that the answer had been "yes" as he quarreled with Whittle.

"I am satisfied that by placing the *Louisiana* on the Fort St. Philip side, about a half mile below the raft, where she would be under the protection of the cross fire of both forts, she would enfilade the position of the enemy's fleet and drive them off, when the men in the forts could get some rest and make repairs," Lovell asserted.

"I have confidence in the officers in command of our fleet below," countered Whittle, "and I do not like to interfere with them."

"Mitchell has already refused to make the desired change," Lovell stated.

"The vessel isn't entirely ready with her motive power," Whittle explained, "and by placing her there I am afraid she will be lost."

"I don't ask that the *Louisiana* be sent down amid the enemy's fleet," Lovell continued, "but that she be towed down and placed in position as a battery. And the necessity is such that it will be better to lose the *Louisiana* than the city of New Orleans."[77] Reluctantly, Whittle scratched out a telegram and handed it to Lovell:

Can you not occupy a position below Fort St. Philip, so as to enfilade the mortar boats of the enemy and give time to the garrison to repair damage at Fort Jackson: See General Duncan on the subject. Higgins will go and point out the position. As I understand it, it is covered by the fire of the two forts, and would require that the bomb vessels should be readjusted to get your range. Strain a point to effect this.[78]

Lovell handed the message back and Whittle asked: "Will that do?"

"Nothing," said Lovell, "short of placing the *Louisiana* in the position indicated will answer my purpose. I am going down in a special boat to the forts this afternoon. Why don't you come and judge for yourself?" Whittle declined. There was too much in the office that demanded his attention, he told the General.[79]

Just about 11:00 P.M. Commander Mitchell telegraphed Whittle that he would move against the Union Navy the next night. Lt. George Shryock went ashore to inform General Duncan of this.[80]

"Tell Commander Mitchell that there will be no tomorrow for New Orleans unless he immediately takes up the position assigned to him with the *Louisiana*," Higgins replied coldly. "If he does not do so the city is gone, and he will be responsible to the country for its loss. The forts are powerless to prevent it."[81]

The mortars, firing their ponderous projectiles in complete safety, continued to eat away at the nerves of the Fort Jackson garrison. A perfect shower of the huge shells poured in and around the fortification, visible from the time they climbed above the trees until they fell, buried themselves, and exploded. Casualties were slight, but the continuous concussion of so many great shells brought mortar crumbling from between bricks, weakening casemates, and shattering the morale of those who had to endure the continuous explosion of the shells. Clarence Cary, midshipman assigned to the *Mississippi*, paid a brief visit to the fort in the midst of Porter's bombardment, endured the shelling for an hour, and took his leave. Rowing back up the river alone, under fire for a mile and a half, he was surprised to come upon an alligator who had been struck in the head by a piece of shell "and was dying under protest."[82]

That evening Duncan sent a message to Mitchell, asking him to "Please keep the river well lit up with fire rafts tonight, as the attack may be made at any time."[83] Mitchell sent Acting Master Charles B. Fairbanks downriver in Launch No. 6. He was to fire his boat-howitzer and send up a rocket if the Federals made an advance.[84]

Toward midnight Lieutenant H. B. Caldwell of the U.S. gunboat *Itasca* was rowed up the river to the chain, eluding Fairbanks, to make sure the gap hadn't been repaired. It hadn't.[85]

At 3:30 Duncan dispatched a final note to Mitchell:

As I anticipated, and informed you yesterday, the enemy are taking up their positions at the present moment, with their large ships, on the Fort St. Philip shore, to operate against Fort Jackson. They are placing themselves boldly, with their lights at their mastheads. You are assuming a fearful responsibility if you do not come at once to our assistance with the *Louisiana* and the fleet. I can say no more.[86]

The movement was more than just an operation against Fort Jackson. At 2:00 A.M. two red lanterns were hoisted to the *Hartford's* mizzen peak and the fleet, guided by the *Cayuga*, raised anchor and steamed off, heading for New Orleans. Sailors grumbled because Farragut hadn't allowed them a grog ration before battle.

Shortly after 3:30 A.M., Sargeant Herman in the water

battery at Fort Jackson sighted the dim shapes of Farragut's war fleet moving through the darkness. He informed Captain William B. Robertson.[87] Acting Master Fairbanks, downriver, had seen the Federal navy on the move. Instead of sounding the alarm, he had deserted to the swamps. Rumors later filtered up to Commander Mitchell that he had been tracked down by several staunch Confederates and killed for his treachery, but he was later reported as arriving with the New Orleans military refugees at the Jackson Naval Station. From there he disappeared from the pages of history.[88]

At 3:40 A.M. the water battery roared the first salutation to the advancing Northern navy. Forts Jackson and St. Philip joined fire, guns at each fortress stuttering one by one into activity. Between the first few shots came the sounds that went with servicing the great guns — shouted commands, the slap of wood rammer and swab handles in gun barrels, metal shot being pushed home, and guns elevating, traversing, being run in and out. Gun after gun came alive to join the fray and in minutes the first stammer of fire had turned to a rolling, thundering roar directed at the vague shapes now probing for the opening in the chain. Muzzle flashes illuminated walls and bastions, cast quick reflections on a rushing black river. Smoke began to gather, billow, and roll. Said Captain Robertson:

I do not believe there ever was a grander spectacle witnessed before in the world than that displayed during the great artilllery duel which then followed. The mortar-shells shot upward from the mortar-boats, rushed to the apexes of their flight, flashing the lights of their fuses as they revolved, paused an instant, and then descended upon our works like a hundred meteors, or burst in mid-air, hurling their jagged fragments in every direction. The guns on both sides kept up a continual roar for nearly an hour, without a moment's intermission, and produced a shimmering illumination . . . beautiful and grand . . . in its effects upon the eye . . .[89]

The flickering light of the muzzle flashes, coupled with the constant movement of the Federal fleet, made the ships almost impossible to hit.

Five minutes after the first shots from the water battery, the lead gunboat — *Cayuga* — drew abreast of Fort St. Philip and began the Union end of the engagement with charges of grape and canister.

Just after 3:00 A.M. General Lovell had arrived from New Orleans to confer with Duncan and inspect the forts. He left by steamer as the guns began, convinced that the city couldn't be held more than 24 hours. "I was well aware," he later stated, "that my batteries of thirty-two-pounders at the lower levees, manned by inexperienced troops, could not detain for any length of time the heavy ships of war of the enemy armed with nine- and eleven-inch guns."[90] E. C. Murray had been on the river, coming down on the transport *Illinois* with a load of supplies for the *Louisiana*. As the guns began the steamer put about and fled back upriver.

As the first guns spoke, Chief Engineer Dearning — Hardy had been transferred to the *Turcarora* — began building a hotter fire under the *Manassas'* boilers: plenty of steam would soon be needed. The ironclad's tender, *Phoenix*, passed a line and pulled the *Manassas'* bow out into the stream. Warley called for steam and the ironclad advanced, gliding through the blackness toward a Federal ship advancing upriver from the shell-streaked area of the forts. The next instant the lieutenant was calling on Dearning to reverse the engines as the River Defense ram *Resolute* crossed the ironclad's path, fleeing upriver with all possible haste. The *Manassas'* bow collided with the *Resolute's* wheelhouse and, as the two ships lay entangled, the Federal slipped by and poured a destructive broadside into the wooden ram. By the time the *Manassas* could break clear, the Federal was gone.

Warley brought the *Manassas* cautiously back into the main stream and slipped downriver, advancing on a big Union sidewheeler steaming diagonally across the water. She was the U.S.S. *Mississippi,* aboard which Warley had made his last cruise with the United States Navy. Pilot William T. Levine pointed her blunt nose and the *Manassas,* with the backing of a swift flood current and the urging of her own propellers, rushed the big Federal.

Aboard the *Mississippi*, artist William Waud, clinging to the foretop, called down to Lt. George Dewey: "Here is a queer-looking customer on our port bow." Dewey espied "what appeared like a back of an enormous turtle, painted lead color."[91] The *Mississippi* put her helm to starboard in an unsuccessful attempt to run the *Manassas* down. She was undoubtedly faster and more agile than the sluggish iron-clad, but was working against the current while the Confederate ran with it. Warley had intended to strike the big Federal's wheelhouse but, in the darkness, pilot Levine's aim was poor. The ironclad struck a glancing blow on the *Mississippi's* quarter, firing her cannon at the same time. The ramming crushed in a four-strake section of planking 7 feet long and 4 inches deep, shearing the heads off 50 copper bolts.[92] The shell came to rest in the *Mississippi's* cabin.[93]

The Federal complained of the ramming by way of a broadside, thrown over the *Manassas'* rounded roof. She then steamed away into the darkness, from all appearances unruffled by her encounter with the long-dreaded ram.

The *Louisiana,* her anchors too difficult to handle, had been moored to the shore, tied in such a position as to render only her bow and starboard batteries effective. With half her full firepower, she commenced firing as the first of Farragut's gunboats appeared, shooting holes in nearly every ship to come within sight. The *Brooklyn* caught one of her shells just a foot above the water line. When Union sailors dug it out later they found that it had failed to explode because the Confederates, in their haste, had forgotten to remove the lead patch covering the fuse. Had it exploded, "it would have blown the whole bow off, and the *Brooklyn* would have gone to the bottom."[94]

An unidentified Union sloop turned lazily toward the *Louisiana,* coming to rest with a thump against the ironclad's bow. McIntosh, thinking they intended to carry the ship by boarding, led a crew to the top to fight them. The sloop, instead, unleashed a heavy broadside at point-blank range. Solid shot rang against the casemate front, denting, twisting, and bending the railroad iron armor, but failing to penetrate. Grape and canister swept the casemate roof, mercilessly cutting down McIntosh and his men. Had the *Louisiana's* gun ports been cut large enough, gunners could have depressed her heavy bow battery and sent solid shot through the bottom of the Federal intruder. Instead, the Confederates had to be content to send their shot and shell crashing through their antagonist above the water line.[95]

The stretch of river immediately above and below the forts had become an inferno, almost all the action concentrated in that area. Clouds of smoke rolled and billowed, luridly illuminated by muzzle flashes, burning bonfires ashore, and flames rising from the hulks of the River Defense Fleet: almost every ram in the army's fleet had been beached and burned by her captain. A big orange moon had risen, but the rolling smoke obscured it from view.

Farragut said of it later: "The smoke was so dense that it was only now and then we could see anything but the flash of the cannon and the blaze of the fire rafts. The passing of Forts Jackson and St. Philip was one of the most awful sights I ever saw."[96]

The *Manassas*, meanwhile, was continuing her futile attempts to halt the Union advance. First Officer Frank Harris spotted the *Pensacola* steaming upriver and called for a full head of steam to ram. As the *Manassas* closed, the *Pensacola's* executive officer, Lt. F. A. Roe, spotted her. The Federal turned quickly, side-stepping the ramming and, as she slid past, fired her after-pivot gun almost in Warley's face. The shot cut off the *Manassas'* flagstaff.[97]

With most of Farragut's fleet now past and steaming triumphantly for New Orleans, Lieutenant Warley determined to attack David Porter's mortar fleet below the forts. The schooners were lying at anchor with steam down and would be easy targets, Warley reasoned, while Farragut's gunboats and sloops were almost all impossible to catch. The *Oneida,* groping through the smoke, caught a brief glimpse of the *Manassas* heading downriver.[98]

As the *Manassas* neared the forts the Confederate guns turned upriver and started firing on her, mistaking her for a Union gunboat, disabled and drifting down. Fort St. Philip fired 75 times before the ironclad could back out of range.[99]

With his course downstream blocked, Warley ordered the *Manassas* north again. Struggling hard against the Mississippi's strong current, the ironclad eventually stumbled onto a large ship which Warley took to be the *Hartford,* Farragut's flagship. (He was mistaken. She was the *Brooklyn.*) First Officer Harris called for ram speed and Levine pointed the ironclad's nose at the big ship. Dearning's stokers threw resin on the fires and the *Manasses* shuddered as her engines strained for speed against the current. A charge was rammed home in the 32-pounder, followed by a dark round iron ball. The gun went out, clanging as the muzzle pushed open the iron port lid. Aboard the Federal, a cry went up: "The ram! The ram!" Officers and seamen, busy fending off a River Defense ram as the *Manassas* approached, rushed to starboard to catch a glimpse of the supposed terrible engine of destruction, and gunners prepared to fight the monster. At a distance of 10 feet the 32-pounder fired. In the next instant the ram struck. Aboard the *Manassas*, everyone but Levine, who was clinging to the wheel, was thrown to the deck. The carronade tipped over, now useless. The gun's lone shot bit through heavy links of chain hung over the *Brooklyn's* side as armor, penetrated the planking, tore through spare rigging piled inside, and lodged itself deep in a pile of sand bags, just short of the boiler.[100] For the second time that night, the *Brooklyn* barely escaped disablement and destruction by a shell. The *Manassas* struck the *Brooklyn's* heavy chain armor just outside a full coal bunker, and the Federals didn't discover any damage until the bunker was emptied. Captain Craven, in his official report, spoke in an offhand way of the *Manassas* "feebly butting" the *Brooklyn*. When the coal bunker was emptied it was discovered that the ram had done enough damage to render the *Brooklyn* completely unseaworthy.[101] J. R. Bartlett, one of the *Brooklyn's* lieutenants, afterwards commented that the full coal bunker was "the only thing that prevented the prow of the *Manassas* from sinking us."[102]

The *Manassas* had suffered, too. Not only was her gun out of commission, but the jolting had just about destroyed her engines. Her boiler had pulled off its mountings, jamming Chief Engineer Dearning against a bulkhead. As the ram backed off, the boiler settled back onto its mounts. The Union gunboat *Iroquois* steamed near. Warley backed the *Manassas* away from the *Brooklyn* and Levine pointed the ironclad's heavy beak toward the gunboat, intending to ram. The Federal put on steam and left the *Manassas* as if the ironclad were at anchor. Two small gunboats sped past, firing as they went. The *Manassas* was powerless to answer.

Having escaped the *Brooklyn*, the *Manassas* limped up-river. She soon stumbled onto a desperate battle: the frail *McRae* was struggling with three Union gunboats. She had been severely cut up, her captain — Huger — was mortally wounded, most of her crew was shot down and, as the iron-clad approached, the gunboat's fire bell was heard to be ringing. The three Federals, sighting the *Manassas,* fled. The *McRae*, severely hurt, dropped downriver, seeking the protection and comfort of the forts.

The *Manassas* continued upriver, searching for Federal stragglers. Instead, she stumbled onto Farragut's entire fleet. Two Federals pulled away from the pack and started toward her, stacks puffing thick clouds of smoke, picking up speed with the strong current. One of them was the *Mississippi*, with whom the *Manassas* had dueled earlier. The other was the gunboat *Kineo*.

Warley saw no way to escape. His ship couldn't run, she couldn't fight, and there was no one to come to her aid. At his command, Levine turned the *Manassas'* head toward the river bank and beached the ironclad. The lieutenant cut the injection pipes, letting her flood, while the crew crawled through the gun port and hatches to disappear into the swamp.

A few Federal sailors pulled to the ram, fired her, and rowed back to the *Mississippi*. The *Mississippi* and *Kineo* stood off and began throwing broadsides at the ram, vent-ing their wrath on the now-helpless wreck. Occasionally they diverted their attention from the *Manassas* long enough to beat the swamp with several charges of grape.

The shock and concussion of exploding shells and pounding solid shot jolted the *Manassas* free from the river bank and she drifted out into the stream. Her metal skin was torn and punctured and she was well ablaze inside. Slowly, aimlessly, she drifted down the Mississippi, gliding, turning with the current. Flames licked wickedly from the shot holes, hatches, and gun port. A carpenter's mate on the Federal *Portsmouth* saw her. "She was what we called played out," he observed.[103] At 7:30 A.M., the fire reached several powder charges stored under Warley's bunk. Mr. Stevenson's gallant little *Manassas* blew her roof off and sank.

In the early hours of the 24th, Commander Sinclair, aboard the unfinished *Mississippi,* received orders to report to Captain William C. Whittle, Sr. at the navy yard.

"The enemy has passed the forts and is coming up the river," said Whittle. "What can be done with the *Mississippi?*"

"We can try to get her up the river," Sinclair replied, "and if this is impossible, burn her."

"Well, use every exertion in your power to get her up, and failing to do so, you will destroy her."[104]

Sinclair returned to the Tifts shipyard and began preparations to take the *Mississippi* upriver. She had no guns — Sinclair would meet them at Jackson four days later, and see them off to Vicksburg, where they would be emplaced in the river batteries. She had no ammunition — the only powder aboard was 1,000 pounds borrowed from Lovell to blow up the ship should she be threatened with capture. Her rudder wasn't installed, her ports were unfinished, and her two outside propellers lay on the wharf. A full plating of armor had been laid on, reaching approximately a third of the way up the casemate, but wasn't bolted down: her final shipment, just arrived, lay aboard several flat cars in the depot of the New Orleans and Jackson Railroad.

Captain Whittle came up from the naval yard and boarded the ironclad to confer with Sinclair. "Save her if you can," he said, "but do not let her fall into the hands of the enemy." Sinclair called on the tugs *Peytona* and *St. Charles* — chartered on the 17th for this purpose — to take the ironclad in tow and pull her up the river. Their captains balked. Sinclair insisted and finally the captains stated that they were unable to, as they were short hands and engineers. Sinclair supplied engineers from the *Mississippi's* staff and hands from the Negroes engaged in loading the ironclad, and the *Peytona* finally passed a line. She pulled the ironclad out into the roaring current (the river was in spring freshet) and both ships, despite the *Peytona's* straining engines, slipped downstream. The ironclad was pulled to the shore and moored. Asa Tift immediately chartered, from Mr. Hyde, the strong steamers *Falls City* and *Edward J. Gay*, to be at the yard before sundown. Tift tried to impress on Hyde the absolute importance of the steamers, to which Hyde replied: "Give yourself no uneasiness about the matter; it will be attended to."

The tug *St. Charles* was finally persuaded to lend a hand and, working close to the river bank out of the rushing current, the two tugs succeeded in pulling the big ram back up to the Tift yard wharf. Asa Tift saw Hyde there again, asked about the promised steamers, and was again reassured.

Col. Beggs of the Committee on Public Safety was aboard the *Mississippi* with the Tift brothers. He informed brother Nelson that he could have two more boats there by four A.M., and Tift shouted across to Sinclair aboard the *Pey-*

tona, relaying the offer. Sinclair invited Beggs aboard the tug; the colonel repeated his offer, and Sinclair accepted with gratitude.

Sinclair, the Brothers Tift, Joseph Pierce, and those naval officers aboard the *Mississippi* kept an uneasy watch down-river. The 75 miles of water between the forts and New Orleans would take time to traverse, but over seven hours had already passed since the early-morning battle, and the smoke of burning cotton and molasses in the city was already clouding the sky to the south. No one knew when the first of the Union sloops and gunboats would push into sight.

Five hundred men were put to work loading armor, equipment, and provisions aboard the *Mississippi,* laboring throughout the day, past the time Hyde's two steamers were due, and far into the night. The *Falls City* and *Edward J. Gay* never arrived. The *City* had fled northward earlier in the day, loaded with provisions and refugees, in company with such steamers as the *Natchez, Potomac* and *Quitman,* all fast ships of far greater strength and power than the little *Peytona* and *St. Charles.* None had offered to lend a hand to the *Mississippi.*

By four the next morning Col. Beggs' promised tugs had failed to arrive. Sinclair waited a little longer, then boarded the *Peytona* and, in company with the Tifts, headed down-river in search of help.[105] Lieutenant James I. Waddell and Constructor Pierce remained aboard the *Mississippi* with instructions to fire her if the Federals made their way up the river.

Soon after Sinclair's departure, five men boarded the ironclad carrying a rope. Their leader demanded: "Where's Tift? Is he aboard?"

"No," replied Waddell.

"He is a traitor, and we brought this rope to hang him."

Waddell, a North Carolina aristocrat with the habit of command, put an abrupt end to the conversation with the brusque reply: "I have laid a train to the magazine, and the vessel will be fired in a few minutes." The hanging party made a hasty departure.[106]

The Tifts and Commander Sinclair, aboard the *Peytona,* steamed three miles downriver to Julia Street, finding the river banks lined all along the way with beached and moored tugs. All were deserted, their crews gone to protect their homes or join in the looting and confusion that raged through the city.[107] Four boats were finally found, the last rounded up as guns roared a few miles downriver as the Federal fleet passed the batteries at Chalmette. Nothing else now stood between Farragut's sloops and the helpless *Mississippi.* The *Peytona* and her four new consorts hurridly fled. On their way up, they met the *Mississippi* coming down. She was in the middle of the stream, drifting with the current. Yellow flames licked from gun ports and hatches, spreading along the planking of her casemate. "She was a formidable ship," said Sinclair, "the finest of the sort I ever saw in my life."[108]

A few hours after the *Mississippi's* demise, Commander David Porter dispatched a note to General Duncan, demanding the surrender of the forts. Duncan answered that he wouldn't surrender without authority from his superiors. Porter's mortars resumed their fire.

The pounding continued all day. Some of the army volunteers assigned to the *Louisiana* boarded the tender *W. Burton,* found some whiskey, and got drunk. This gave Mitchell another point with which to counter Duncan's entreaties to thrust the *Louisiana* into offensive combat before she was ready. Mitchell had agreed to take the ironclad downriver to bombard Porter's "bummers" but, with the volunteers drunk and the rest of the crew exhausted, he wrote Duncan that "These circumstances . . . and excessive difficulty in handling the vessel, will prevent our taking the poition, at least today, that I proposed and was arranged between us this afternoon."[109]

That night the mortar schooners retired. Capable of carrying only 250 shells each, they had withdrawn to replenish their magazines. General Duncan asked Commander Mitchell to move the *Louisiana* above Fort Jackson, where her guns could protect the forts from Farragut's fleet and Ben Butler's army. All the heavy guns of both forts pointed to the lower river, leaving the rear unprotected.

Mitchell was unable to comply with the request. The ironclad's own motive power was incapable of stemming the Mississippi's current and she could not get a tow from any of the nearby tugs. "The *W. Burton* is crippled, and the *Landis* also, and the gunboat *Defiance* [a survivor of Stevenson's River Defense Fleet] will not do anything for us. If she comes within my reach I will deprive her captain of his command by force, if necessary . . . We shall probably remain where we are, and do all we can to defeat the enemy should he attack us again."[110]

April 26 was blessed with quiet. The next day the bummers returned, several of them lobbing their shells from positions within plain sight of Fort St. Philip. At Fort Jackson, soldiers began to desert: nine days and nights of almost continuous bombardment had strained nerves to the breaking point. General Johnson Duncan decided to call it quits.

The situation looked better aboard the *Louisiana*: the propellers were in place and had actually spun a few revolutions to prove that they were working. Commander Mitchell retired that night with the full certainty that the morning of April 28 would see the invincible *Louisiana* steaming about under her own power, crushing any Federal who dared stand before her. Duncan would at last be relieved of the fear of those huge, booming mortars.

As those aboard the *Louisiana* plotted the morning's activities, however, an army officer boarded the Federal *Harriet Lane* to announce to a gloating David Porter that the forts were ready to capitulate. At dawn on the 28th an officer boarded the *Louisiana* and announced the news to an unbelieving John K. Mitchell. The Commander immediately took a boat for Fort Jackson and a conference with the General. Mitchell later recalled: "General Duncan . . . informed me that in his offer to surrender the forts he had disclaimed all control over the forces afloat. This unexpected surrender of these important land defenses seriously comprising the position and safety of my own command, I expressed to General Duncan my deep regret that a precious knowledge of his intentions to surrender had not been communicated with me . . ."[111]

Later in the morning army officers from the forts boarded the *Harriet Lane* to sign the surrender agreement. Commander Porter, in his *Naval History of the Civil War,* stated that he was "surprised" to find that the *Louisiana* wasn't included in the surrender. He shouldn't have been: Col. Higgins had informed him earlier that the army wouldn't be responsible for surrendering the navy.[112]

Mitchell, meanwhile, had called a conference of his officers. The *Louisiana* was unprovisioned and poorly equipped to fight her way through Farragut's fleet and battle the Mississippi's currents all the way to Vicksburg. And it was a moot point whether or not she could survive a Gulf voyage to Mobile or another Confederate port. Mitchell decided to burn her.

Wishing to avoid an explosion while the flag of truce flew, Mitchell ordered the magazine and all charges in the guns drowned: instead of ending her life in one loud and brilliant burst, the *Louisiana* would be left to burn safely and slowly, her woodwork disintegrating under the flames and her hot iron plating settling until only a cloud of steam over the rushing river remained as a last reminder of her presence. The crew and most of the officers boarded the tender *Landis*, leaving Mitchell and Lts. Whittle, Ward, and Wilkinson to set the fire.

When the flames caught, Lt. Whittle and two men were dispatched in a small boat to the *Harriet Lane*. Whittle was to inform Commander Porter that the *Louisiana* was moored to the shore and afire, and that her mooring ropes might burn through, setting her adrift. He was halfway to the *Harriet Lane* when the *Louisiana* exploded. Her magazine had not been drowned effectively.

Commander David Porter, who, through the entire war, displayed an unforgiving hatred of his Southern opponents, found in the explosion of the *Louisiana* an excellent opportunity to kick his enemies while they were down. His reports and writings presented the incident as a planned and deliberately aggressive act by the Confederate Navy against his fleet, executed under a flag of truce. He described a resulting tidal wave that heeled the *Harriet Lane* far over on her side (Confederate officers in the company of Porter at that time reported no such effects and Whittle, in the small boat, mentioned only a gentle swell)[113] and pointedly charged John Mitchell with "setting fire to and blowing up the floating battery *Louisiana* and sending her adrift upon the four vessels of ours that were at anchor while they had a flag of truce flying." In a letter to Sec. Welles he stated that:

Had the *Louisiana* blown up in the midst of our vessels she would have destroyed everyone of them. As it was, good fortune directed her toward Fort St. Philip, when she exploded with great force, scattering fragments all over the work, killing one of their own men in the fort, and landing a large beam close to the tent of Commander McIntosh, who was lying with one arm blown off, another broken, his kneecap shot away, and a leg broken . . . The surgeon in attendance pronounced it the most perfidious act he had ever heard of. The explosion was seen and heard for many miles, and it was supposed that the forts were blown up.[114]

Porter's accusations of dishonorable conduct and the misunderstandings they created added greatly to the hatred and enmity that would exist for years between many of the principals of the battle of New Orleans. When the Confederate naval officers surrendered, Secretary Welles ordered them locked in irons and confined to the hold — treatment worthy of pirates — during their voyage from New Orleans to prison. Commander Mitchell, reminiscing on his own treatment in Union hands, later commented:

The course of Flag-officer Farragut and Commander D. D. Porter in this matter shows them to be servile and degraded tools, well fitted for carrying out the infamous policy of an unprincipled and despotic government.[115]

3

On and Off the Mississippi

On August 24, 1861, President Jefferson Davis went before the Confederate Congress to ask for naval appropriations. Chief among the navy's needs were a pair of iron-clad gunboats to defend the Mississippi River. The legislators listened to Davis' plea, one of the few times they would hear the Chief Executive speak on behalf of the navy, and granted $160,000 for two ironclads to be built at Memphis.[1]

Contracts for the vessels were let to John T. Shirley and Prime Emmerson. Shirley's ship was to be called the *Tennessee* while Emmerson's would carry the name *Arkansas*. Construction was started in October of 1861, with an optimistic December 24 set as the completion date.

In addition to the above appropriation for two Mississippi River ironclads, $50,000 was handed down ear-marked for the construction of gunboats to defend the Cumberland and Tennessee Rivers. Lieutenant Issac N. Brown was sent to Nashville to purchase and arm steamers for river defense.

110

He immediately bought three, the *James Wood, James Johnson,* and *Dunbar,* for conversion to vessels of war.[2] He authorized the conversion of two of four steamers offered for sale by R. B. Cheatham, mayor of Nashville, and work was immediately begun to convert the steamer *Eastport,* at Cerro Gordo, to an ironclad. She had been cut down to her main deck, a casemate frame constructed, and all of her backing laid down, ready to receive her armor, when Lt. S. Ludyard Phelps, U.S.N., began a fast push up the Tennessee River in early February, 1862. With the gunboats *Tyler, Lexington,* and *Conestoga,* he created a major panic on Tennessee's in-state river system, forcing the burning of the steamers *Appleton Belle* and *Lynn Boyd* at the mouth of the Duck River, the *Sam Kirkman, Julius,* and *Time* (the latter with $100,000 of government stores aboard) at Florence, Alabama, and the sinking of the *Dunbar* in Cypress Creek. The *Muscle* and *Sallie Ward* were captured.[3] At Cerro Gordo, the Confederates cut the *Eastport's* suction pipes and scuttled her to keep her out of Federal hands.[4] Phelps, however, had her raised and sent her back to Cairo, Illinois, where she was completed and mustered in Federal service.[5] She eventually struck a torpedo on the Red River and was so badly damaged that Admiral Porter had her destroyed.[6]

Before the construction of either of the Memphis ships could begin, Shirley and Emmerson had to build shipyards, as the Tifts had at New Orleans. Emmerson chose Fort Pickering as his site.[7] He set up two sawmills there to cut pine planking, having his oak timber cut at five outside mills and hauled in.

Ships' carpenters, so necessary in constructing floating equipment, were not to be found in the vicinity of Memphis. Shirley and Emmerson advertised at St. Louis, New Orleans,

Mobile, and Nashville with little result. They turned to the army, asking for ships' carpenters and a hundred laborers. General Leonidas Polk sent six or eight men.[8] He refused further help, even under pleas from Secretary Mallory.

Shirley, meanwhile, was experiencing difficulties. His share of the $160,000 was far from enough. To finance the building of the *Tennessee* he was forced to sell his house and land.

As October lengthened into November it became clear that neither ship would be finished by the December 24 deadline. The *Arkansas* grew slowly, her hull and deck gradually coming into existance, a casemate frame surmounting the deck, and plank backing going down on the frame. The *Tennessee*, however, had barely been started. Her keel had been laid and that was all.

Iron for armor was in small supply in Memphis. A little was procured within the city, but most had to come from Arkansas. Work crews picked it up at various places along the river in 50- and 100-pound lots. Up the Cumberland River, bolts and spikes were being rolled to tack the finished iron plates to the *Arkansas'* backing. Loaded aboard a train for Memphis, they got as far as Nashville, where they were seized for use on an ironclad building there.[9]

In March came news of the abandonment of Columbus, Kentucky. In April came even more distressing news: Island No. 10, with over 2,000 Confederates, had been surrendered. All that stood between Memphis and Union occupation was Fort Pillow and a floatilla of converted river boats. They were not expected to stand long against the Union ironclad gunboats.

With Memphis threatened with capture it was decided to move the ironclads down to a safer area. Moving the

Tennessee was impossible: she was only a frame with very little of her planking on. Work continued until June 5 when, at the last minute, she was burned to prevent her capture. Shirley had put close to $76,000 into the ship. He was a financially ruined man.[10]

The *Arkansas* was in condition to run. Her hull and casemate backing were completed and her engines — built in Memphis — were in place, though her propeller shafts, forged and turned at Leeds in New Orleans, were not connected. Lt. Charles McBlair took command with orders to have her towed to New Orleans, completed, and used in consort with the ironclads *Manassas, Mississippi,* and *Louisiana* against the Federal squadron massing south of there. But on April 25 McBlair received word that New Orleans was in Federal hands: the *Arkansas* appeared trapped. But in the long stretch of river between Memphis and New Orleans a refuge was found; at the little hamlet of Greenwood, Mississippi, 160 miles up the river from Yazoo City.

Greenwood proved to be a plantation town with one rickety dock. McBlair tied the incomplete *Arkansas* there. A barge followed, loaded with most of the ironclad's armor plate. Not far from Greenwood it hit a snag, ripped out its bottom, and sent the entire load of iron into the mud at the bottom of the Yazoo.

On May 26, Lt. Issac Brown received orders to report to Greenwood and relieve McBlair of command of the *Arkansas.* From the time of the loss of his Tennessee gunboats until the fall of New Orleans, Brown had been stationed at Algiers, working on several small ironclad gunboats. He arrived at Greenwood on May 28 and found the *Arkansas* in deplorable condition. No work had been done on the ram since she had left Memphis. Her armor was still at the bottom of the Yazoo: no one had bothered to try to raise it. Aboard the ship itself, ten cannon lay scattered haphazardly over the deck: there was not a sign of her gun carriages and no one seemed to know anything about them. Planks and timbers littered the deck along with her carriagless guns, and the few men on board seemed content to leave the ship as it was. Evidently, McBlair had little inclination to finish the *Arkansas*.

There is no record of Issac Brown's immediate reaction to the state of affairs that existed aboard this seemingly worthless hulk, but he probably searched out McBlair with a good deal of his rage in evidence. Lt. McBlair's inaction, stormed Brown in a dispatch, was "practical treason."[11] And McBlair seemed in no hurry to leave once relieved. Brown "came near shooting him" to get him out of the way. "He has gone to Richmond to denounce me, no doubt," said Brown, "but I care not what they say of me there so long as it is evident here that I am trying my best to get ready to strike the enemies of my country and of mankind." Brown, ambitious and energetic, was going to be a dangerous man for the Union.

The morning after Issac Brown took over, a gang of 100 carpenters and laborers, commandeered from neighboring army encampments, began the task of putting the ram in fighting shape. The lieutenant had collected 200 men altogether and was working them around the clock in two shifts.[12] He also borrowed a number of oxen and field hands from neighboring plantations. He even managed, in the backwoods of Mississippi, to find a diving bell. Within two days all the armor was raised from the sunken barge.

Brown floated the *Arkansas* downriver to Yazoo City, which contained a "navy yard" of sorts. A log raft had been placed across the river at Liverpool Landing and batteries were erected ashore. These should effectively halt any

Federal gunboats that got the notion of poking their noses upriver. The makeshift gunboats *Polk* and *Livingston* — all that remained of Commodore Hollins' river floatilla — and the *Van Dorn* were on the river under the command of Commander Robert F. Pinkney. Brown sent Lt. Charles W. (Savez) Read down to Liverpool with orders to have the gunboats armored with cotton bales and anchored just below the raft, bows downstream and steam up, ready to fight anything that pushed up the river. Pinkney flatly refused to comply with these or any other suggestions from Brown. He would await orders from Captain William F. Lynch at Jackson, just ordered to the command of all Confederate Naval Forces on the Western Waters.

Immediately after arriving at Yazoo City, Lt. Brown contracted with two men in Jackson for gun carriages. Neither man had any experience in the construction of gun carriages. Nevertheless, five carriages were soon delivered by each man and the *Arkansas'* guns were mounted.

Fourteen forges were set up aboard ship and ashore and the armor plating began to go on. It was soon found that the iron sent from Memphis was far from enough. Wagons were sent shuttling back and forth between the river and the railroad, where they picked up additional iron. A drill press was set up aboard the steamer *Capitol,* and it satisfactorily served to punch holes in the railroad iron that was to armor the *Arkansas.*

It wasn't long before the Federals, hearing tales of a Confederate ram being built, decided that a reconnaissance up the Yazoo was in order. The Ellet rams *Monarch* and *Lancaster* were soon pushing up the river. Cutting through the muddy brown water, they rounded a bend and came face to face with three Confederate gunboats: the *Polk, Livingston,* and *Van Dorn.*

With not a spark in the fire boxes or a pound of steam

pressure in the boilers of any of the three ships, Pinkney fired them all. The Federals sat happily by, admiring the sight of the three Rebels afire, until the *Van Dorn* blew up with such force as to nearly sink both the Yanks. The Federals, satisfied with the destruction of three Confederate gunboats without firing a shot, turned and headed back down the river. Later in the day, the *Arkansas* — for whom the rams had been searching — arrived, having completed a trial run from Yazoo City to Liverpool. Brown and his officers were stunned by Pinkney's "cowardly work" and suggested that the commander deserve an immediate court-martial.

Captain William F. Lynch, on his arrival at Vicksburg, came up to make a personal inspection of the *Arkansas*. He reported to Secretary Mallory that the ram was "very inferior to the *Merrimac* in every particular. The iron with which she is covered is worn and indifferent, taken from railroad track, and is poorly secured to the vessel; boiler iron on stern and counter; her smokestack is sheet iron." The boiler plate armor — "for appearance sake" — had been improvised because the machinery that was supposed to bend the armor plate to fit at the corners of the casemate and deck had never arrived. A double layer of one-inch bar-iron covered the pilot house, while the casemate top was planked up and overlaid with a half-inch layer of iron. If the *Arkansas* carried poor quality armor, she attempted to make up for it with a fierce bite. Her battery, mounted on carriages made of green wood that had already begun to warp, consisted of:

Bow—two 8-inch Columbiads; Starboard—one 9-inch Dahlgren, one 6-inch rifle, and one 32-pounder; Port—one 9-inch Dahlgren, one 6-inch rifle, and one 32-pounder; Stern—two 6-inch rifles;

Her gun commanders were:

Lt. John Grimball—starboard bow Columbiad and starboard 9-inch gun; Lt. A. D. Wharton—starboard 6-inch rifle and starboard 32-pounder; Lt. George W. Gift—port bow Columbiad and port 9-inch gun; Lt. Alphonso Barbot—port 6-inch rifle and port 32-pounder; Lt. Charles W. Read—stern 6-inch rifles.

Masters John L. Phillips and Samuel Milliken were in charge of the two powder divisions.[13]

To augment her guns the *Arkansas* carried fixed to her bow the sharp iron ram which had become a standard feature on Confederate ironclads. On her trial trip the ironclad's engines — brand new — pushed her at a speed of six knots in still water. Against the current she did only four. Brown later said of the engines:

We had at first some trust in these, not having discovered the way they soon showed of stopping on the center at wrong times and places; and as they never both stopped of themselves at the same time, the effect was, when one did so, to turn the vessel round, despite the rudder. Once, in the presence of the enemy, we made a circle, whilst trying to make the automatic stopper keep time with its sister-screw.[14]

She was 165 feet in length, 35 feet abeam, and drew 14 feet of water.

With the *Arkansas* nearing completion, Brown began looking for a crew. About 200 men were needed. Of these, over half came from the crews of Pinkney's burned gunboats. The difference was made up by 60 men from General M. Jeff Thompson's Missouri cavalry under Captain Harris, and a few Louisiana artillerists from General Martin L. Smith's command. The Missourians had never been aboard a warship before and had never handled a heavy naval gun, but they would learn. Training began on July 11.

Since the beginning of summer the water in the Mississippi and in her tributaries had been falling steadily. The water had been shoal under the *Arkansas* at Greenwood and had dropped alarmingly at Yazoo City and Liverpool Landing. There was some doubt that the *Arkansas* could spend the summer as far upriver as Yazoo City, and the only other substantial and permanent berth within reach was Vicksburg. The bluff city, last bastion of Confederate defense on the Mississippi, was under seige by the Union army and the combined fleets of Farragut and Porter up from New Orleans, and Davis, down from St. Louis. Davis' fleet consisted of ironclad gunboats, most of them slightly superior to the *Arkansas* in speed, though light in armor. His flagship, the *Benton,* had terrorized Hollins' flotilla from New Madrid to Memphis. Davis had six of the iron boats above Vicksburg. Farragut's fleet, ten heavy sloops of war and swarms of gunboats, was the same that had forced the destruction of the *Manassas, Louisiana,* and *Mississippi* at New Orleans. Also present were the seven wooden rams that had broken the back of the Confederate flotilla in the battle at Memphis. This was the array the *Arkansas* would have to cut through to gain the safety of Vicksburg's frowning batteries.

With this armada before Vicksburg, General Earl Van Dorn wrote General Daniel Ruggles at Yazoo City, urging that the *Arkansas* at least make an attempt to get to the city. "It is better," he wrote, "to die game and do some destruction than to lie by and be burned up in the Yazoo." Ruggles, a Massachusetts Confederate who had served briefly at New Orleans while Brown was there, mentioned the note to the lieutenant. Brown's anger flared at the inference that he would burn the ship rather than seek active combat and he replied to Van Dorn with: "I regret to find that by implication it is thought I would prefer to burn the *Arkansas* in Yazoo River than to hurling the vessel against the enemy."

As a matter of fact, Issac Brown was of the opinion that the *Arkansas* should hold the Yazoo. There were several fast steamers in good repair on the river and the valley was fertile, capable of furnishing needed provisions for the defenders of Vicksburg and the armies in Virginia and Tennessee. In addition, a navy yard of sorts had been constructed and equipped at Yazoo City.[15] He sent Savez Read to Vicksburg to convey these thoughts to General Van Dorn. Read left Liverpool Landing on horseback at sunset and, riding all night, reached Vicksburg around 8:00 A.M. He chanced upon a friend, Col. Withers, and the two had breakfast. The colonel then accompanied him to see Van Dorn. Hearing Read out, Van Dorn stated that he "thoroughly appreciated" the importance of holding the Yazoo River but, as the *Arkansas* could be used only in deep water, he thought it advisable to get her into the Mississippi as soon as possible. He suggested that the *Arkansas* cut her way through the armada above Vicksburg, strike the sloop *Brooklyn* and the squadron of mortar schooners lying below the town, then leave the Mississippi and make for Mobile.

After the interview, Withers offered to guide Read on a reconnaissance of the Federal fleet. Read accepted and the pair departed for Vicksburg, arriving near the fleet's location in late afternoon. A fight through briars and vines in a "dense and entangled" woods brought them to the riverbank, where Read put his field glasses to use in looking over the ocean-going sloops of war and the river ironclads.

A man of war's cutter landed nearby, but the Rebels remained undetected.

Read left Vicksburg at dusk, riding until 2:00 A.M. A planter lodged him until sunup, when he continued his ride to Yazoo City. Brown had returned there for additional work on the *Arkansas*.[16] There were 37 Federal warships in sight of Vicksburg, Read told the *Arkansas'* commander, and "plenty more up the river." Van Dorn directed Brown to run the *Arkansas* through the Federals and bring her in to Vicksburg.

Obstructions in the river would have to be removed before the *Arkansas* could get down to the Mississippi. When Brown queried as to how long it would take to open a passage, he was told it would require at least a week. Double-checking, Brown sent Lts. Gift, Grimball, and Read to the obstructions. They reported that a passage could be cleared in half an hour.

Captain Lynch came down from Yazoo City with the intention of going along. "Well, Commodore," said Brown, "I will be glad if you go down with us, but as this vessel is too small for two captains, if you go I will take charge of a gun and attend to that." Lynch replied: "Very well, Captain, you may go; I will stay. May God bless you!"[17]

On the morning of July 14, the *Arkansas* slid slowly away from Satartia Bar and headed downriver. Officers and crew knew they would soon enter a battle for their lives, with the odds stacked heavily against them.

Twenty miles below Satartia Bar, someone discovered that a steam leak had soaked all the powder in the *Arkansas'* magazines. The ironclad was immediately pulled to shore and moored to a tree. The crew grabbed blankets, tarpaulins, and everything else of the sort that was available and filed past the magazine, each receiving a load of soggy powder. They stepped off the ship and walked to a nearby clearing — site of an old lumber mill — where the powder was spread on the blankets to dry in the hot July sun. Had a few Federal gunboats poked their noses up the Yazoo at that time, they would have been pleasantly surprised to find the big Confederate tugging lazily at her moorings, her crew off in the forest, and not a grain of powder for her guns. Luckily, there were no Federals stirring on the Yazoo that day.

With the help of the blazing sun, the powder was soon dried to the point of ignition and was thrown back aboard, the leak having been stopped. Again the *Arkansas* eased out into the dark waters of the Yazoo and, at midnight, anchored at Haines Bluff, only a few miles from the Mississippi.

During the night, two men deserted. They soon appeared aboard the U.S. ironclad *Essex* and poured out the entire story of the *Arkansas* and her proposed dash through the Federal fleets. Farragut and Davis were soon given the story. They met briefly with General Williams, commanding the forces ashore, and no one, least of all Farragut, seemed overly worried. They had all been hearing for months of the coming of the great Rebel ram and all were quite tired of the mention of her.[18] On July 10, Farragut had written Secretary Welles asking that his fleet be sent to Texas or Mobile, leaving Davis' ironclads to guard Vicksburg. He had mentioned then that the *Arkansas* was up the Yazoo, "from whence I do not think she will ever come forth."[19]

At dawn on July 15, the *Arkansas* pulled away from Haines Bluff and started down the final stretch of the Yazoo. At the mouth of the river, other ships were astir, ascending the river. They were the ironclad *Carondelet,* the Ellet ram *Queen of the West,* and the tinclad *Tyler.* The *Carondelet* was commanded by Henry Walke, friend and messmate of Brown's from the Old Navy.[20] As they entered the Yazoo, the *Arkansas*, for whom they were searching, was a few miles upstream, aground and straining hard to get free. The thrust of her propellers, worked both forward and back, finally tugged her free.

It must have been with shocked surprise that Brown spotted the Federals, three abreast, coming up the river. But he quickly descended to the gun deck, ordered his men to stations, and made the customary pre-battle speech:

Gentlemen, in seeking combat as we now do, we must win or perish. Should I fall, whoever succeeds to the command will do so with the resolution to go through the enemy's fleet, or go to the bottom. Should they carry us by boarding, the ship must be blown up, on no account must it fall into the hands of the enemy. Go to your guns.[21]

The Confederate was quickly readied for action. Gun crews stripped to the waist and tied bandanas around their heads to keep the sweat out of their eyes. The deck was sanded, pistols and cutlasses were distributed, muskets loaded, and the magazine and shell rooms inspected. Rammers, sponges, vent drills, and all the other equipment needed for operating the big naval guns were made ready. The *Arkansas* and the three Federals closed rapidly.

The Federals came on quickly, then, as the *Carondelet* fired her bow guns, all three turned and headed downriver.

The *Arkansas* had yet to fire. The small gun ports allowed little elevation or laterial training; therefore, the guns' trunnions had been marked the day before and the gunnery officers had agreed not to fire until the target moved into the sights of the guns.[22]

The retreating Federals kept up a hot fire with their stern guns. Shot banged on the *Arkansas'* casemate front and raised water spouts alongside. An Irishman with more curiosity than caution struck his head out of a gun port for a better view. A cannon ball beheaded him. Lt. Henry K. Stevens, fearing that the sight of the headless corpse would demoralize the crew, started to push the body out of the gun port. He called on one of the crewmen to help. The man gave Stevens a look of anguish and cried: "Oh, I can't do it, sir, he's my brother."[23]

The *Arkansas* was gaining on the Federals. Lt. Gift sighted down the long barrel of his Columbiad. The muzzle pointed just behind the junction of the water with the *Tyler's* stern. Slowly, the muzzle seemed to climb, moving farther up the Federal's stern as the *Arkansas* closed the distance. Gift steadied himself, then fired. The shell, with a five-second fuse, cut through the gunboat, killing her pilot, then burst in the engine room.[24] Grimball's Columbiad now took up the fire. Gift's gun recoiled off its mounts with the first shot and was out of action for five or ten minutes. Grimball's bow gun, officered by Robert McCalla, made up for it.

As the *Arkansas* closed the distance, the action became general. The *Queen of the West* ranged up on the *Arkansas'* starboard side to ram. Dabney Scales punctured her with a 9-inch shell, quickly followed the A.D. Wharton at the 6-inch rifle, and R. H. Bacot with the 32-pounder. The *Queen,* receiving full measure the offering of the starboard battery, abandoned all further thoughts of combat and ran.

Brown took up a position on the casemate roof, fully exposed to all fire. The *Tyler,* keeping pace with the *Carondelet*, bristled with sharpshooters, all blazing away at the *Arkansas*. Their shots spattered around Brown. A ball finally struck him in the head and toppled him through the open hatch. He regained consciousness to find himself being carried off by several men. Putting his hand to the wound and drawing it away, he convinced himself that he wasn't seriously hurt when he failed to find any brains mixed with the blood on his hand. He sent his bearers back to their guns and again took his place atop the roof.

The *Arkansas* now brought her full attention to the *Carondelet*, on which she was gaining. The bow guns were firing solid shot propelled by 15-pound powder charges. The heavy wrought-iron projectiles went all the way through the Federal ironclad.

A shot from the *Tyler* struck at Brown's feet, penetrating the pilot house. It cut the wheel, mortally wounding Chief Pilot John Hodges and disabling Yazoo River pilot James R. Shacklett. Mississippi River pilot James Brady — "a Missourian of nerve and equal to the duty" — took the wheel, and Brown directed him to "keep the iron-clad ahead."[25]

Gift, his gun back in action, spotted a man standing outside the casement on the *Carondelet's* port sill, loading a stern chaser. The ships were so close that he could have easily recognized the man had he known him. With the muzzle of his gun pointing in the general direction of the *Carondelet's* stern, the lieutenant pulled the lanyard. The big Columbiad roared and recoiled hard, emitting a huge cloud of blue-gray smoke. When the smoke cleared the man, the gun, and part of the *Carondelet's* deck had vanished.[26]

The *Carondelet* was a shambles. Eight big 64-pound shot from the bow Columbiads had penetrated the casemate, creating havoc in the Federal's interior. Three projectiles tore a path through Walke's cabin, the wheelhouse, the steerage cabin, and lodged in a bulkhead, just short of penetrating the boilers. Three times the wheel ropes were shot away, leaving the *Carondelet* to run a sometimes-erratic course that allowed the *Arkansas* to make considerable gains. The backing bell and speaking tubes were shot away. Steam pipes, cold water pipes, and the steam exhaust were severed and the steam gage smashed, allowing escaping steam to billow through the ship. Boats were destroyed, davits knocked off, and the gunboat's bulkheads, cabins, and interior generally shot to pieces. The striking force of the big projectiles, traveling the length of the entire ship, led Walke to believe that he had been hit in the bow at least three times before he had turned to flee, though the *Arkansas* hadn't begun firing until she was well up on the *Carondelet's* stern.[27]

The Confederate's ram bow was practically pushing through the Federal's stern when pilot Brady informed Brown that they were in danger of grounding. The *Arkansas* put her helm slightly to starboard to pass the *Carondelet* on the Federal's starboard side. Lt. Henry Stevens, the Connecticut Rebel, strolled along the port broadside battery, checking to see that all guns were depressed to send their shots through the Yankee's side and out the bottom of her hull. The *Carondelet*, her wheel ropes at last irreparable, grounded against the river bank among the willows. The *Arkansas*' engines stopped and she glided past the Federal, delivering her broadside as she passed. Lt. Brown, still standing on the casemate roof as his ship passed the Yankee, reported no signs of life aboard. He called out to his old messmate, Walke, but received no reply.[28] Said Brown: "We left him hanging onto the willows."[29]

It took approximately an hour for the *Arkansas* to steam the distance from the *Carondelet's* wreckage to the mouth of the Yazoo. She was little more than 500 yards behind the *Tyler* most of this time, banging away occasionally and receiving a stubborn return fire from the timberclad's 30-pounder Parrot rifle and the sharpshooters. As the ironclad entered Old River — a lake formed by a cut-off — just prior to entering the Mississippi, Brown inspected the engine room. He found the temperature there hovering between 120° and 130° and the black gang, unable, with the smokestack already riddled, to keep up the 100 lbs. of steam pressure they had promised, beginning to pass out. Stevens, however, had already organized relief gangs and began sending them in at 15-minute intervals.[30]

Emerging from the Yazoo, the Confederates came face to face with a sight calculated to chill the heart and weaken the backbone of even the most daring. Lined along the east side of the river lay Farragut's magnificent fleet of heavy sloops of war. The stretch of river between this line and the east bank was packed with a mass of rams and Davis' ironclads. On the west side of the river lay the gunboats. Drawn up on the west bank were several batteries of field artillery and troops of sharpshooters. The end of this corridor was blocked by a large ram and a big ironclad flying Flag Officer Davis' pennant. She was the *Benton*.

The odds were indeed staggering. There was no possible course, however, except to push on, straight into the guns of this armada, and batter through to the safety of Vicksburg.

The *Arkansas* moved slowly downriver toward the waiting Federals. The sun beat down, unbearably hot. Not a shot had been fired. Several Federal ships moved about uneasily. No wind stirred and the river was silent.

The eyes of everyone who could see the arena of battle soon became focused on the Federal gunboat *Kineo,* as she advanced along the river bank, evidently intending to be the first to engage the ironclad.

She bore a large number "6" on her funnel. Savez Read bore a special hatred for the No. 6 gunboat of Farragut's fleet, a hatred known throughout the ship. He had served aboard the *McRae* at New Orleans and had become de-

voted to his commander, Thomas Huger. Huger had been
mortally wounded during the battle and Read had seen,
by the light of muzzle flashes, the "No. 6" painted on the
boat that had fired the fatal shot. The news from Gift,
carried aft by a powder monkey, that No. 6 was in the
fleet and advancing to engage, brought Read obvious delight. "He came leisurely and carelessly forward, swinging
a primer lanyard, cool and calm. On seeing No. 6 his eyes
brightened and he smiled as if he were going to join company with some friends instead of enemies."[31] The *Kineo*
carried an 11-inch gun and two 12-pounders, and clearly
desired the honor of having the first shot at this bold Rebel.
She moved out into the middle of the stream, put on steam,
and cut across the *Arkansas'* port bow, firing a charge of
grape from her 11-inch gun. The heavy little iron balls
bounced harmlessly off the *Arkansas'* iron side. Aboard the
Arkansas, Brady gave the wheel a sharp turn and pointed
the Confederate's bow directly at the No. 6. Gift turned an
8-inch shell loose into Read's arch enemy, then Brady
swung the ship back around, allowing the contents of the
port broadside to also be presented to the Yankee.

As if the *Kineo's* attack had been the awaited signal, the
entire Federal armada opened fire. The air, a moment before calm and still, was suddenly filled with flying iron in
the form of round shot, conical solid, shell, grape, canister,
and musket ball. They banged and skidded on the *Arkansas'* armor, striking once and richocheting off to fall to the
water, spent. Shell fragments beat the water around the
ironclad into a white froth.

The *Arkansas* was, by this time, coming abreast of Farragut's line of sloops. Each Federal delivered to the ram a
full broadside, then, as the *Arkansas* passed, closed in
behind to block any attempted retreat by the Confederates.
The Rebel's broadsides fired as fast as her guns could be

loaded and run out. They didn't have to worry about pointing: there was no place the guns could be trained where a Yankee didn't lay in the way of their shells. The stern guns had a field day with the ships closing in behind.

Brown noticed that the rams behind Farragut's ships were getting up steam to speed out between the big sloops and hit the Confederate as she passed. "Brady," the Lieutenant said, "shave that line of men-of-war as close as you can, so that the rams will not have room to gather headway in coming out to strike us." Brady did just as ordered, cramping the rams, but putting the *Arkansas* practically at the gun muzzles of the big Federal sloops.[32]

The Union ram *Lancaster*, sunk once at Memphis by the Confederate ram *General Price*, moved directly across the *Arkansas'* path. Brady asked if he should run her down. "Go through him, Brady," Brown answered. Gift had other ideas. He planted one of his 8-inch shells squarely in the wooden ram's mud drum, filling her engine room with steam and scalding water. Part of the *Lancaster's* crew and a company of sharpshooters had taken refuge there. They came pouring out of hatches and port holes, tearing off their clothes and screaming like fiends. This was the only shot the *Lancaster* received during the fight. It killed 18 and wounded 10.

Just after Gift's magnificent shot into the *Lancaster*, a shot cut down the *Arkansas'* colors. Dabney Scales jumped quickly to the shot-swept roof, knotted the severed halyard, and ran them up again. As he returned to the deck, they were shot down again. He was about to return to repeat the task, but was forbidden by Lt. Brown.

Ceaselessly battered by heavy shot, the *Arkansas'* armor was finally pierced. A solid shot from one of Farragut's sloops came through and lodged near Gift's Columbiad, knocking over a man engaged in picking up a shot. The

The *Merrimack* and Gosport Navy Yard in flames. (*Secret Service of the Confederate States in Europe,* Thomas Yoseloff, New York)

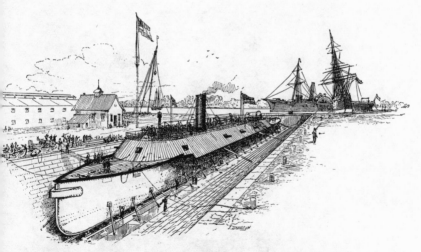

The *Merrimack* being converted into the ironclad *Virginia* at Gosport. (*Battles and Leaders of the Civil War,* Thomas Yoseloff, New York)

Commander John M. Brooke, C.S.N. (*History of the Confederate States Navy*, Rogers and Sherwood, New York)

Captain French Forrest, C.S.N. (*History of the Confederate States Navy*, Rogers and Sherwood, New York)

The *Virginia* completed, commissioned, and afloat. Note the two 12-pounder howitzers mounted on her casemate top. (*Official Records of the Union and Confederate Navies in the War of the Rebellion*, U. S. Government Printing Office, Washington, D. C.)

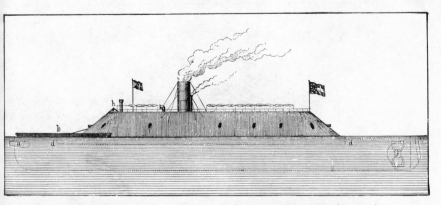

The *Virginia*, sketched the day before battle. (*Battles and Leaders of the Civil War*, Thomas Yoseloff, New York)

On the *Virginia's* gun deck. An artist's conception of combat from inside the dark casemate. (*Battles and Leaders of the Civil War,* Thomas Yoseloff, New York)

Commander Catsby ap R. Jones. (*History of the Confederate States Navy,* Rogers and Sherwood, New York)

The duel between the *Monitor* and the *Virginia*. (*Battles and Leaders of the Civil War*, Thomas Yoseloff, New York.)

Captain Sidney Smith Lee, C.S.N. (*History of the Confederate States Navy,* Rogers and Sherwood, New York)

Captain George N. Hollins, C.S.N. (*History of the Confederate States Navy,* Rogers and Sherwood, New York)

The *Virginia's* commanders: Adm. Franklin Buchanan; Capt.
Josiah Tattnall, C.S.N. (*Battles and Leaders of the Civil War,*
Thomas Yoseloff, New York)

The *C.S.S. Manassas*. (*Official Records of the Union and Confederate Navies in the War of the Rebellion*, U. S. Government Printing Office)

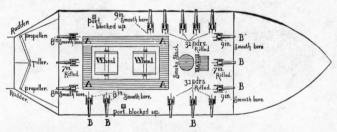

Deck plan of the *C.S.S. Louisiana*. (*Battles and Leaders of the Civil War*, Thomas Yoseloff, New York)

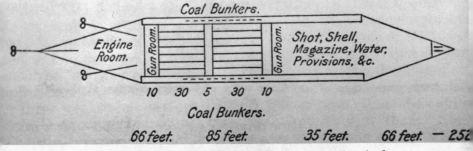

Coal Bunkers.

Engine Room.

Gun Room.

Gun Room.

Shot, Shell, Magazine, Water, Provisions, &c.

10   30   5   30   10

Coal Bunkers.

66 feet.   85 feet.   35 feet.   66 feet. — 252

Diagram of the *C.S.S. Mississippi*. (*Official Records of the Union and Confederate Navies in the War of the Rebellion*, U. S. Government Printing Office)

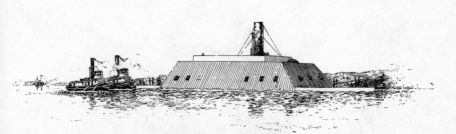

The *Louisiana*, still unfinished, on her way down to Fort St. Philip. (*Battles and Leaders of the Civil War*, Thomas Yoseloff, New York)

Lt. Alexander F. Warley, C.S.N. (*Battles and Leaders of the Civil War,* Thomas Yoseloff, New York)

Comm. John K. Mitchell, C.S.N. (*Battles and Leaders of the Civil War,* Thomas Yoseloff, New York)

Captain William C. Whittle, C.S.N. (*History of the Confederate States Navy,* Rogers and Sherwood, New York)

David Porter's mortar schooners engaged in night firing against Fort Jackson. (*Battles and Leaders of the Civil War,* Thomas Yoseloff, New York)

The sloop *U.S.S. Mississippi* and the gunboat *Kineo* running down on the *Manassas*. (*Battles and Leaders of the Civil War,* Thomas Yoseloff, New York)

Commander Charles F. McIntosh, C.S.N. (*History of the Confederate States Navy,* Rogers and Sherwood, New York)

The *Manassas* about to ram the *Brooklyn*. (*Battles and Leaders of the Civil War*, Thomas Yoseloff, New York)

Lieutenant James I. Waddell, C.S.N. (*History of the Confederate States Navy*, Rogers and Sherwood, New York)

The Battle of Memphis. On the riverbank at right is the burning frame of the *C.S.S. Tennessee*. (*Battles and Leaders of the Civil War*, Thomas Yoseloff, New York)

Commander Issac N. Brown, C.S.N. (*History of the Confederate States Navy,* Rogers and Sherwood, New York)

The *C.S.S. Arkansas.* (*Official Records of the Union and Confederate Navies in the War of the Rebellion,* U. S. Government Printing Office)

The *C.S.S. Palmetto State.* (*Official Records of the Union and Confederate Navies in the War of the Rebellion,* U. S. Government Printing Office)

Captain John R. Tucker, C.S.N. (*History of the Confederate States Navy,* Rogers and Sherwood, New York)

sailor got up, rubbed his hip, and remarked that a shot would "hardly strike twice in the same place." He had just uttered the words when a shell came through the breach made by the preceding shot, lodged in one of the cotton bales used to pad the armor, and exploded. When the smoke cleared, Gift found himself standing with his cap gone and his hair and beard singed. Sixteen men had been killed and wounded by the explosion. In his division, only Gift, Quartermaster Curtis, and one of the Missouri cavalry captains were left standing. The three of them succeeded in firing the Columbiad once more. The same bad luck soon befell the port 9-inch gun, putting Gift's entire command out of action. A solid shot hit just above the Dahlgren's port, breaking through and bringing with it a hail of wood and iron splinters. The mass showered the gun deck, taking out the Dahlgren's entire crew, breaking Gift's left arm, wounding some of the men at Dabney Scales' starboard Dahlgren, and riddling the smokestack, filling the humid casemate with suffocating smoke.

The *Arkansas* was, by this time, almost through the Union gauntlet. The only obstacle left was the ironclad *Benton*. Beyond that ship waited the welcome, protective cover of Vickburg's heavy batteries. The *Arkansas* put on all the steam she could muster and headed for the Federal's broadside, intending to ram. The *Benton*, rather than be run down, moved out of the way. As the Confederate passed, they unloaded the contents of their remaining bow gun, their starboard broadside, and their stern guns into Admiral Davis' stern gun ports. The *Benton* then took up the chase, steaming after the Rebel at a leisurely pace until she came within range of the Vicksburg batteries. A roaring salvo from the big guns on the hill forced her to back off. A Chicago *Times* correspondent commented on the *Benton's* pursuit:

The *Benton* waked up then and made a valorous rush at nothing, and got punctured for her pains. She might as well have rushed at the moon. She poked her nose around the corner, when there was nothing in the world to shoot at, and received the full fire of the batteries and was glad enough to get back again, like a gander charging to protect his geese, after the danger is all past, and perchance running his nose into a hornet's nest.[33]

Porter's mortar fleet, lying below Vicksburg under Commander William B. Renshaw, panicked. The *Sidney C. Jones*, aground, was burned.[34] The army ashore fired their commissary stores, boarded transports, and fled downriver in company with the bummers.[35]

The *Arkansas* was in sad condition. Her crew was maimed and mangled, gaping holes had been punched in her armor, her ram bow was broken, her smokestack riddled, iron plating cracked in places, and her pilot house was stove in. But she was victorious! She had single-handedly fought three powerful fleets and was still alive to brag about it. As she steamed toward the city, battered and bleeding, the hills swarmed with soldiers and civilians, cheering and waving sheets and flags, their hearts bursting with pride and joy. It was glorious! As Lt. Gift said:

It was the first and only square, fair, and equal stand-up and knock-down fight between the two navies that the Confederates came out first-best. From the beginning our ship was handled with more pluck, decision, and judgement than theirs (the *Tyler* excepted);[36]

The *Arkansas* moored opposite city hall and army officers came aboard to inspect the craft. What they saw must have made them gasp. The guns, beautifully served throughout both battles, were still hot and smoking. Around them stood or slumped those of the gun crews that were able to remain on their feet, fighting off waves of faintness from heat and exhaustion. They were stripped to the waist and perfectly black with powder smoke. Men, writhing in agony, were being carried off on stretchers. Other forms lay still and silent in the blood-soaked sand on the deck. Two large holes were opened in the armor, the woodwork around one scorched by an explosion. Chunks and splinters of wood and iron littered the deck. The smokestack, both inside the casemate and out, had the appearance of a nutmeg grater.

Ten dead and fifteen wounded were taken out and the Missouri and Louisiana boys returned to their commands, leaving the *Arkansas'* crew skeletal. The ironclad dropped down to a coal depot to refill her bunkers. The bummers, convinced that the *Arkansas* had had her fill of combat for the day and would not attack, returned to their stations. They began lobbing their 13-inch, 200-pound shells toward the ironclad, displaying extremely poor gunnery. The *Westfield*, Renshaw's gunboat, came closest to hitting the ironclad, sending several of her flat trajectory shots splashing nearby.[37]

David Farragut was fighting mad. He had a right to be. Either of the fleets above Vicksburg should have been capable of destroying the *Arkansas*. Yet the ironclad had run through, dealing destruction right and left and treating the United States Navy to its most humiliating defeat of the war.

Farragut fired off a quick dispatch to Davis:

As the boy says, "I told you so" . . . I will get the squadron underway as soon as the steam is up, and run down in line— the ships in line with your ironclad vessels. We must go close to him and smash him in. It will be warm work, but we must do it; he must be destroyed . . . We will go down in line of battle, and when passed we will turn about and come up again. Be sure to fire into the wharfboat. She is the place where they make their ordnance incendiary preparations.[38]

Cooler heads prevailed, however. A night attack could be made with one fleet — either Farragut's or Davis' — achieving the same results without risking the sacrifice of the entire force to the big guns in the hills.[39]

A reconnaissance was started. The *Benton* got too close again and the Confederates sent two shots plunging through her armor, killing three men. [40] Farragut conceded the rashness of a daylight attack under the powerful batteries and agreed to wait for sundown. His fleet would go down in the darkness in double line, ships to the inside next to the city and gunboats on the outside. ". . . no one will do wrong," said Farragut, "who lays his vessel alongside of the enemy or tackles with the ram. The ram must be destroyed."[41]

As night fell, Davis' fleet steamed down and opened fire on the Confederate batteries above the city. Farragut's fleet, their guns well supplied with solid shot and heavy anchors hoist to the yardarms to drop onto the Confederate's deck, steamed slowly downriver. As they came near the place of the *Arkansas'* anchorage, Federal gunners prepared for revenge. But she wasn't there. Brown, anticipating an attack, had shifted positions. Against the bluff, the ram was hard to see. The dismayed Northerners didn't spot her until she opened fire on them. The *Hartford*, finding the plucky ram by her gun flashes, stood in close and caught the full contents of the ironclad's broadside. The Federal returned a roaring salvo of her own. One of her 11-inch solid shot struck a few inches above the *Arkansas'* water line, penetrating into the engine room, where it cut two men in half, wounded several others, and dismounted the engines. Continuing on its course, it cut through into the dispensary, smashing medicines, and lodging in the opposite wall. Its position could be easily found from the outside by the lump it made under the armor.

Ship after ship passed, pouring broadsides into the *Arkansas*, taking a few shots in return, and moving on. Pilot Charles Gilmore was killed, and James Brady wounded. The *Arkansas* remained stationary during the whole attack, taking the bludgeon blows of the 9- and 11-inch guns, and when the last ship had passed, she was still afloat. "We got down very well," said Farragut, "except that it was just what I supposed from the first would be the case, that we started too late. It was so late when we got off the town that there was nothing to be seen of the ram. I looked with all the eyes in my head to no purpose. We could see nothing but the flash of the enemy's guns to fire at."[42] The Federals suffered 27 killed and wounded in the attack. The *Winona* had been shot through and was run ashore to keep from sinking. The *Sumter* had been hulled twice.[43] Said Farragut: "I shall take another chance at the ram . . . and I will continue to take chances to try to destroy her until my squadron is destroyed or she is."[44] Davis advised caution.

. . . you will not be surprised that, having myself learned a lesson of patience at Fort Pillow and witnessed its exercise at Columbus and Island No. 10, I should be unwilling to put in jeopardy all the great triumphs and interests which are placed in my keeping. I have watched eight rams for a month, and now find it no hard task to watch one. I think patience as great a virtue as boldness, and feel anxious, above all things, to save that portion of the Republic which lies adjacent to and dependent upon the Mississippi from an alarm which would interrupt its business, destroy its peace, and affect the public credit at home and abroad.

. . . I am as eager as yourself to put an end to this impudent rascal's existence. I have given a great deal of thought to it to-day. I have even laid down a plan of proceeding. We can not do anything until the *Essex* can get up steam . . . and we ought to have the *Sumter* above to do her ramming with effect.[45]

Farragut suggested that "A few shells now and then would disturb the people at work on the ram very much . . ." Davis agreed and passed the message on to Porter. Early the next morning, the mortar boats opened fire again. If the 9- and 11-inch flat trajectory shots couldn't sink the *Arkansas,* surely one of these huge 13-inch explosive shells, falling from great heights, could smash easily through the ram's fragile roof plating and exit through the bottom of the hull, sinking her. The only trick was to hit the Confederate. When the shells began falling too near she changed position, crewmen hauling her along the shore by hand to confuse Federal gunners. Still, the big shells came close, several bursting directly over the ram. Of the shelling, Brown commented:

I know of no more effective way of curing a man of the weakness of thinking that he is without the feeling of fear than for him, on a dark night, to watch two or three of these double-fused descending shells, all near each other, and seeming as though they would strike him between the eyes.[46]

Farragut, on the other hand, enjoyed the spectacle immensely. In a dispatch he told Davis: "Do tell the captain that the shelling is magnificent. They are falling all around him and I expect one to fall on board every moment."[47]

Commander Brown (his run through the fleets had earned him a promotion) relinquished his command for a day to Captain Lynch. With the "wonder" ship under his personal command for the first time and her dismounted engines repaired, the captain went searching for action. Pulling away from the moorings, he pushed the *Arkansas* up the river to give some of the mortars lying with Davis' fleet a taste of their own medicine. The action he craved was not to be his on that day, however. As soon as the Federals spotted the Confederate coming up the river, their ironclads took the mortar boats in tow and fled, soon leaving the slower *Arkansas* behind. With coal in short supply and no Federals willing to do battle, Lynch returned the ironclad to Vicksburg. Brown returned to command the next day.

At 4:00 A.M. on July 22, Flag Officer Davis' ironclads moved downriver to bombard the upper Confederate batteries. Rear Admiral Farragut's fleet, downriver, was to have begun a bombardment of the lower batteries in conjunction with Davis' efforts, but remained silent. Their crews were at battle stations with guns cast loose and they moved about mysteriously, as if preparing to ascend the river for another attack on the ironclad. They made no such advance, however. After a half-hour of bombardment, the ironclad *Essex*, commanded by Wm. D. (Dirty Bill) Porter, came steaming down the river, followed at an interval by the *Queen of the West*. The Federals couldn't have picked a more opportune moment to strike the *Arkansas*: only 28 men were aboard the ironclad, the rest were either dead or in the hospital, sick, wounded, or worn out to the point of collapse.[48]

Grimball opened the ball with a shell from his Columbiad. The *Essex* didn't answer, but kept on coming, all ports tightly closed. Scales, commanding Gift's Columbiad, fired next, also failing to bring a reply. Gift, his arm broken in the *Arkansas'* first day of combat, was standing by.

Brown soon saw the *Essex's* intention: she was going to ram a hole in the *Arkansas'* side. Brown, however, would not be beaten at his own game. Noting that the *Essex* was squared across the bow like a flatboat — not the ideal shape for ramming — he payed out his bow hawser and let his sharp ram bow ride out to point at the *Essex*. If the Federal struck his bow, it would be she, not the *Arkansas,* that went to the bottom. But Porter had come downstream with the intention of ramming, and he was going to do just that. Pulling farther out in the river and coming in to avoid the *Arkansas'* sharp bow, he determined to strike the Confederate at an angle. As the *Essex* came in, her three bow gun-port covers opened and her guns were run out. Only a few of the *Arkansas'* guns could be brought to bear. As the *Essex* closed, the *Arkansas* cut loose. The *Essex's* bow guns roared in return. A 10-inch shot from one of them struck near the port bow Columbiad, ripped off a piece of armor, and drove it diagonally through the ship, splitting it on the breach of the starboard stern rifle, killing and wounding 12 men. An instant later the *Essex* struck. The Federal rasped alongside the Confederate's side and came to rest piled up on a mud bank just astern of the *Arkansas*. The entire crew (now down to 16 men) rushed aft. By this time a small amount of steam had been worked up in the boilers and, while the crew cleared away the wreckage of wood and iron around the stern guns, Brown revolved his port screw a few times, nosing his bow back into the river bank and sliding his stern out to bring his guns to bear on the grounded Federal. The two stern rifles began to roar, bouncing shots off the stranded *Essex*. The Federal didn't reply, but kept her ports tightly closed and strained to get off the bank. She finally slid free and headed downriver. She had gotten her fill of the *Arkansas*.

The cry went up that the *Queen of the West* was now approaching, and the crew raced back to the bow guns. Brown payed out his bow hawser again, bringing his sharp bow out against the *Queen*. The wooden Union ram followed the *Essex's* lead, rushing in at an angle to avoid being cut down by the *Arkansas'* bow. Gift was at the guns now, working with one arm. He sighted the port 32-pounder so that, as the *Queen* plunged past its muzzle, he could put a shot right into her boilers. He watched intently as the *Queen's* bow charged nearer. At the point where the Federal's boilers should be lined up with the cannon's long barrel, he pulled the lockstring. The old cannon's vent had been enlarged, however, and, to Gift's dismay, the primer "drew out" without firing the gun. A man standing nearby picked up the primer, replaced it in the vent, and hammered it once with a compressor lever, igniting the charge. The shot struck the *Queen,* but her vulnerable boilers were well past.[49]

The *Queen* was coming in at full speed with the current at her back; and even though she struck a glancing blow, she tore a minor hole in the *Arkansas'* side and set both ships trembling throughout. The *Queen* followed the same path as had the *Essex,* skating the length of the *Arkansas'* side and piling up on the mud bank at the Confederate's stern. The crew again raced aft to man the stern guns and Brown again ordered the ship ahead on the port screw, bringing the bow in and the stern out. The Confederates had time to send a few shells through the Federal before she got off the bank. She immediately grounded again, but was off in a few seconds and moving out into the river for another attack. Brown sent his gun crews rushing from the 6-inch rifles to pour the contents of the ram's port broadside into the Federal. The three big shells discouraged the *Queen* from any further combat and she broke off the engagement.

One of the *Essex's* guns had been loaded with marbles. The Confederates picked up hundreds of them on the

Arkansas' deck.[50] Had a charge of them come through a gun port, it would have been as deadly as canister.

After its fourth fight in nine days, the *Arkansas* was finally put in for a major overhaul. Commander Brown asked for and received a furlough to visit his family, who were refugees in Grenada, Mississippi. On his arrival at that city, he was taken violently ill, the effects of three months of performing superhuman tasks and winning impossible victories on too little food and sleep.

While Brown was flat on his back, General Earl Van Dorn decided to recapture Baton Rouge, capital of Louisiana. General John Breckenridge was dispatched with several thousand men to effect its liberation. Van Dorn ordered the *Arkansas* along to destroy any Federal gunboats that might cover the Federal army if Breckenridge backed them against the river. Lt. Stevens, left in command of the ironclad in Brown's absence, wrote the commander, informing him of his orders. Brown immediately replied, ordering Stevens to leave the *Arkansas* at Vicksburg. Her engines had become quite contrary, he said, and there was danger of them quitting at a critical moment. Van Dorn and Captain Lynch countermanded Brown's orders and, after raising a crew, the *Arkansas* slid away from the Vicksburg bluffs at 2:00 A.M. on a Sunday morning.[51]

The *Arkansas'* chief engineer, George W. City, had completely broken down in health — the result of his long and harrowing vigil over the ironclad's machinery. The only person that could be found to replace him was a young man from the army. The young fellow did his best to keep the engines in running condition, but he had worked only with paddlewheel steamers and was unfamiliar with the intricacies of the screw propeller and short-stroke engines. The task was beyond him. By the time the *Arkansas* had arrived at the mouth of the Red River, the engines had become so unmanagable that Stevens called a halt and held a council to decide whether or not to go on. The engineer stated that he thought the engines would hold out, so the lieutenant decided to chance it.

A few miles below Port Hudson the engineer called a halt to make final adjustments. Gift and Bacot went ashore to see if they could learn something of the movements of the armies. Enquiring at a farm house, they were informed that their old antagonist, the *Essex,* along with several wooden gunboats, was on the water at Baton Rouge. Breckenridge was to make the attack at dawn the next day.

At daylight the rattle of musketry and the roar of artillery announced that the battle had begun. The *Arkansas* cast off and went steaming down the river, her engines straining to the limit. She was late. The sounds of combat soon ceased and an ominous hush settled over the land and river.

Coming around a bend and into sight of Baton Rouge, the crew could see that the Confederates had driven the Federals from their positions and had them backed up to the river. The only thing that kept them from driving the Yankees right into the water were the heavy batteries of the *Essex* and her consorts.

The key to the battle seemed to be the *Essex.* If she could be destroyed, it would be an easy matter to take care of the wooden gunboats, leaving the Union army caught between the *Arkansas* and Breckenridge's army.

Stevens ordered his men to battle stations. The words had hardly been uttered when the starboard engine broke down. It quit so suddenly that the helmsman was unable to compensate and the *Arkansas* was run aground. Apprehensively, crewmen pulled the engine apart and went to work on it with files and chisels while officers kept watch on the *Essex.* Luckily, the Federal ironclad made no move to come out and fight and, after several hours work, the engine was reassembled. It proved to be in working order. Some railroad iron was thrown overboard to lighten the ship, the engines were backed, and the *Arkansas* slid off into deep water. She had not gone 100 yards when the same engine broke down again. An inspection revealed a broken crank-pin. The ironclad was pulled to shore and moored, and a forge was set up on deck to make a new pin. The operation took all night.

At daylight the next morning the enemy got underway and began moving upriver toward the *Arkansas,* the *Essex* leading. The last bolts were being tightened down, the final touches being put on the *Arkansas'* engines as the Federal opened up. Slowly the *Arkansas* turned and steamed up the river. Stevens' plan was to get a good start, come barreling down the river, and cut the *Essex* in half. The *Arkansas* was traveling up the river, away from the Federals, when the port engine broke down, again running the ironclad aground on some submerged cypress stumps near the river bank.[52] Lt. Read's stern rifles opened a slow fire. The Federals replied, neither side scoring a hit. It appeared that the *Arkansas'* engines were beyond suitable repair, hopelessly unreliable for battle. The *Essex* would probably come up-river eventually, take a position on which none of the *Arkansas'* guns could be brought to bear, and pound the Confederate to pieces. Stevens contemplated his chances and came to the conclusion that any attempt to defend the ram in her present state could only result in the useless sacrifice of her entire crew. The only course left open was to destroy the ship.

The crew walked out on the deck and stepped from the bow onto dry land. Stevens, Read, Midshipmen Bacot, Scales, Talbott, and Gunner Travers remained aboard to destroy the ship.[53] Her machinery was broken with axes.

Cartridges were scattered around and shells were placed between the guns. All guns were loaded and run out. Cotton padding was pulled out and mattresses in the wardroom were torn up. Both cotton and mattresses were then set afire. In the process of firing the ship, a grenade exploded in Lt. Stevens' hands, burning them badly.[54]

The officers, after firing the *Arkansas,* followed the crew ashore. As the flames began licking at her deck, the ironclad floated free. The current swung her around and she set a straight course for the *Essex,* seemingly bent on destroying her antagonist without human help. Flames licked through gun ports and her guns roared as the fire reached them. The Federals, unnerved by the *Arkansas'* advance, beat a hasty retreat. The *Arkansas* followed leisurely, loudly proclaiming with each explosion of a shell or gun that she still ruled the Mississippi. In the midst of her glorious advance the flames reached her magazine and, with a thunderous roar, she destroyed herself.

Issac Brown, his illness vanished and his command destroyed, gathered the remains of the *Arkansas'* crew and returned to the site of his first meeting with the *Arkansas* — Yazoo City — to take over the navy yard.

Earl Van Dorn was pursuaded to loan out enlisted men skilled as carpenters and mechanics, and Brown's shipyard company, working with assets totalling five saw and planing mills, a machine shop, and carpenter and blacksmith shops, laid down keels for three ironclads.[55] Two, the *Mobile* and *Republic,* were to be fast screw gunboats, similar in armament, armor, and configuration to the *Arkansas.* The other, forever after known as *"The Unnamed Monster,"* was to be a giant, the biggest warship ever built inland — 310 feet in length with 4½ inches of armor.[56] She would resemble the *Louisiana* and was to be powered by four engines driving four wheels and two propellers.

To stave off the ever-prowling Federal gunboats, Brown and his shipyard workers and the men from the ships took over the defense of the Yazoo, "rather by inference than by direct orders." They were on their own — the Navy Department occupied with greener pastures — and could build as they pleased with whatever materials fell to hand, but would have to defend themselves on their own hook. Brown, with Masters Ewing (possibly Francis M., reported at Jackson station in August, 1862, then fading from the records) and McDaniel (perhaps one Z. McDaniel, whose sole entry in Confederate naval records reads "Special duty, Mississippi River defenses, 1862") improvised several torpedoes and proceeded to mine the river. They mounted a 6-inch gun atop Haines Bluff and obstructed the river just below it with piles of logs and railroad ties. The army again lent a hand, emplacing several guns along with the 6-inch piece to create a small battery.

By mid-December, 1862, the battery had grown considerably, mounting 18 heavy naval guns to protect the ever-growing navy yard and the three rams building upriver.[57] On December 12, a Union flotilla, including the ironclads *Carondelet, Cairo, Pittsburg,* and the tinclads *Signal* and *Marmora,* pushed up the Yazoo to sweep the river of torpedoes. The expedition cleared out several rifle pits ashore, but ended when the *Cairo* ran afoul of one of Brown's torpedoes and sank.[58] Torpedoes and the Haines Bluff battery could not completely protect Yazoo City, however. W. T. Sherman's troops eventually came inland, taking the battery from the rear, and Brown was forced to destroy the yard and the three ironclads in late May, 1863.[59] Along with the yard, the three ironclads, and numerous steamers in the river, the little *Ivy* went up in flames.

In the spring of 1862, several steamers took advantage of the seasonal floods to escape New Orleans and the threat of capture by Farragut's invasion fleet. Among those to leave the Crescent City were the *J. A. Cotton,* which found its way to the Teche River. The *Cotton,* built for the Bayou Sara trade, was a large river steamer of the classic lines captained by E. W. Fuller, a long-time western steamboat man. A staunch Confederate with an excellent knowledge of the river, Fuller had briefly commanded the armed tug *Music* and the captured *Queen of the West;* and now he determined to convert his steamer into a gunboat — preferably, because of her frail construction, an ironclad. To accomplish this, he sought the help of Major J. L. Brent, Chief of Artillery and Ordnance on General Richard Taylor's staff. Together, the two men undertook the task of transforming the unarmed and unarmored river steamer into an ironclad gunboat of some formidability.

Timbers and planking went up on the *Cotton's* deck, forming a casemate backing. This was padded with cotton bales, then plated with railroad iron. A 32-pounder and two 24-pounders, all smoothbores, were mounted on the hurricane deck. The casemate extended aft far enough to give only partial protection to her engines and boilers.

The *Cotton* was by no means a first-class ironclad. A good rolling broadside from a Union ship of the line like the *Minnesota,* with her 8-, 9-, and 10-inch guns, would have reduced her in an instant to a shattered hulk. But the *Cotton* was never meant to stand against 44-gun frigates and ocean-going sloops. She was intended to operate, rather, in the backwaters of Louisiana. Her purpose was to hold the interior against marauding Federal gunboats, a task which, with some verve in handling, she could have been able to accomplish.

The *J. A. Cotton* was never a commissioned naval vessel.

Captain Fuller himself was a civilian. He applied for rank in the Confederate Navy and was nominated for a lieutenant's commission in January, 1863, just six months before his death. As for her crew, they were — in the main — army volunteers. There was, however, a slight touch of navy aboard. Several officers had been assigned to the ironclad to teach the men the art of handling the guns. Among them was Henry K. Stevens, late of the *Arkansas*.

In October, 1862 Union General Weitzel emerged from New Orleans with his force and set out on a mission with a dual purpose: wreak as much destruction as possible along the bayou country of Louisiana; and destroy the gunboat *Cotton*. The Federals, receiving their information from contrabands, deserters, and other questionable sources, had been led to believe that the *Cotton* was quite as formidable as the *Virginia* or *Mississippi*.

On the evening of Saturday, November 1, 1862, the *Cotton* was lying peacefully at anchor in Berwick's Bay, approximately 90 miles west of New Orleans, when the smoke of several steamers was spotted. Steam was raised and the ironclad began preparing for action when the source of the smoke, a group of Federal gunboats acting in conjunction with Weitzel's land forces, entered the bay. They immediately opened fire and the *Cotton* retreated. She backed into the river, keeping her bow to the enemy, protecting her unarmored stern. The river was narrow with no room for the ironclad to turn once she backed in. She kept an orderly retreat, backing slowly in front of the cautiously advancing Federals. Union shot whistled close and raised water spouts nearby, but the *Cotton* reserved her fire, backing carefully, trying to keep from running aground.

As the ironclad turned into the Atchafalaya River she fired her first and only shot of the engagement. The ball struck one of the gunboats in the nose, crushing its planking.

The Federals continued their pursuit for perhaps a half an hour, then gave up and reversed their course to take up anchorage in the bay. The *Cotton* continued on her way, turned into the Teche River, and steamed to the Fuselier plantation, where she moored for the night.

The next morning Fuller received a communication requesting him to take his ship to Numa Cornay's bridge and make a stand against the advancing Federals, holding there as long as possible, then retreating to the next bridge.[60] If he found it impossible to halt the Yankees, he was to sink the *Cotton* in the river as an obstrucion to halt their gunboats.

On the morning of November 3, four Federal gunboats, led by the *Kinsman*,* began an advance up the Teche River in search of the *Cotton*. Officers aboard the *Kinsman* soon spotted the smoke of the ironclad a short distance up the river and hastily prepared to open an engagement. Gunners swung the bow pivot gun, a mean-looking Parrott rifle, to bear on the smudge of the *Cotton's* smoke.

At 2:00 in the afternoon the Federals caught sight of the *Cotton* and pushed forward to attack, confident in their 4-to-1 advantage of numbers. The *Cotton,* instead off retreating, halted and cleared for action. The Federals slowed, taken aback by the ironclad's sudden change in attitude. They quickly opened fire, however, filling the air with flying shells, and were just as quickly answered by the guns of the *Cotton*.

Fifteen minutes of hot, destructive fire proved too much for one of the Federals. She pulled out of the fight and dropped downriver to lick her wounds. A second gunboat was not to be cowed by the ironclad's accurate fire. She

---

* The *Kinsman* was commanded by Thomas McKean Buchanan, brother of Admiral Franklin Buchanan, CSN.

advanced cautiously, creeping along the river bank. The Confederates let her come within 200 yards before opening up on her with every gun that could be brought to bear. Three shots struck her near the water line and she ran her head up on shore, leaving only her pivot gun in a position to engage.

In the face of withering Confederate fire, Union firing slacked off. It became increasingly evident that the wooden-hulled Federals had found more than they could handle in the *Cotton*. Aboard the ironclad, Fuller had probably already marked this engagement down as the *Cotton's* first victory when he was informed that the guns had just fired their last cartridge. She had nothing more with which to fight.

With victory snatched from her grasp, the *Cotton* began another backing retreat. A few sacks were found on board. They were improvised as cartridges and fired at the half-heartedly pursuing Federals to stave them off. When the sacks were gone, legs were cut from the pantaloons of some of the crew and filled with powder. But few of these were needed. The Federals broke off the engagement and fell back down the river.

Confederate gunnery had been nothing short of excellent. Even Lt. Comm. Buchanan praised the Southerners' firing in his official report. His ship, the *Kinsman*, had been struck eight times. The *Estralla* and *Diana* both ended the engagement carrying three Confederate shot.[61]

Buchanan's gunboats spent November 4 in making repairs. The next day they again ascended the river and opened fire on the *Cotton* from behind a point of land out of range of the *Cotton's* guns. When two of the gunboats finally ventured into the open, however, they drew a fierce fire from the Confederates. The two Yanks remained in range, trading shots with the *Cotton* for about 35 minutes, at which time all four Federals retired. The ironclad's un-armored cabin roof sustained a minor crack from a shell. Otherwise, there was no damage.

On November 6 the gunboats again opened a slow fire from long range. No damage was done and the *Cotton* failed to reply. This ended the ironclad's action for the year.

On January 14, 1863, General Weitzel made a combined land-water attack on the Confederate shore batteries along the river, and on the *Cotton,* anchored near them. The *Cotton* held her ground, her guns giving a good account of themselves, until a heavy force of infantry and light artillery was spotted coming up abreast of her on shore. The iron-clad's moorings were slipped and she began another backing retreat . . . but she wasn't quick enough. Federal soldiers leveled muskets and sent sheets of leaden ball pouring through gun ports and unarmored woodwork. The gallant Lieutenant Stevens fell, "fighting like a hero, brave as a lion . . ."[62] All over the deck, gunners were cut down by the terrible, sythe-like sweeps of musketry. The pilots were killed. A ball smashed Captain Fuller's arm. He backed the *Cotton* up the river and out of danger, steering with his feet. The ironclad tied up out of range of Union guns and Fuller and the rest of the wounded were transferred to the steamer *Gossamer*.

Lieutenant E. T. King, second in command, took the *Cotton* back downriver toward the scene of the fighting. A skeleton crew was at the guns when a Federal battery, masked by woods and in a position where the *Cotton* couldn't bring a gun to bear, opened a hot fire. The cabin was riddled immediately. The iron armor turned shot, shell, and grape, but the gun ports had no shutters, and a shell or charge of grape was likely to come through at any minute, destroying everything within the casemate. Ambushed and badly surprised, King reversed the *Cotton's* wheels and retreated, backing her upstream again to the point at which he had taken command.

The battle ceased at nightfall. General Mouton, commanding the Confederate forces, was of the opinion that his command was too weak to make a successful stand against Weitzel's force of 4,500, and decided to retreat. The *Cotton,* unable to retreat farther up the shallow river and threatened with capture where she lay, was fired and scuttled. The next day Weitzel withdrew, the *Cotton* destroyed and his campaign closed.

In mid-1863 another menace to Union control along the lower Mississippi appeared. She was the ironclad *Missouri*, being constructed on the Red River.

The *Missouri's* general design followed closely that of the ironclad *Arkansas*. She was 183 feet in length, 33 feet abeam, and drew around 8½ feet of water. Her casemate backing was of yellow pine, 23 inches thick. The entire casemate was 130 feet, 6 inches in length, 33 feet in width, and 11½ feet high. She was pierced for ten guns — two gun ports forward, two aft, and three to each broadside — on the ordnance plan of the *Arkansas*. Her armor consisted of railroad T-rails, in a thickness of 4½ inches, held to the backing with railroad spikes. They had been laid too far apart to be solid to any degree, and the shells and conical solid of Farragut's 9- and 10-inch guns would probably have made her casemate a death trap. Her pilot house was situated at the front of the casemate, rising 19 inches above the roof.

Unlike the screw-propelled *Arkansas,* the *Missouri* was driven by a wheel set in the stern of the casemate. Although it was sunk well into a recess, over 8 feet of it remained exposed above the casemate roof. She was powered by two engines, each with a stroke of 7 feet, 6 inches, and a cylinder bore of 24 inches diameter. Her boilers — four of them — were 40 inches in diameter and 26 feet long. A new innovation was added to make living aboard her a little more bearable — a fan blower.

Though the *Missouri* was pierced for ten guns, she acquired only three; an 11-inch Dahlgren mounted on a pivot carriage to fire from the bow and starboard broadside, a 32-pounder seige gun mounted to fire through the bow and the port broadside, and a 9-inch Dahlgren pivoted to fire through the stern and either broadside. Rumors in the Federal navy had it that these guns were all taken from the *Indianola,* a Union ironclad captured and burned by the Confederates near Natchez in February, 1863. Confederate reports, however, indicate that the guns originally belonged to David Porter's old flagship, the *Harriet Lane,* captured at Galveston, Texas.[63] The *Missouri's* magazine and shell rooms were located forward.

Lieutenant Jonathan H. Carter was given command of the ironclad. His orders directed him to take the ship downriver as soon as possible to cooperate with General Dick Taylor's Army of Western Louisiana. Taylor was a man who, unlike some army officers, was able to rise above service prejudice and would do everything in his power to insure cooperation between the army and navy. General Edmund Kirby Smith would later say of Carter: "He is a determined man, and, I think, will fight his vessel desperately."[64] Between the two of them — Carter and Taylor — the *Missouri* should have wreaked some destruction on the lower Mississippi.

In September, 1864, Lt. Carter and a part of the *Missouri's* crew took part in an attempt to capture the U.S. gunboat *Rattler.* Acting Master D. W. Glenny, commanding the *Rattler,* appears to have been enamoured with a Mississippi belle, Miss Winnie Wilcox of Rodney. Word in Federal circles had it that he was engaged in the cotton-smuggling business with the Rebels. At any rate, his sympathies for the Union appear to have been luke-warm, at best.

In early August, Glenny, through a planter named Briscoe, communicated with Col. Issac F. Harrison, C.S.A., offering to set up the capture of the *Rattler* for $2,000 and 100 bales of cotton.[65] He proposed to take two boats — with most of the *Rattler's* crew — ashore on an expedition and have them captured. The Confederates would then take possession of the boats, and board and capture the *Rattler.* Harrison agreed to the scheme and a Federal prisoner later stated that he had overheard the Confederates say that Glenny had gotten his money, but not the cotton.[66] Carter, after taking the *Rattler,* was to proceed downriver with her and capture a few more Federals. Kirby Smith, commanding the Army of the Trans-Mississippi, hoped his men might be able to make a safe river crossing once several of the Federal boats were in hand and a stretch of the river under Confederate control.[67]

In early September several Negroes boarded the *Rattler* to inform Glenny that, on the night of September 4, two sons — Confederate officers — would be visiting at the home of their father, Joshua Jones. Glenny organized an expedition and, on that night, set out in the cutter with a large portion of his gunboat's crew. They landed, leaving the two Negroes with the cutter, and started inland. Carter's men ambushed them almost immediately. The Federals were easily overpowered, and Carter and his men were soon in the cutter, pulling for the *Rattler.* A gig had put out, however, and spotted the cutter coming in. The officer of the gig hailed, and Carter, surprised, answered with a vague "aye, aye." Suspicious, the gig's officer opened fire and called on the *Rattler* to bring a gun to bear, warning that they were about to be boarded. The cutter put about, the expedition a failure.

Glenny soon reappeared in Vicksburg, and Major General N. J. T. Dana wrote Glenny's commanding officer, Lt. Comm. Thomas O. Selfridge, that Glenny was telling people he was free on parole, and was required

To keep his vessel out of the way and not use his guns on the enemy. They say that he is on most intimate terms with James and other rebels in his vicinity, and was captured under the most suspicious circumstances.

He has considerable money . . .[68]

The "suspicious circumstances" of Glenny's capture led to Selfridge's placing him under close arrest aboard the *Rattler*. Glenny wrote to Miss Wilcox, giving the letter to a friend to mail, but the friend turned it, instead, over to Selfridge. The lieutenant opened it and read:

The insult that has been put upon me by the servant of an imbecile Government has sunk deep into my heart. I now live for one purpose, and that is deep, bitter revenge. I will sacrifice home, kindred, aye, my dearest friends, to accomplish my aim. Like a snake I will sting when least expected, and my name shall be a terror to every Yankee. The haunts of old oceans are too familiar to me to fear their fast cruisers, for will not my bonny barque be equally swift? . . . There are other brave hearts that will sail under my orders who are now serving under the Federal Government. You, who are the only being that I claim as a friend, will not, I hope despise me. Do not call me a traitor; remember that I have been true and faithful to the Federals till they wrongfully abused me . . .[69]

On the night of November 3, Glenny escaped from the *Rattler* along with the officer of the deck, his close friend, Acting Ensign E. P. Nellis. They slipped off in a skiff tied to the *Rattler's* stern, to disappear forever.[70]

Kirby Smith, late in the year, sent an officer and several men from the *Missouri* down to mine the river below Grand Encore.[71]

On April 4, 1865, the *Missouri* arrived in Alexandria. Bad luck and circumstances had prevented Carter's fulfilling the hopes that Kirby Smith had had for the *Missouri,* but the mere presence of the beast, enlarged out of all proportion by the ever-active rumor mill, kept the Federals worried, as evidenced by a telegram of April 29 from Major W. Hoffman, warning Brigadier General Cameron to keep an especially sharp lookout, as rumor had it that the *Missouri* would soon be down to go into combat.

But the *Missouri* remained idle, and on June 3, 1865, with the war played out in all sectors, Lt. Comm. W. E. Fitzhugh, U.S.N., formally received from Lt. Carter the surrender of the C.S.S. *Missouri* and the parole of her officers and men.

The *Missouri's* officers were:

Captain—Lt. J. H. Carter; Lts.—F. M. Roby, Wm. Crain, R. B. Larmour, J. C. Holcomb; Passed Midshipman—Wm. H. Shaw; Masters—E. Alexander, Robert Benthall, J. M. Douglass; Acting Master's Mate—Robert Ackman; Asst. Surgeon—John E. Duffie; Assist Paymaster—W. A. Hearn; 2nd Assist Engineers—C. Covert, John E. Ensard, F. P. Jones, A. Clayton, J. W. Dorsey; 3rd Assist Engineers—M. J. Duty, U. H. Quirk; Acting Carpenter—C. Moore; Pilots—Benoist W. Ray, Proctor Ankrim, Joseph Baisseau.

4

The Charleston Squadron

A government contract led to the laying, in January of 1862, of the keel for an ironclad at Charleston, South Carolina. Completed that summer, she carried 4 inches of armor and was armed with an 80-pound rifle forward, a 60-pound rifle aft, and an 8-inch shell gun in each broadside. Her length was approximately 150 feet, she was 35 feet abeam, and drew 12 feet of water. She was christened the C.S.S. *Palmetto State*.[1]

In March of 1862, James Eason, owner of Charleston's largest iron foundry, was awarded by the state of South Carolina a contract for the construction of a second ironclad at that port "for the defense of Charleston harbor."[2]

Eason laid his ship's keel behind the city post office. When finished, she was 135 feet in length, 35 feet abeam, and drew about 12 feet of water. Her casemate backing consisted of 22 inches of oak and pine, overlaid with two 2-inch layers of armor, covering her hull for a distance of 5 feet below the water line and sweeping forward to encase her ram bow. Five hundred tons of iron were used in plating her. She was to be driven by a single engine with a cylinder 30 inches in diameter and a stroke of 26 inches, turning a three-blade propeller 8 feet in diameter.

Her battery consisted of two 9-inch Dahlgrens and four 32-pounders converted by rifling and banding to fire 60-pound shot. She was launched in August and christened the C.S.S. *Chicora*.[3]

Duncan N. Ingraham was assigned to command the Charleston squadron. Officers of the ironclads were:

Palmetto State

Lt. Commander—John Rutledge; Lts.—W. H. Parker, Philip Porcher, George S. Shryock, Robert J. Brown; Master—F. T. Chew; Surgeon—A. M. Lynah; Paymaster—John S. Banks; Chief Engineer—M. P. Jordan; Assist. Engineers—J. J. Darcy, Wm. Ahern, John C. Johnson; Midshipmen—C. F. Seiver, W. P. Hamilton, C. Cary; Boatswain—T. Wilson; Gunner—George M. Thompson; Pilots—G. D. Gladden, Andrew Johnson.

Chicora

Commander—John Tucker; Lts.—George H. Bier, Wm. T. Glassell, Wm. H. Hall; Master—A. M. Mason; Acting Master—John Payne; Passed Midshipman—Joseph Claybrook; Midshipmen—R. H. Bacot, Palmer Sanders, Roger Pinkney; Surgeon—Wm. Mason Turner; Engineers—Hugh Clark, J. W. Tombs, J. J. Lyell, Wm. F. Jones; Gunner—E. R. Johnson; Carpenter—James F. Weaver; Acting Paymaster—E. A. West; Pilots—Thomas Payne, James Aldert.

Some distinguished South Carolina names appeared in the ironclads' rosters—Flag Officer Ingraham, for instance, and John Rutledge, and the *Chicora's* young midshipman, Roger Pinkney. And talent, both old and new and all of it well proved, was much in evidence. John Tucker and William H. Parker were down from the James River Squadron. George Shryock and Clarence Cary were aboard the *Palmetto State,* both having witnessed ironclads at their worst at New Orleans. And R. H. Bacot, a battle-tested young veteran who had served the gallant *Arkansas'* starboard 32-pounder, was aboard the *Chicora.* A. F. Warley would soon be in Charleston, along with Bacot's fiery ex-commander, Issac Brown. For the first time, the Confederacy had two fully operational ironclads on the water in a single port and an assembly of talent that would be able to use them to their fullest advantage.

In December of 1862, the keel for a third ironclad was laid at Charleston, again under Eason's supervision. She was to be 180 feet in length and 36 feet abeam, with a 12½ foot depth of hold. Her engine's cylinder diameter was 36 inches; her propeller's diameter was 8½ feet, and 600 tons of iron were required to give her a 4-inch plating of armor. She was to carry six guns — four Brooke rifles firing shot ranging in weight from 90 to 110 pounds, and two 9-inch smoothbores.

Her construction was financed largely by the womenfolk of Charleston, through contributions of jewelry and their fund-raising fairs, bazaars, and similar entertainments. Accordingly, though she was officially the C.S.S. *Charleston,* she was popularly known as "The Ladies Iron-Clad Gunboat."

At 11:00 on the night of January 30, 1863, the *Chicora* and *Palmetto State* cast off their moorings and, in company with the gunboats *Ettiwan, Clinch,* and *Chesterfield,* turned towards the bar at the mouth of the harbor. Fog hung thick and cold in the night, obscuring details of the five ships and casting hazy halos around the signal lights with which they identified themselves to Confederate gunners at the fortifications ringing the harbor.

Near the hour of 2:00 A.M., the squadron dropped anchor behind the bar, the pilots stating that the tide was not yet high enough to permit the ironclads to cross in safety. They remained there until 4:40, when the whole squadron upped anchor, gliding through the fog and out into the Atlantic in search of United States' blockaders. For the first time, Confederate ironclads were leaving the inland waters, penetrating the ocean itself in search of combat.

The squadron fanned out, cruising eastward with the wooden gunboats hanging back — the heavily armed blockaders were a bit more than the converted commercial steamers cared to tackle — and presently blundered into the blockading fleet. Those searching the fog through the viewing slits in the *Palmetto State's* pilot house made out the bulk of a squarish stationary object dead ahead, and the flagship put on steam to ram. In the dim glow of battle lanterns on the gun deck, Philip Porcher* — immaculate in white gloves, an unlighted cigar between his teeth — supervised with an air of detachment the preparation and pointing of the squat black 80-pounder rifle nestled in the bow.[4]

The vague squarish object in the water took form as the ram closed the distance. Its lines lengthened and masts and a smoke funnel could be seen rising from the deck to disappear in the fog. As yet, no hail had been given, no sign of activity showed itself aboard the still target as the *Palmetto State,* engine hissing and pounding, plunged closer. The blockader loomed larger; a trace of anchor chain could

---

* Lieutenant Philip Porcher, a native of South Carolina and former lieutenant, U.S. Navy, was lost at sea when the blockade runner *Helen*, carrying cotton to Nassau under his command, foundered in a storm, May 10, 1864.

be seen reaching vaguely down and out from the bow and the bulk of life boats could be distinguished. Suddenly a lookout hailed: "What steamer is that? Drop your anchor; you will be into us!" A Confederate officer returned triumphantly: "This is the Confederate States steamer *Palmetto State!*" The ironclad surged the remaining few yards and the two ships met, the ram's iron-sheathed bow snapping planking and driving deep into the blockader's innards. Phil Porcher's 80-pounder roared, its shell piercing the Federal's condenser and steam drum, traveling on to kill a gunner in his room, and blasting a 5-foot hole in the opposite wall of the ship.

She proved to be the *Mercedita,* Captain Stellwagen commanding. Second in command Lt. Abbot was paddled out to the ironclad in a small boat to surrender the ship, as Stellwagen wasn't quite awake yet. The lieutenant reported that the *Mercedita* was sinking and that she didn't have enough boats for her men. In their haste to get his lifeboat launched, Lt. Abbot's men had forgotten to cork the drain hole and, as a result, their own boat was taking water. Abbot asked if he and his boat's crew might be taken aboard. Flag Officer Ingraham refused — there was no room for prisoners aboard the *Palmetto State*. He sent the Federals back aboard the *Mercedita* — she had yet to sink and looked to be in little danger of it — and stood for the *Chicora,* who had become engaged with several enemy vessels.

The *Chicora* opened her end of the encounter at 5:20 A.M., coming to grips with a schooner-rigged steamer, propeller driven, that the Confederates were unable to identify.* The ironclad fired off a few rounds in this fellow's direction, then turned her attention to a large side-wheeler — the

---

* Probably the *Augusta*, which reported catching several large-caliber shells in her hull.

Quaker City — bearing down on her port bow. The Yank came boldly on until, at a range of about 100 yards, the *Chicora* let fly with her bow gun, then rounded to, offering 120 pounds worth of shot from her two-gun broadside and a 9-inch shell from the stern-chaser.

The first shot from the *Palmetto State,* followed by the *Chicora's* first barrage from the general vicinity of the *Keystone State's* anchorage, led the blockaders to suppose that a blockade runner had been sighted trying to slip out. The *Quaker City,* looking for the supposed fugitive, had rushed at a dim shape lying in the water and was astonished beyond words when the supposedly fleeing "runner" sent a 9-inch shell whistling overhead. A gun crew managed to get off a shot from the ready Parrott rifle as the Confederate pitched three more large-caliber shells her way. The blockader's captain reported that one of these

entered . . . amidships about seven feet above the water line, cutting away a portion of the guard beam and a guard brace, and then on its course through the ship's side exploding in the engine room, carrying away there the starboard entabulature brace, air-pump dome, and air-pump guide rod, and making sad havoc with the bulkheads.[5]

The *Quaker City* turned and fled.

A large side-wheeler stepped boldly out of the mist and a screw sloop, half hidden in the haze, stood off to take stock of the situation. The side-wheeler — she was the *Keystone State* — rounded to at a fairly close range, giving the Confederate both broadsides. The *Chicora* replied with a single shot, an incendiary shell from her bow gun. It struck just forward of the Federal's port paddle wheel house, setting the ship afire and disabling the wheel. The blockader immediately ceased firing and hauled down her flag.

Captain Tucker ordered Lt. Bier to take a small boat,

board the *Keystone State,* and bring her in to Charleston harbor as a prize. A boat was lowered and Bier and his crew were in the process of manning the bobbing craft when it was discovered that the *Keystone State,* despite the fact that she had surrendered, was getting underway, working her starboard wheel. The prize crew was immediately gotten back aboard, the boat was secured, and the *Chicora* gave chase.

The *Memphis,* a captured blockade runner now armed for Federal duty and under the command of Lt. P. G. Wartmouth, had stumbled on the scene expecting, like the *Quaker City,* to help catch a runner going out. Instead, she found the *Keystone State,* afire with her flag down, dead in the water. The *Memphis* passed a line and started pulling, out of sight of the Confederates, drawing the surrendered blockader off to safety.[6] It amounted to a legitimate recapture without, as yet, any more belligerent action on the part of the *Keystone State.* All, so far, was strictly within the rules of honorable warfare.

Tucker, watching the distance between his ironclad and the *Keystone State* widen, hesitated to resume fire, as the Yankee still had her flag down. Perhaps, he thought, the fire and damage prevented the Federals from stopping the blockader. Perhaps she was out of control. Then, with the *Chicora* fast falling behind, the *Keystone State* raised her flag and resumed firing. Tucker was furious. "Their commander," he later said, "by this faithless act, had placed himself above the pale of civilized warfare." The *Keystone State* was soon lost in the fog.

The frustrated *Chicora* turned and vented her wrath on two schooners, a brig, and a bark-rigged propeller. She tried to come to close quarters with each, but the Federals would have none of it. The Confederate at last turned her attention to a dimly seen steam sloop, engaging her at long range. She was probably the *Housatonic,* destined to become the victim of the world's first successful submarine attack. While the ironclad was at this, the flagship signaled her to break off action.

The squadron anchored, at 8:45 A.M., at the entrance to the beach channel. They remained seven hours, waiting for sufficient water to carry them across the bar.

That afternoon Baron de St. Andre and Senor Moncada — foreign consuls from France and Spain, accompanied by General Ripley — boarded the gunboat *Clinch* and started a tour of inspection. They crossed the bar and headed for the blockaders' usual anchorage, venturing far beyond the usual blockade stations. They saw not a sign of a sail, even with a telescope. The *Mercedita,* presumably safely surrendered and left on her own, had fled immediately for Port Royal. The *Memphis,* towing the *Keystone State* through the thinning morning haze, was not far behind,[7] and the entire blockading squadron had followed.

Mr. Bunce — British consul — had made the same tour earlier in the day aboard the British corvette *Petrel,* then in Charleston harbor. That evening the three consuls met and declared that, according to the international rules of war, the blockade off Charleston harbor was officially broken. Communications to that effect were sent to the three governments represented and the disbursement of the blockading fleet off Charleston was proclaimed by the Confederate government, making Charleston, for 30 days, a free and open port. But despite international rules, the blockaders soon began to reappear, resuming the blockade.

The first announcement of the breaking of the blockade set Charleston wild with rejoicing — rejoicing that faded with the return of the grim Federal steamers. But the Secession City did not forget the heroism of the Confederate sailors who had made the attempt. Dances and dinners in homes and in halls, by private citizens and civic groups, hosted the officers and crewmen of the *Chicora* and the *Palmetto State*. On February 3 a special service was held in St. Philip's church in their honor. Glory, praise, and public notoriety were hollow rewards for some, however. Gloomy James Tombs, second assistant engineer aboard the *Chicora*, said of the raid and its aftermath:

The upshot of the engagement was a grand bit of glory, but not a prize or ship destroyed, and when we passed back over the bar and back into Charleston we all felt disappointed at the night's work. We did not accomplish as much as our sister ship, the *Palmetto State*. They say we raised the blockade, but we all felt we would have rather raised hell and sunk the ships.[8]

The ironclads' attack seemed to awaken the north to the fact that the armored warriors reported for so long to be building in Charleston were now both operational and deadly. To keep the two home-grown rams in check, the Federals stationed off Charleston harbor the most powerful ironclad fleet ever assembled anywhere. Consisting of the monitors *Weekhawken, Passaic, Montauk, Patapsco, Catskill, Nantucket, Nahunt,* and *Keokuk,* it was led by the big armored steam-frigate *New Ironsides*. The original *Monitor* was to have been among the squadron, but she had foundered at sea.

In March of 1863, Flag Officer Duncan N. Ingraham was relieved of his command afloat and given command of the Charleston Naval Station. Captain John R. Tucker was given command of the squadron. The *Palmetto State* lost her title as flagship and Tucker's pennant went up on the *Chicora*.

One of the main Union designs of the third year of war

was the capture of Charleston. The Hotbed of Secession — especially the fort that sat like a wart on the surface of its harbor — was a symbol of defiance for the South, an open wound in the pride of the North. The capture of the Secession City would be every bit as much a moral victory as would the capture of Richmond. The Federals wanted the port badly.

Harbor defenses were strong. Pierre Beauregard had come to Charleston just before the war's outbreak, bringing a professional's approach to the placement of guns for the reduction of Fort Sumter. His handiwork showed him to be a master at his trade and, when the fort had fallen, the forts and emplacements encircling the harbor proved to be competent defense against invasion from without as well as defiance from within. He was back now, building new batteries, moving or strengthening old ones, and sewing the harbor with all manner of mines and entangling booby traps, together with aiming stakes to help Confederate gunners find the range at given points in the channel and harbor.

Samuel F. Du Pont, admiral commanding the blockading squadron off the Charleston bar, had a fair idea of the harbor's strength. The ideal campaign for the fall of Charleston, as he saw it, called for a thrust by the army from Charleston's rear, supported by the navy at the harbor's mouth. The Washington Government saw it differently. A quick thrust by the navy should turn the trick in jig time, they said. Wooden ships had forced the surrenders of New Orleans and Port Royal, and the Mississippi River ironclads had conquered the forts in the upper Mississippi. Surely a competent commander with eight invulnerable monitors and the armored frigate *New Ironsides* — the most powerful ship in the world — could do the same at Charleston. Why waste time with seige operations?

Accordingly, on April 7, the entire Federal ironclad

squadron steamed into Charleston harbor. Their immediate objective was the reduction of Fort Sumter, the sturdy symbol of defiance thought to be the key to the entire Charleston defenses. As the monitors came in, the ironclads *Chicora* and *Palmetto State* got up steam and proceeded to a point between Fort Sumter and Cummings Point. They halted there, watching the monitors advance. According to orders, they were to go into action only if the Federals passed Fort Sumter and threatened the city proper.*

The mighty *New Ironsides,* too great of draft to follow her monitors in close, dropped anchor too far from Sumter to render her fire effective. The monitors closed in on the fort, all reaching predetermined stations about three o'clock. A ranging shot was thrown from Sumter and the battle was joined.

Confederate fire was heavy. The monitors had placed themselves between Sumter, in mid-harbor, and Fort Moultrie and adjoining batteries on Sullivan's Island to the northeast. Sumter's northeast face was soon padded with thick clouds of smoke. Fort Moultrie was similarly wreathed. The blue-gray clouds drifted down and flattened on the water, eventually to be blown away by the wind. Near misses raised water spouts around the cluster of monitors and the water immediately surrounding them frothed a spotty white with fragments of shattered shells and, soon, flying shards of splintered armor.

It soon became evident that the monitors were getting the worst of it. Although their 11- and 15-inch shots brought great masses of the fort's masonry sliding into the harbor,

---

* Yet, on November 14, 1863, Gen. Beauregard, with full knowlege of these orders, attempted a slur on the rams by stating that: "The best proof of the total failure of the three iron-clad gunboats, *Chicora, Palmetto State*, and *Charleston* . . . is that . . . they did not fire one shot in defense of Fort Sumter during the naval attack of the 7th of April last."

the monitors themselves were sent reeling by the heavy projectiles that fell on them in torrents. Union fire slacked off when Confederate shot bent turret tracks, preventing the thick-skinned circular gun boxes from turning. Several of the heavy iron port shutters were jammed closed. At length, the light failing and the tide going out, the ironclads withdrew. They had all been injured. Great chunks of armor were missing from some; deck armor was splintered and cracked on others. None of the single-turret regular monitors were really disabled — all could still get about under their own power — but five of the seven were unable to put down an effective fire. The freak *Keokuk* (a turtle-deck affair with two stationary turrets) had been hulled repeatedly and her twin turrets pierced. She filled and sank just outside the bar. The Confederates, in a daring expedition, soon recovered most of her equipment. One of her guns was mounted at Fort Sumter. Her rammers, sponges, and battle lanterns were put into service aboard the *Chicora*.[9]

On August 7, two boats loaded with volunteers from the *Chicora* and *Palmetto State,* commanded by Lieutenants A. F. Warley and John Payne, joined a few men from the 25th South Carolina Infantry in an attempt to capture several Federal guard boats that took stations nightly between James and Morris Islands. The Confederates surprised the Yankee sailors and, in the skirmish that followed, killed two Yanks and wounded five others, capturing a boat and twelve prisoners.[10]

The night of September 8 saw a small boat attack launched against Fort Sumter. Four hundred sailors and marines in a number of boats were towed in toward the fort by a tug and, about 800 yards out, cast loose. The Federals closed slowly and quietly on the dark and silent fortress, hoping for a surprise.

There was no surprise. As the first boats beached on the tiny rim of foundation extending into the water from the fort's walls, the night came alive with noise, smoke, flame, and flying metal. Confederates swarmed the parapet, sending down fire balls, hand grenades, and showers of musketry. The *Chicora,* anchored nearby, was quickly on the scene. Canister, grape, and shell spewed from her gun muzzles, killing Federals as they flattened themselves against Sumter's damp brick wall.

Of the 400, about 120 landed. All were killed or taken prisoner. The rest put about and headed out to sea and the *Chicora* returned to her guard station. The night was quiet again.

The *Charleston* was launched late in 1863. She was ready for service in 1864 and was added to the fleet under the command of Issac Brown. Captain Tucker moved his flag from the *Chicora,* making the stronger *Charleston* flagship of the squadron. Commander Thomas T. Hunter was ordered to the command of the *Chicora* and Commander James H. Rochelle assumed command of the *Palmetto State.*

A major point in the Union campaign for the conquest of Charleston was the occupation of Confederate-held Morris Island, a point from which their huge Parrott rifles could batter Fort Sumter down about the ears of its defenders. Battery Wagner, a sand-and palmetto log work at the tip of the island, was subjected to several frontal assaults, then naval shelling from the monitors. It finally fell under sustained seige operations. The *Charleston's* guns covered the evacuation. The fort's garrison was removed by boats from the *Chicora.*

With a vastly superior ironclad flotilla guarding the wooden blockaders outside the bar, the three armored Rebels could do little but carry out minor defensive duties. One of them took station in the channel near Sumter each night, acting as a guard boat.

All three ironclads were soon fitted with spar torpedoes — copper cylinders filled with 90 pounds of gunpowder, fitted to the end of a long spar. These were mounted at the ironclad's bows, triced up in the air when not in action. In combat, they could be lowered to about 6 feet beneath the water's surface and rammed against an enemy vessel, blowing a hole in her bottom. The *Palmetto State's* armament had been more than doubled. Two additional gun ports had been cut in each side and she now mounted ten big 7-inch rifles, four in each broadside and a bow and stern chaser. The additional weight (approximately 13,000 pounds per gun) increased her draft, decreasing her speed and maneuverability.

On the night of February 26, 1864, the *Charleston* was briefly invaded by Union sailors when a picket boat from the U.S.S. *Nipsic,* manned by an officer and five men, was captured by a Confederate boat. The Federals were housed aboard the *Charleston* before being sent off to prison.[11]

A fourth ironclad was to make her appearance in Charleston waters, F. M. Jones receiving the contract from the Confederate Government. She was to be a monster — 216 feet in length, 51 feet abeam, and drawing over 15 feet of water. She was to be protected by 6 inches of armor and would be pierced for eight guns. Jones was to give her two noncondensing engines, brand new from the Columbus naval works, each of a 36-inch cylinder diameter with a 24-inch stroke, turning a 10′ 8″ propeller on an 8-inch shaft.[12] Steam was provided by five cylindrical flued boilers, each 20 feet in length and 4 feet in diameter, heated by furnaces with a surface grate area of 129 square feet. Her engines could turn at a maximum of 40 rpm, and she could make 4 knots turning 32. Her cost, including later repairs, came to $193,480.[13]

Named the *Columbia* (although occasionally referred to as the *Ashley*), the fourth ironclad was destined to little fame in the Charleston area. She was launched on March 10, 1864, and was yet to be completed when, on January 12, 1865, she was run aground on a sunken wreck near Fort Moultrie. The weight of her armor cracked her keel when the tide went out.

Two other ironclads were well underway by the fall of 1864, one launched in late October and moved out of range of the occasional Federal shells that fell around the construction site. They were to mount four guns each, encased in and protected by 6 inches of armor. By early November they were reported as completed through their woodwork, propellers and shafts installed, engines nearly ready at Columbus, and awaiting their armor.

Armor starvation was becoming acute in the fall of 1864. Chief naval constructor John L. Porter reported to Mallory that:

It will be seen that everything has been done to get up an ironclad fleet of vessels which could possibly be done under the circumstances, but in consequence of the loss of our iron and coal regions, with the rolling mills at Atlanta, our supply of iron has been very limited. The mills at Richmond are capable of rolling any quantity, but the material is not on hand, and the amount now necessary to complete vessels already built would be equal to 4,230 tons, as follows:

	Tons
At Richmond, for two vessels	575
At Wilmington, for one vessel (1-inch plate)	150
At Charleston, for two vessels	800

At Savannah, for two vessels 750
At Columbus, for one vessel 280
At Mobile, for three vessels 1,250
On the Bigbee [Tombigbee], for one vessel 425
    Total .... 4,230[14]

In February of 1865 Sherman left Savannah and cut into the interior of South Carolina. Threatened from the rear, the port of Charleston was no longer tenable. Preparations were made to evacuate. Fort Sumter, having stood for four long years against everything the Federals could throw at her, was deserted. The crews of the ironclads were landed, provisioned, armed, and formed as infantry. Under Rochell's command, they set off toward Wilmington, North Carolina, and would soon be fighting with General Lee in the Confederacy's last days.

As the sailors marched away, Lt. Bowen, executive officer of the *Palmetto State,* fired the *Charleston, Palmetto State,* and *Chicora.* They burned for several hours, then exploded. He had evidently forgotten about the *Columbia,* for the Federals found her, still aground, when they entered the city.[15] Rear Admiral John A. Dahlgren inspected her, pronouncing the craft "a remarkably fine, powerful vessel . . . a really formidable customer, and very strongly built, with great capacity as a ram. She would have stood a good fight with one of our ironclads."[16] She was floated off the wreck, repaired, and, on May 25, sent to Hampton Roads.

5

The Savannah Squadron
and the Muskogee

On November 12, 1861, the steamer *Fingal* chanced the blockade off the South Atlantic coast and made port at Savannah, Georgia, bringing in what was to be the biggest single shipment of war materials ever run in to the Confederacy. Stevedores at the Savannah docks unloaded a cargo reported as consisting of 10,000 British Enfield rifles, 1,000,000 ball cartridges, 2,000,000 precussion caps, 3,000 cavalry sabers, 1,000 carbines with cutlass bayonets and 1,000 rounds of ammunition per carbine, 500 revolvers with cartridges, several large-caliber rifled cannon, several smaller cannon, 400 barrels of powder (some of which was destined for the *Virginia*), assorted medical stores, and material for uniforms.[1]

Lieutenant James D. Bulloch, the Confederacy's chief secret service agent in Europe, had purchased the *Fingal* nearly new. She had loaded in Greenock, Scotland, and sailed on October 10. Four nights later, in a driving storm, she had proved her worth as a ram by running down and seriously damaging an Austrian coal brig.[2]

Her war goods delivered in Savannah, the blockade runner gorged herself on cotton bales and prepared for the run out. She would never make it. Since her celebrated arrival, no less than five Federal warships had appeared and Savannah was bottled up tight.

Like nearly every other Southern seaport and river town — from Norfolk to Pensacola, from New Orleans to Nashville — Savannah desired an ironclad as a defense against a Union water-borne invasion. As the *Fingal* was big and relatively fast — and couldn't get out — it was decided to convert her. The project was begun by cutting her down to her main deck, which was then overlaid with a wood backing and iron plating to a thickness of one foot. A casemate frame was erected amidships, overlaid with a thick wood backing, then covered with a 4-inch iron sheath in two 2-inch layers, all inclined at an angle of 30°. She was armed with a 7-inch Brooke rifle at bow and stern and a 6-inch Brooke in each broadside. Her 7-inch guns were pivoted, enabling them to be fought in broadside. Charles Girard, an agent of Napoleon III visiting the Confederacy in 1863, described the Confederate Brooke gun and its projectile.

. . . an attentive observer would not fail to notice the circular bands or rings, closely joined to the gun, which are meant to make it more resistant under the expansive force of a strong powder charge.* As to their groove, it is on an inclined plane rather than in a straight furrow.

---

* The Brooke's breech was clasped in three of these bands, preheated, slipped over the breech, then allowed to shrink as they cooled for added strength. The Parrott gun accomplished the same end with a single casing covering the entire breech, while the Dahlgren was thickened at its breech—bottle shaped—to achieve the same strength.

The projectiles are made of forged iron, cast iron being as we know, greatly inferior to that type of metal. Those which I had the opportunity to examine were adapted to a caliber of 7 inches. Their shape is oblong, cylindrical for most of their length, with the exception of the head, which is slightly conical and cut around with a bevelled edge. The rear end, which fits into the breech of the gun, has a wide circular groove, enclosing a centrally-placed rim, and holds a copper disc whose edges are juxtaposed metal, one about a third of the way down from the front, the other near the rear. They are designed to fit into the grooves of the gun. The average length of these cannon balls is 12 English inches; their rear diameter 6 94/100; the front diameter, 6 87/100; and their weight from 116 to 120 pounds.

From a distance of 260 yards, with a charge of 20 pounds of powder, these projectiles will penetrate four iron plates, each 2 inches thick, plus 18 inches of oak, placed together against a clay cliff. In its blast, the cannon ball will also completely shatter the entire thickness of the wood mentioned here.[3]

An iron ram was secured to the ironclad's already-dangerous prow and a spar torpedo gave her additional lethalness. Her length was 204 feet, her beam 41 feet, and her draft 15 feet 5 inches. The conversion was the work of Nelson and Asa Tift, late of Millandon's shipyard, New Orleans. The ironclad was rechristened the *Atlanta* and command was given to Commander William McBlair.[4]

The United States Army received its first glimpse of the *Atlanta* when, on July 31, 1862, the ironclad cruised down the Savannah River's South Channel toward Tybee Island, showing herself to Union-held Fort Pulaski. The Federals had been well aware of the building of the *Atlanta* and Northern editorial pages had carried the usual flood of demands that the Federal Government do something about this new menace. But when the *Atlanta* made it known that she was afloat and active, the Northern press screamed panic. The New York *Herald's* correspondent commented that: "Unless some monitor comes to our succor, the fair weather yachts [Union blockaders] now reposing on the placid bosom of the Savannah River, have before them an excellent opportunity of learning what it is to be blown out of the water."[5] The *Atlanta,* in Northern minds, like the *Virginia*, the *Manassas*, the *Cotton*, and others, became a terrible engine of destruction, capable of sweeping the coast from Florida to Maine, destroying or driving off all the ships of the North and South Atlantic Blockading Squadrons, opening the entire Confederate coast to foreign trade, and laying the Atlantic shore from Delaware to Maine under tribute. The truth of the matter was that, due to the defects seemingly inherent in nearly all of the cobbled-up Confederate armorclads, she was not nearly so formidable as the Federals and her own countrymen supposed. She steered poorly; her speed was, at best, six knots; her excessive draft limited her effectiveness for harbor defense; her miserably constructed gun ports, just like those of the *Louisiana* and *Arkansas,* had been cut too small to allow proper lateral training and elevation; and she was, like most ironclads both North and South, an uncomfortable ship, poorly ventilated. H. B. Littlepage, in a letter dated February 16, 1863 to Catsby Jones, described living conditions aboard the ram.

There is no ventilation below at all, and I think it will be impossible for us to live on her in the summer. I would defy anyone in the world to tell when it is day or when night if he is confined below without any way of marking time. When we go to sleep there is nothing between us and the water outside except a thin shell of iron about five-eighths of an inch in thickness. I would venture to say that if a person were blindfolded and carried below and then turned loose he would imagine himself in a swamp, for the water is trickling in all the time and everything is so damp.

With the *Atlanta's* appearance above Pulaski, Gideon Welles and the Federal Government sat up and took notice of the dire threats and somber warnings being issued by the Northern press. Several monitors soon appeared among Savannah's blockaders.

In July Captain Josiah Tattnall reappeared in Savannah, cleared by a Court of Inquiry of charges that he had needlessly destroyed the *Virginia*.

The new year found Tattnall, flag officer of the Savannah squadron, formulating plans for an attack on the Federal monitors. It would be wisest, he concluded, to engage them at long range, hoping to dislocate their turrets through the jarring impact of his 7-inch Brooke bolts while somehow keeping clear of their 11- and 15-inch missiles. Surely, he placed extreme faith in Confederate gunnery, assuming that the backwoods army draftees that would comprise his crew could strike, at long range, the narrow, rounded turret of a monitor while the twice-as-large Union rifled bolts thrown by professional naval gunners would sail over and around his long casemate with its half-as-thick armor. But the feasability of the plan was never tested: the whole operation collapsed when it was found impossible to get the *Atlanta* through the South Channel without removing obstructions placed there to halt prowling Federal men of war.

In February the monitors attacked Fort McAllister, a strong earthwork located on Genesis Point, south of Savannah. As guns began to roar, the *Atlanta* steamed downriver, anchoring near Couston's Bluff to add her battery to the guns of a fort situated there. The monitors, however, concentrated on Fort McAllister. The fort returned their fire well, hitting the Federals several times, but failing to inflict any damage. The *Atlanta* saw no action.

At 1:30 P.M., February 16, 1863, Commander McBlair

died. On February 18 Commander Arthur Sinclair,* who was to have commanded the *Mississippi* at New Orleans, assumed command, relinquishing it to Commander William A. Webb on May 2. Webb had commanded the gunboat *Teaser* during the *Virginia's* duels in Hampton Roads, and had since served at the Charleston naval station. He commanded all naval forces afloat at Savannah until Captain William W. Hunter took the flag. Tattnall now commanded the station. Officers assigned to the *Atlanta* were:

Captain—Comm. Wm. A. Webb; Lts.—J. W. Alexander, Alphonse Barbot, Geo. H. Arledge; Master—Thomas L. Wragg; Passed Assist. Surgeon—R. J. Freeman; 1st Assist. Engineer— E. J. Johnson; 2nd Assist. Engineer—Wm. J. Morrell; 3rd Assist. Engineer—Leslie King; Midshipmen—J. A. G. Williamson, J. A. Peters; Master's Mate—Wm. McBlair; Gunner— Thomas B. Travers; Paymaster—Wm. B. Micou; Paymaster's Clerk—G. W. Carey; Lt. of Marines—James Thurston; Pilot— James Fleetwood.

Commander Webb devised a plan of battle exactly opposite to that proposed by Tattnall. The *Atlanta* would come to close quarters with the monitors, when she would stand a fair chance of blowing the bottom out of one with her spar torpedo, hoping to either ram the other or put a shell through an open gunport.

At 3:30 A.M. on July 17, 1863, the fires in her furnace illuminating the inner lip of her squat funnel, the *Atlanta* slipped her moorings and turned her head down the Savannah River. Accompanying her was the wooden gunboat *Isondiga,* Lt. Joel S. Kennard commanding, along to engage any of the wooden blockaders that might show themselves.

---

* Sinclair was to drown in the foundering of the blockade runner *Leila* on January 14, 1865.

The *Atlanta's* two opponents, the *Weehawken* and the *Nahant,* lay at anchor farther downriver, both armored with ten inches of hard, high-grade iron and each mounting an 11-inch and a 15-inch rifle.

In naval circles of the time, the casemated type of craft was considered superior to a turreted craft because of the big broadsides that could be discharged from a long casemate side: a casemated ship could throw more metal per salvo than a turreted craft. In the upcoming engagement, however, there could be no doubt that the situation was reversed. The *Atlanta* could bring to bear, at most, three guns of 6- and 7-inch caliber. A single monitor could bring to bear at all times two guns of 11- and 15-inch caliber. The factor that was essential for a casemated craft's superiority — weight of metal — was, in this case, decidedly on the side of the monitor. And there were two of them. The monitors were, in fact, superior in all departments — armament, armor, speed, maneuverability, and crew. While the *Atlanta's* officers might equal their Union counterparts in experience, training, and ability and perhaps even exceed them in nerve and mettle, the advantage of a good crew must be thrown to the Union side of the balance. The Federal crews were seasoned in ironclad warfare and had spent their lives before the war on merchant vessels or U.S. ships of war. All, to a man, were professional sailors. In contrast, the crew of the *Atlanta* could boast of only 40 true sailors, the majority of them rather indifferent to the Confederate cause. The bigger part of the crew had been recruited from Georgia infantry. The only ones that could really be counted on were Lieutenant James Thurston's 28 marines.

Webb's plan called for a quick and hard-pressed attack, taking the monitors by surprise, then sinking or capturing the whole Savannah blockading squadron. The *Atlanta* would then put to sea, heading for Charleston. She would surprise and destroy the entire blockading squadron off that port, then stand down the coast, raising the blockade all the way to Fernandina, Florida.

With all sounds muffled and ports tightly closed against the escaping light of battle lanterns, the *Atlanta,* trailed by the *Isondiga,* slid through the predawn dark into Wassaw Sound. Down the sound a monitor, urged by the current, tugged gently at its anchor. The squat, gray Confederate lowered her torpedo, its slender staff kicking up a frothing false wake before the ram bow, and turned for the monitor, putting on steam. She ran onto a sandbar, grounding no farther than ¾ of a mile from the apparently unaroused Federal.

It took 15 agonizing minutes to get the *Atlanta* free of her imprisoning rip. During that time the mild gray of coming dawn had tinged the eastern sky, while the monitor gave no outward sign of being aware of the Rebel's presence. As the ironclad slid free, Webb ordered the helmsman to bring her into a deeper channel. The ship's wheel turned in compliance, but the flood tide was pushing the big ironclad the wrong way and, with her keel in the mud, the *Atlanta's* steering was contrary. She grounded again. This time, the monitor (she was the *Weehawken*) upped her anchor — clots of thick smoke belching from stacks that were being lowered flush with the deck — and began moving. Webb ordered Lt. Barbot to open fire, hoping the whistling Brooke bolts would suggest the use of caution on the Federal's part, keeping her at long range until the *Atlanta* could get free. The *Weehawken,* however, was not to be bluffed. She came boldly on. Just in time, the *Atlanta* slid off her mud bank, only to ground again — hard — and heel over, in such a position that her guns could not be brought to bear on anything. They pointed awkwardly at the sky and a gunner sighting down the long black barrel of the lethal, yet useless, 6-inch rifle could see the tops of the trees on the river bank, now bathed in molten gold sunlight, and the haze in the early western sky throwing back the garish red and gold of the sun rising across the river.

The *Weehawken* steamed leisurely past and, at a range of 300 yards, delivered the contents of her huge guns. The 11-inch shot missed; the 15-inch bolt was better aimed. It struck solidly above a port shutter near the pilot house. The heavy projectile smashed through the *Atlanta's* armor with disconcerting ease, bringing in a hail of wood and iron splinters that swept down the entire crew of Lt. Thurston's broadside gun. The mass raked the deck, also wounding half the crew of Lt. Barbot's gun, while the concussion of the blow knocked shot and shell from their racks, sending them rolling down the canted deck. A near panic seized the conscripts at the sight of the bolt's destruction. The ironclad's engines strained hard to bring her off the mud bar, but it was all to no avail. She was stuck fast.

After an interval, the monitor's 11-inch gun roared again. Its bolt struck, starting several timbers and causing the ram to leak, but failed to penetrate. A second shot from the 15-inch gun quickly followed. It smacked a port shutter, broke it in half, ripped off several great chunks of iron and wood, and tossed the whole mess inside, bringing down half the crew of another gun.

A sort of silence, broken only by the muffled clanking of the *Atlanta's* straining engines, settled over Wassaw Sound while the monitor's guns were reloaded. Then the 15-inch gun boomed again, sending a screaming projectile through the corner of the Confederate's pilot house, ripping off the roof and wounding both pilots.[6]

The *Atlanta,* as far as Webb was concerned, was finished. She was hard and fast aground under the guns of the *Weehawken,* with the *Nahant* coming up on her. She was unable to make any pretense at defense, and the Federals were turning her casemate into a slaughter house. The only course left was surrender. The Confederate banner came down and Webb addressed his crew.

I have surrendered our vessel because circumstances over which I have no control have compelled me to do so. I know that you started on this expedition with high hopes, and you have been disappointed. I most earnestly wish that it had been otherwise, but Providence, for some reason, has interfered with our plans, and we have failed of success. You all know that, if we had not run aground, the result would have been different, and now that a regard for your lives has influenced me in this surrender, I would advise you to submit quietly to the fate which has overtaken us. I hope we all may soon be returned to our homes and meet again in common brotherhood.[7]

The Federals made prisoners of 165 men. They were confined to Fort Lafayette in New York harbor. The *Atlanta* was towed to the Philadelphia Navy Yard, repaired, and, in February, 1864, returned to duty as part of the Federal North Atlantic Blockading Squadron.

Lieutenant Washington Gwathmey, C.S.N., was on duty with the army when orders from the Secretary of War dated July 10, 1863, ordered him to proceed to Savannah and report to Flag Officer W. W. Hunter for assignment to duty. On arriving in Savannah, the lieutenant found himself in command of the ironclad C.S.S. *Georgia.*[8] She was large — 260 feet in length, 60 feet abeam, capped by a big casemate standing 12 feet high. Her battery varied — reported at four, five, and nine guns ranging from 6-inch rifles and

32-pounders to 8-inch Columbiads and 9-inch Dahlgrens — as the army borrowed, returned, then borrowed again from her armament to bolster their own batteries ashore.[9] She was almost useless, an absolute failure as a naval vessel, because her weak and cranky engines could not create enough horsepower to set the great beast in motion. She was moored northeast of the city off Fort Jackson, near the big bend in the Savannah River where a few of her guns could bear on both the North and South Channels. Stone-filled cribs surrounded her to protect from ramming or torpedoing by Union raiders, and a big timber — one of the cross-braces from her launching way — hung down from her keel. It had stuck there as she was launched and was never removed.[10] Her 82-man crew was composed of conscripts but, under Gwathmey's predecessor, Lieutenant J. Pembroke Jones, they had been well drilled and disciplined.

The ironclads *Savannah* and *Milledgeville*, both built under government contract at H. F. Willink's shipyard, were constructed along lines similar to those of the *Atlanta*. The *Savannah* was completed soon after the *Atlanta's* capture. She drew 12½ feet of water and carried a battery identical in size and mounting to that of her unfortunate predecessor. The *Milledgeville* was to house four guns in a short casemate plated with 6 inches of iron. Her engines, constructed at Columbus by Chief Engineer Warner, were sent up and installed, and she was armored up over her knuckle and launched in late November, 1864. Another vessel similar in dimensions and configuration was underway at the neighboring yard of Krenson & Hawkes, but her engines were not completed in time and there was never enough iron available to begin her armoring.[11]

As December, 1864, descended on Savannah, so descended Sherman. He had cut savagely through the state, marking his trail with fire, destruction, and despair. Now he was before Savannah, drawing up his troops to lash the city into submission and so complete his eastward plunge. General William J. Hardee, commanding the district composed of Florida, Georgia, and South Carolina, prepared to retreat in the face of the overwhelming Federal hordes. While he gathered the remnants of a Confederate army about him and sent his meager supplies rattling north in wagons, Sherman laid seige to the city.

On December 20, in what amounted to a covering action for Hardee's retreating army, the *Savannah* engaged in her first fight. She steamed downriver and anchored near Hutchinson's Island, opening a bombardment on the Federal army's left flank. Confederate shore batteries joined in as Hardee and his army crossed to Hutchinson's Island, then marched across Union Causeway and onto South Carolina soil.

That night Commodore Tattnall began destroying all naval stores lest they fall into Union hands. The ironclad *Georgia* was fired at her moorings. She burned hotly and soon blew up. The *Milledgeville,* only a month launched, was burned to the water's edge and sunk in the middle of the river. Only the *Savannah* remained afloat.[12]

The next day, when Sherman completed the investment of the port and occupied the surrounding fortifications, the ironclad *Savannah* was still on the water, without a port of safety or a friend for miles around.

As the Stars and Stripes went up over Fort Jackson, the Stars and Bars climbed the *Savannah's* flagstaff, snapping out in the brisk December wind in bold defiance of the hostile force occupying its home port. Looking for a fight, the ironclad got underway and headed downriver, reversing her screw to drift to a halt near Fort Jackson. Both of her 7-inch rifles were shifted to broadside with her 6-inch gun, and the Rebel sailors opened fire. Federal artillerists hurriedly manned guns that had so lately spoken under Confederate hands and, for a short time, kept up a lively return fire against the ironclad, doing her no damage. The vengeful, screaming shells of the *Savannah's* rifles soon took effect, however, sending the Yanks scurrying for cover. The Confederates shelled the fort for several hours, then broke off the engagement and returned upriver.[13]

After dark, Captain W. T. Brent, commanding the *Savannah,* ran his charge aground on the South Carolina shore, where Commodore Tattnall awaited him. The crew was landed with small arms and provisions, and waited silently ashore while officers applied a slow match to the gallant ironclad's magazine. The group then shouldered their muskets and set off behind Tattnall and Brent, heading for Hardeeville where Confederate forces were gathering. Behind, her nose in the shallows, lay the abandoned *Savannah.* A little after 10:00 P.M. she ended her life with a roar that shook houses for miles around.

Perhaps the most striking example of iron starvation in the Confederate naval yards is presented in the attempts to get the C.S.S. *Muskogee* afloat and completed at Columbus. Built under the direction of, and for the command of, Lieutenant Augustus McLaughlin, she had been frequently reported as a center-wheeler like the *Louisiana* and *Missouri,* but appears, instead, to have been a twin-screw vessel, her engines prepared by Chief Engineer Warner. Pierced to mount six guns behind 4 inches of armor, she was reported, on November 30, 1863, as being "ready to launch," her machinery complete. She appeared again, five months later, in one of Mallory's memorandums as "delayed for iron armor. Machinery read." By November 5, 1864, the Columbus yard had "a sufficiency of iron on hand to put the armor on the knuckle [a 2-inch plating], which will enable them to launch, but not enough to complete the armor." She was still on the stocks, but was to be launched "so soon as the river rises."[14]

The year between the completion of the ironclad's wood-work and machinery and the arrival of the iron to armor her knuckle was whiled away with various experiments meant to decrease her draft. Mallory spoke of her as a "lightdraft" vessel, but the statements of exchanged Union prisoners that she drew a mere 6 feet are hardly credible.

She was never to see action. The shallow depth of the Chattahoochee kept marauding Federals out and, just as effectively, kept the "lightdraft" *Muskogee* locked in. She was finally afloat, still awaiting the last of her armor, when fired and sunk at the war's end.[15]

6

North Carolina Waters

Orders dated January 15, 1864, directed Commander James Wallace Cooke to proceed to Edwards Ferry, on the Roanoke River in North Carolina, and complete and take command of the ironclad under construction there. The Navy Department had chosen him, it said, because of his "acquaintance with the people and resources of the district." Not mentioned, but perhaps just as much behind the department's choice, was Cooke's reputation as a fighter. He had commanded the gunboat *Ellis* during the struggle for Hatteras Inlet and its chain of islands early in the war. His reluctance to retreat before the Union fleet had cost him several wounds and a term in a Federal prison, but the months in the stockade seemed only to have whetted his appetite for fighting.

The site chosen for the construction of the ironclad — to be called the *Albemarle* — was a corn field on the farm of William Ruffin Smith. The ship was, in fact, almost a Smith family project. Peter Evans Smith, son of William Ruffin, was superintendent of construction. Yellow pine planking for the craft was cut on the farm of son B. G. Smith, captain of the Scotland Neck Mounted Riflemen, and son Charles served as courier for the builders. When he became old enough to enter the army, cousin Frank J. took the post.[1]

The *Albemarle* was the offspring of one Gilbert Elliott. Like Cooke, he had fought at and was captured in the Hatteras Islands affair. In prison he had spent his time making drawings of gunboats, several of them ironclad. On release he had been assigned to duty at the Drewry's Bluff batteries below Richmond with the 17th North Carolina. Still in his teens, he grew a beard to add a few years to his face, and took some of his sketches to Richmond. John L. Porter viewed them, created some professional plans and specifications from them, and got Elliott detached on naval service, assigned to the corn fields and river banks of North Carolina to build ironclads.[2] The structure rising in William Smith's corn field was not his first attempt. Acting as agent for J. C. Martin of Elizabeth City, Elliott had secured two previous contracts for ironclads to be constructed in North Carolina. One, contracted for on April 16, 1862, simply faded from the records. The second, the contract signed on September 17 of the same year, was burned on the stocks at Tarboro exactly 13 months later when the town was threatened by raiding Union cavalry.[3]

In mid-February Captain Robert D. Minor, a lieutenant commanding a gun on the old *Virginia* and, of late, commander of the Naval Ordnance Works lying in the south part of Richmond, was ordered to North Carolina to hurry work on the *Albemarle* and her sister ship, the *Neuse,* building 70 miles to the south at Whitehall on the Neuse River, under the direction of Howard and Ellis of New Bern.[4] He had been offered command of the *Neuse,* but had declined to devote his time to the rapid completion of both ships.[5] And work did go rapidly on the *Albemarle* — up to a point. Residents of the upper Roanoke proved highly receptive to the idea of helping the Southern Confederacy — never popular in North Carolina — build a warship. A large gang of workmen was recruited, and the hull, casemate frame, and armor backing were completed in good time. Engines and armor proved harder to come by. Not that iron wasn't, for once, available. Tredegars were little more than 100 miles north, and a smaller rolling mill had been established at Wilmington. But the Confederacy's railroad system was in a dilapidated state, and those leading into the interior of North Carolina were among the worst of a bad lot, so that when the armor was rolled and ready for delivery, it was almost impossible to get it to its destination.

Commander Cooke had been on the road attempting to procure iron for his ram, not only from the rolling mills in Richmond and Wilmington, but from small foundries and even scrap piles all over North Carolina and southern Virginia. He got promises of iron — from Richmond, from Wilmington, from Charlotte, and from all the scrap piles in between — and saw it aboard trains leaving for Halifax, a rail center 25 miles upstream from Edwards Ferry. Between the point of departure and the point of arrival, however, the flat cars loaded with great gray slabs of armor plate always seemed to disappear. Like countless other shipments of naval supplies riding the rails from Atlanta to New Orleans, from Columbia to Charleston, from Columbus to Savannah, or from any of the rolling mills and naval ordnance works to any port in the Confederacy, the *Albemarle's* iron — all of it — had been side-tracked to various spurs to sit, rusting, while the builders at Edwards Ferry sat idle. Flag Officer William F. Lynch, over from the lost Mississippi River to try his luck a second time in North Carolina waters, aired his disgust in a letter to Mallory.

the rights of the navy are not respected, its wants are utterly disregarded, and it is in the power of an acting assistant quartermaster to cause our transportation to be set aside at will. The importance of completing the iron-clads on the Neuse and the Roanoke does not seem to be comprehended.

On March 7, finally, the first 14 carloads of armor plate arrived in Halifax. The wooden *Albemarle,* logs under her hull acting as a path of rollers all the way to the water's edge, was dragged into the river by horses and men and towed upstream to Halifax to be armored. Work picked up again and her armor — once Peter Smith had invented a drill that poked holes in her plates at the rate of four minutes per hole rather than twenty per hole — went on at a goodly rate.[6]

The naval works at Charlotte, set up with machinery salvaged from Norfolk, turned out two propeller shafts for the *Albemarle,* and two engines were procured, supposed to put out 200 horsepower each through 18-inch cylinders. Her ram was oak, not iron, and her frame was caulked with cotton, her seams sealed with tar.[7]

The *Albemarle's* ironcladding was half-completed and her boilers, engines, and propellers installed but still disconnected, when a communication arrived from Major General Robert F. Hoke. His small army was making preparations to strike Federal-held Plymouth, and he wondered if the *Albemarle* might be able to lend a hand. Cooke replied that the *Albemarle* could be ready for action "in 15 days, with ten additional mechanics." The mechanics arrived and preparations for combat were begun.

The construction of an ironclad anywhere in the Confederacy was seldom a matter unknown to Union naval forces in that particular area. The building of the *Albemarle* and *Neuse* was no exception. But Admiral S. P. Lee, commanding the North Atlantic Blockading Squadron, was, from all appearances, singularly unperturbed at the threat posed by the Rebels' make-shift iron gunboats. He suggested to the commanders of his light-draft blockaders in Albemarle Sound that, when the *Albemarle* made her appearance, two of them draw alongside her, slip ropes, chains, and cables across her to tie her down, and blast her into submission.

Captain Charles W. Flusser, U.S.N., had met Commander Cooke before. He had been aboard the Federal gunboat *Commodore Perry* at Elizabeth City and had boarded the Confederate *Ellis* to find Cooke fighting like a madman, though carrying a bullet in his arm and bayonet wound in his leg. Flusser had saved the Confederate from execution and taken him prisoner.[8] A Kentuckian, Flusser had two brothers fighting for the Confederacy, and had been begged, to no avail, by George N. Hollins to come south when the war broke out.[9] He now commanded the squadron in Albemarle Sound from the double-ender *Miami* and, apparently, shared Admiral Lee's opinion of the *Albemarle*. He lashed his ship to the gunboat *Southfield* with a chain and was determined to take the ram exactly as Lee had suggested, telling his immediate superior, Commodore H. K. Davenport: "You need not be uneasy as to the result."

Since April 1, the *Albemarle* had resided at the little hamlet of Hamilton, where Cooke and his men suffered from poor food and bad water while work progressed on the ram. She was 158 feet in length, 35 feet abeam, and drew only 8 feet of water. He armament consisted of two 100-pounder English Armstrong guns at bow and stern, pivoted to fire straight on or in broadside.

On Sunday evening, April 17, the *Albemarle,* in company with the steamer *Cotton Planter,* left Hamilton, headed for Plymouth. She drifted backwards downstream, chains and anchors hanging from her bow to control her in the current.

The trip was quiet and without consequence until, near 10:00 P.M., the main coupling bolts of one of the propeller shafts pulled loose. The ship was moored to shore and new bolts were forged. The process took six hours, after which the *Albemarle* resumed her journey downriver. She was stopped again when her rudderhead broke, causing a delay of four hours.

Cooke, his crew, and mechanics spent the next day in finishing the ironclad as the ship drifted, stern foremost, downstream. At 10:30 that night she tied up three miles from Plymouth, above a row of obstructions.

Cooke found himself with absolutely no knowledge of the strength of Federal defenses between the obstructions and Plymouth. As to Hoke's intentions, he was entirely in the dark. To remedy the lack of intelligence, Gilbert Elliott, pilot John Luck, and two crewmen set out in a small boat. Keeping to the shadows of the north bank, the boat drifted downstream, Elliott taking soundings over the obstructions. From the row of pilings driven in the river bottom, the Confederates could see Federal transports departing Plymouth, removing Yankee women and children from the danger of a coming battle.

Toward midnight Elliott and Luck returned to the *Albemarle.* They reported two Federal earthworks along the river. The first, Fort Gray, mounted a 200-pounder Parrott rifle, which they felt could be passed without difficulty. The *Albemarle* could cross the obstructions in safety due to the Roanoke being at an unusually high flood stage.[10]

It was 2:30 Tuesday morning when the *Albemarle* got underway, bow foremost this time, the chains and anchors gone, with steam up and her propellers turning. The *Cotton Planter* remained above the obstructions:[11] a 200-pounder rifle was too much to be faced by a converted merchant steamer. The ram slipped slowly downriver, ports closed and all lights masked and, at 3:00 A.M., glided over the obstructions without mishap. Fort Gray opened fire immediately, but their gunnery was poor and the *Albemarle* cruised past without being hit.

The Union gunboat *Ceres* was the first of the Federal flotilla to sight the *Albemarle*. She hastened to inform the *Miami*, sped downriver to warn the gunboat *Whitehead*, then wisely took her wooden walls as far as possible from the coming contest.

The *Albemarle* advanced easily, pushed by a strong current. The *Miami* and *Southfield* came up to take the center of the arena, guns and crews ready, the chain between them slack and dark and wet, waiting for the Confederate to come charging into their trap. Cooke, however, had no intention of being trapped. Perhaps forewarned as to Flusser's plan of battle, he guided the *Albermarle* as close to the river bank as he dared, leaving no room for a gunboat to get between the ironclad and the shore. It was a reversal for Flusser. His plan had been completely foiled, and now his wooden gunboats would have to stand and slug it out with the *Albemarle*.

The *Albemarle* slid leisurely down the shoreline, gradually closing the distance between herself and the united *Miami* and *Southfield*. Suddenly, with a speed that took the Federals by surprise, she turned and dashed into deep water, burying 10 feet of her prow in the *Southfield's* side. In three minutes the *Southfield* was disappearing below the waves, the *Abemarle's* bow still in her. The ironclad's deck tilted, bringing water gushing through the bow port and leaving her guns useless. Part of her crew rushed up through the hatches, crowding the roof. From there they opened a heavy musketry fire on the *Miami*. Comrades on the gun deck handed up loaded muskets, taking and reloading empty ones in return. Here the Confederates suffered their only casualty: a man named Harris was killed by a pistol ball.[12]

The sinking *Southfield* hit bottom and rolled over, releasing her grip on the *Albemarle's* bow and allowing the Confederate to bob upright again. The Southern riflemen abandoned their position on the roof, slipping through to the gun deck to man the big Armstrong rifles. The guns swung to broadside and a shell crashed through the *Miami*. She answered with a hot fire that sent solid shot and shell bouncing off the ram's solid armor. Captain Flusser pointed the pivot gun and fired it himself. The shell struck the *Albemarle*, ricocheted back aboard the *Miami* and exploded, killing Flusser where he stood. Acting Volunteer Lieutenant Charles A. French — late of the *Southfield*[13] —took command and the *Miami* retreated, leaving the *Albemarle* in possession of the field.

Gilbert Elliott and pilot James B. Hopkins went ashore, pulling a small boat up a creek behind the town, to determine Hoke's battle plans and ascertain just what part the *Albemarle* was to play in the recapture of Plymouth. They found Hoke, conferred with him, and hurried a dispatch back to Cooke.[14]

As dawn broke the *Albemarle* dropped anchor and trained both guns on Fort Williams, an earthwork that was the key to Plymouth's defenses. Repeated frontal assaults had proven it nearly impregnable from land, but its river face was all but defenseless: the fort had relied on the gunboats' big naval cannon for adequate defense from the water. With the gunboats disbursed, the *Albemarle* could, at leisure, shoot Fort Williams to pieces.

All day Tuesday, all Tuesday night, and half of Wednesday, the ironclad's big guns directed a slow, deliberate, and well-aimed fire against the earthwork. At noon on Wednesday, April 20, the fort surrendered. Col. John Taylor Wood, who had served the *Virginia's* after gun as a naval lieutenant, reported to President Davis: "Heaven has crowned our efforts with success. General Hoke has captured this point with 1,600 prisoners, 25 pieces of artillery, and navy cooperation." Cooke's official report read, in part: "In truth, sir, I can take no credit to myself for the success of the *Albemarle* in her engagements, for, with such efficient and energetic officers, failure was almost impossible."

The *Albemarle's* share in the captured stores was 200 tons of good anthracite coal. She suffered nine broken plates on her outer layer of armor and lost one man.

On May 17, the Confederate Congress passed a joint resolution of thanks to General Hoke, Commander Cooke, and their officers and men. Cooke was later promoted to captain.[15]

On May 4, Commander Cooke received orders from Captain Robert F. Pinkney (who had, to Issac Brown's dismay, burned the gunboats *Polk, Livingston* and *Van Dorn* in the Yazoo, and had now assumed command of the naval defenses of North Carolina) to convoy the steamers *Bombshell* and *Cotton Planter* to the Alligator River. The *Cotton Planter* carried a detachment of sharpshooters. The trio left Plymouth at noon.[16]

The gunboats *Commodore Hull, Miami, Ceres,* and the army transport *Trumpeter*, had just entered the Roanoke for the purpose of mining the river[17] when the Confederates were spotted coming down. The *Trumpeter* made a hasty withdrawal to call up the flotilla and the gunboats began falling back gradually, keeping the Confederates in sight. The *Cotton Planter* turned back toward *Plymouth* and the *Albemarle* and the little *Bombshell* stood out onto Albemarle Sound. They pushed the Union trio back gradually until the Federal flotilla hove in sight, when the three joined it and the whole blockading squadron came on, the main body in a double line, the *Miami, Ceres,* and *Commodore Hull* spread across its front.

As the distance between the opposing forces closed, the *Bombshell* opened the ball with a shot from her "heavy" gun. One of the Federals answered, her projectile failing to find its mark. The *Albemarle's* bow gun spoke, the shot striking the after section of the *Mattabesset.* The gun roared again, the second shot's course following that of the first, dropping spars, rigging, and six writhing bodies in a tangle around the Federal's after-pivot gun.[18] The antagonists then closed and the battle was joined in earnest. The *Miami* charged down as if to ram, then sheared off, delivering a broadside against the *Albemarle's* armored side. The *Ceres* and *Commodore Hull* followed, running the same pattern, while the double line of warriors steamed straight in and engaged without maneuvering. The *Albemarle* shifted her bow gun to starboard, her stern gun to port, and began firing slowly. The *Miami, Ceres,* and *Commodore Hull* turned and tried their maneuver again, each picking up 100 more pounds of Confederate shot. The *Sassacus* rounded-to, sending several broadsides into the *Bombshell.* The little boat hauled down her flag.

The blockading flotilla drifted around the *Albemarle,* firing 100-pound shot under double charges. The *Mattabasset,* at a range of 150 yards, delivered a broadside that knocked 23 inches from the underside of the Armstrong[19] firing out the *Albemarle's* port side. The gun ceased firing and her port shutters were closed. This left only one opening — the gun port through which the bow gun was firing — to provide ventilation for the entire ship. Cooke had ordered the hatches closed, fearing Union musketry and grenades. The Confederates sweltered.[20]

As the afternoon sun began to touch the horizon, the *Sassacus* came barreling in under a tremendous head of steam, intent on cutting the *Albemarle* in half. At a speed estimated at nine to eleven knots (although her officers later admitted that it may have been no more than five),[21] she struck the *Albemarle* at right angles on the Confederate's armored knuckle, heeling the ironclad over. A torrent of water cascaded in the open port and the crew became, momentarily, apprehensive. Cooke was reported to have rallied them, crying: "Stand to your guns! If we sink, let us perform our duty and go down like brave men." A crewman, however, remembered that "Captain Cooke was standing in the hatch and was knocked down. He looked kinder scared like."[22] The *Sassacus'* bow was stove in and her splintered jaws gripped the *Albemarle's* knuckle like a vise while her wheels backed furiously, trying to pull free.[23] The ironclad then got underway. The movement brought the *Sassacus* swinging around to bang broadside-to-broadside against the ironclad. From this position the *Sassacus'* entire broadside was depressed to strike the Rebel's armor at right angles. But when the guns roared, their shells shattered from the concussion against the *Albemarle's* armor and the solid shot went bounding off to sink in the sound. The *Albemarle's* stern-chaser returned to action, swinging back to port to send a projectile through the gunboat's side. The shot pierced the Federal's boiler, wreathing her in a cloud of steam. Thirteen men were scalded in the hissing, swirling mass of vapor. The Federal now wrenched free and drifted out of the fight, badly hurt.

Slowly, the *Albemarle* turned and headed for Plymouth. The Federal flotilla turned with her, as if glued to her iron sides. They kept pace — a mass of wood, iron, smoke, flame, noise, and fighting men — all steaming leisurely toward a setting sun that painted a broad stripe of rich gold across the vast black surface of Albemarle Sound. Only occasionally did the *Albemarle's* bow gun answer the heavy bombardment battering her casemate.

Federal shot had so riddled the ironclad's smokestack as to almost completely destroy her draft. Bulkheads, butter, bacon, and lard were burned in an effort to keep up the steam needed to get the ship back to her moorings.

The Federals made a few final efforts to halt and destroy the *Albemarle*. The *Miami* attempted to use a spar torpedo with which she had been armed; she failed. The *Mattabesset* tried to lay a seine over the Confederate's propeller; she also failed. The ironclad continued, slow but undaunted, steaming toward Plymouth.

One by one the Federal gunboats dropped from the group until, finally, only two remained. These eventually dropped off and sat, watching the *Albemarle* draw slowly away until they were joined by two more. The four pulled close together, evidently in conference, presenting a target too tempting to resist. The *Albemarle* yawed to bring her bow gun to bear and sent a shell screaming off, the crew listening delightedly to the distant splinter of wood that told of the projectile's finding its mark. Like disturbed hornets, the four gunboats broke and charged, swarming down on the *Albemarle* to strike her again. The fighting finally died at 7:30, when the ironclad fired a final gun at her departing antagonists.

Signs of Federal damage became evident when the next tide littered the shore with large wood splinters, big fragments of copper sheathing, gun rammers, window sashes, hatches, cabin fixtures, bits and pieces of fine furniture, and several smashed launches.

The *Albemarle* had sufferd seven broken plates, her after-gun muzzle was shot away, and her smokestack was shot to pieces. On reaching Plymouth, she was put in for repairs. Cooke's health broke and he was replaced by John N. Maffitt.

Maffitt began preparing for an immediate attack on the Federals, but the army remonstrated. Should the *Albemarle* be lost, they said, Plymouth would again fall to the Federals.[24] Maffitt listened and the *Albemarle* remained on the defensive.

On May 24 the ironclad appeared, guarding a rowboat[25] dragging for torpedoes. The gunboat *Whitehead* sighted her, fired one shot, and retreated.

The next night five crewmen from the *Wyalusing* attempted to destroy the *Albemarle*. They ascended the middle river in a small boat, then waded the swamp to a spot up and across the river from the *Albemarle's* moorings, carrying with them two 100-pound torpedoes. They harnessed the torpedoes together, set them adrift and, with guide lines, tried to lay them across the *Albemarle's* bow. They had gottten them into an almost perfect position when the guide line rasped against a nearby schooner. A sentry fired at the noise, setting off a volley, and the Federal sailors abandoned the effort. All five escaped.[26]

The Federal Government asked John Ericsson to design for them a sort of light draft monitor, an ironclad carrying only one heavy gun and drawing but 4 feet of water, to operate in the shallow North Carolina inlets against such vessels as the *Albemarle* and *Neuse*. Ericsson figured and calculated, then told Gideon Welles that it couldn't be done. The Navy Department presented their problem to Alban Stimers, who drew up plans for just the craft they needed. Twenty of these light-draft monitors were started, and all were in advanced stages of construction when the first was launched. It was found that, with fuel, provisions, and ordnance aboard, they would ride with their decks just 7 inches below water. Due to a slight miscalculation in a clerk's mathematics, all 20 were worth nothing as heavy-gunned ironclads. They were finally commissioned as iron-hulled gunboats, mounting one unprotected 9-inch gun on deck instead of in a turret.

Melancton Smith, assuming Federal naval command in the Roanoke area, mined the river's mouth with electric torpedoes to be fired from pits dug in the shore. Early in July a Confederate raiding party carried off the sailors standing by in the firing pits. Their boat was found, but there was no trace of the sailors.[27]

A final effort to destroy the ironclad was made, based on the success of the Confederate torpedo boats in use in Charleston. Steam-driven, these boats rode low in the water — almost invisible in darkness or fog — their only arma-ment a spar torpedo at the bow. Several New York en-gineers had gone to Charleston to study the little boats and their method of attack, then went to Washington to sell their ideas to the government. Gideon Welles listened and was impressed, and the engineers went back to New York to procure suitable boats. Three steam launches — wooden rather than iron like the Charleston "Davids" and open with a higher freeboard than the Confederate torpedo boats — were sent south. One foundered at sea, another was driven ashore in Virginia and captured. Only Lieutenant William B. Cushing's launch arrived safely. It was fitted with a torpedo and preparations were made for an attack.

John Maffitt relinquished command of the *Albemarle* on September 9, ordered to Wilmington to command the blockade runner *Owl*. Alexander F. Warley, late of the

Manassas and *Chicora*, succeeded him. On September 23, he took the ironclad downriver. The *Valley City* sighted her[28] at the mouth of the Roanoke, fired a shot, and retreated. No one came up to challenge the Confederate, and she ventured no farther.

Illness ate into the Albemarle's crew, reducing it until only 60 effectives — hardly enough to man the ship — were left aboard. She was left moored to the shore, awaiting a crew. Warley kept up the morale of those remaining by sending them out, ten at a time, to engage in guerilla activities against the enemy. Meanwhile, people downriver had reported that they had seen and heard a steam launch maneuvering about. Warley suspected its purpose and had a cordon of cypress logs floated around the immobile ironclad. Several field guns were pulled up on shore and the guard was doubled.[29] Warley, however, placed little stock in these defensive measures and began forecasting an end for the *Albemarle*.

In the dark, rainy early morning of October 27, Lt. William Cushing's launch slipped past a Confederate picket station set up on the wreck of the *Southfield*. Cautiously, quietly, the launch worked its way upriver, hunting for the blunt outline of the *Albemarle*. She soon found it against the south shore and turned toward the ironclad, picking up some speed. She was closing in warily, hunting for hidden defenses, when the *Albemarle's* Officer of the Deck sighted her and gave hail. A shot, then a volley, of musketry spattered the water. A bonfire sprang up on shore, revealing the stationary *Albemarle* and the cruising torpedo launch in its flickering, uncertain light.

The first hail brought the *Albemarle's* crew running to their posts. Sighting the launch, they shifted a gun to bear, loading with grape. They depressed the piece as far as possible (but not far enough), took a quick sighting, fired, then grabbed muskets and rushed to the roof.

Cushing's launch hesitated a moment, then set her course and put on steam. She struck the cordon of logs at full speed, jumped it, and brought her torpedo rasping against the *Albemarle's* hull. A muffled explosion sent an enormous geyser shooting skyward, falling to swamp the launch. Several crewmen cried out in surrender while Cushing and a few others went overboard to escape.

Aboard the *Albemarle*, Warley called his carpenter and ordered him below to ascertain the damage done. The fellow disappeared into the hold but was soon back, reporting that there was a hole in the ironclad's hull "big enough to drive a wagon in." Crewmen manned pumps and a donkey engine was started, helping to clear the water. It was to no avail: she was taking water fast and sinking. Her crew soon crowded the roof, dismal, while the ironclad rested on the shallow bottom, her casemate partially out of the water. She would not trouble the Federals again.[30]

By late October, 1864, the company of Smith & Elliott was hard at work on a four-gun ironclad of relatively light draft, building at Edwards Ferry. She was never completed.[31]

Ordered to cooperate with the army in the recapture of New Bern, the *Neuse*, finally completed at Whitehall, was on her way to the engagement when run aground on April 22. Lieutenant Benjamin Pollard Loyall, commanding her, was transferred to the naval school ship *Patrick Henry* on the James, and Captain Robert F. Pinkney, up from Savannah, assumed temporary command. He went on to relieve Wm. F. Lynch as commander of North Carolina's naval defenses, and was replaced aboard the *Neuse* by Captain Joseph Price. Lt. William Sharp, late of the *Pat-*

rick Henry and *Beaufort* and then commanding the Kinston naval station, had held command of her briefly in the interim. She was still aground when Hardee's retreat before Sherman left Kinston undefended, opening the entire area and forcing her destruction.[32]

In the spring of 1862, two ironclads identical in size and armament were begun at the yard of Berry and Brother in Wilmington, N. C. Carrying the Brooke-Porter casemate on the squarish Tift hull, they were both approximately the size of the *Albemarle*, their casemates pierced for four guns.[33] By December of 1863, the first, the *North Carolina*, had been completed. The second, the *Raleigh*, had her machinery installed and was being armored. By late winter she was finished.[34] Both mounted a 6.4-inch Brooke rifle at bow and stern, and a pair of smoothbores in broadside. The *Raleigh*, with a crew of 169 men, 23 officers and 25 marines, was commanded by Lt. J. Pembroke Jones. The *North Carolina*, carrying 140 crewmen, 21 officers, and 12 marines, was, at this time, commanded by Lt. Patrick Mc-Carrick. By late fall of 1864 a third armored vessel was reported under construction there, this one 226 feet in length and, hopefully, "of such draft of water as will enable her to go in and out of the harbor at all times." Her machinery was new and ready to be installed, built at the Columbus naval works under the supervision of Chief Engineer Warner. Like so many others, she was never to reach completion.[35]

At 7:30 P.M. of May 6, 1864, the *Raleigh,* in company with the gunboats *Yadkin* and *Equator*, escorted several blockade runners down the Cape Fear River to Fort Fisher. The blockader *Britannia* sighted them at the fort and stood off to await developments.

As the darkness thickened the *Raleigh* crossed the bar

and stepped into open sea to strike the blockade or, if nothing else, at least create a diversion for the benefit of the runners. She made immediately for the *Britannia*, intending to ram. The Federal, however, had other ideas. She sent up a cluster of rockets, got off a shot from her 30-pounder Parrott, then put about and retreated, keeping up a running fire with her 24-pounder howitzer. The *Raleigh* returned with her bow gun. Her first shot put out the fleeing Federal's binnical light. The second shot missed, passing close over the blockader's starboard side. The *Britannia* burned a blue light in signal to the fleet as the *Raleigh* fired again.

The bigger part of the Union fleet, meanwhile, had gotten underway when the rocket cluster had gone up, thinking the *Britannia* had cornered a blockade runner. They steamed toward the action, but bypassed the two combatants in the dark and steamed back out again.

The *Britannia* took evasive action, weaving left and right in an attempt to lose the deadly ironclad. The Confederate held a true course and gained. At the last moment the Federal slipped into shallow water where the Confederate couldn't follow, and the *Raleigh* abandoned pursuit. She stood out to sea and stumbled across the *Nansemond*. The Federal, surprised by the ironclad looming up unexpectedly out of the dark, turned and fled, banging away in fear with her after howitzer. The *Raleigh* sent back a vigorous fire, but the Federal had the advantage of speed and was soon out of range.

The next ship to exchange fire with the *Raleigh* was the *Howquah*. Under the impression that a blockade runner was being run down, she had come rushing in when the *Britannia's* signal rockets went up, spent a considerable time exploring the darkness, and then blundered onto the *Raleigh*. She fired a quick shot that brought a geyser of water splashing down on the cold iron plate of the *Raleigh's* slanting side, then put about and retraced her course, the *Raleigh* close behind. The Confederate's bow gun roared, the shell exploding on the blockader's starboard quarter. The ironclad then commenced to yaw to starboard and port, affording her broadside guns a chance. The maneuvers cost her dearly in speed, however, and the *Howquah* was soon out of sight.

As morning began to break, the Federals swarmed into the *Raleigh's* vicinity in rather alarming numbers. At 5:00, the *Mount Vernon* sighted the Confederate. She stood off and eyed the ironclad. Twenty minutes later the *Fahkee* and *Niphon* hove in sight and followed the *Mount Vernon's* example, staying well clear of the Rebel's menacing ram, big rifles, and shell guns. At 5:30, the *Mount Vernon* summoned up the courage to steam in a little closer and deliver four shots. All fell short.

At 6:15, the *Kansas* arrived on the scene. She chanced two shots, then ran. The *Raleigh* drifted, eyeing her antagonists, weighing her chances. None of the blockaders would come within range and, with their superior steaming qualities, the *Raleigh* might chase them all over the ocean without ever being able to close to effective range. Rather than waste a day's worth of precious coal, she turned and stood in to shore.[36]

A shoreside battery fired off a jaunty nine-gun salute as the *Raleigh* crossed the bar. Minutes later she struck a point called "The Rip,"[37] and the weight of her armor broke her back. Her guns and armor were removed, her boilers saved and sent to the gunboat *Chattahoochee* at Columbus, and she was partially burned. Years later, at low water, small boys fishing from the beach could see her charred ribs reaching skyward from The Rip.

A court of inquiry under George Hollins convened in

Wilmington on June 6 to investigate the loss. Its findings were that:

in the opinion of the court the loss of the *Raleigh* can not be attributed to negligence or inattention on the part of anyone on board of her, and every effort was made to save said vessel. We further find that the *Raleigh* could have remained outside the bar of Cape Fear River for a few hours with apparent safety but, in the opinion of the court, it would have been improper; and, in view of all the circumstances, her commanding officer was justified in attempting to go back into the harbor when he did.

It is further the opinion of the court that the draft of water of the *Raleigh* was too great, even lightened as she had been for this occasion, to render her passage of the bar, except under favorable circumstances, a safe operation, particularly as her strength seems to have been insufficient to enable her to sustain the weight of her armor long enough to permit every practicable means of lightening her to be exhausted.[38]

The *North Carolina* was no more a success than the ironclad *Georgia*. She was awkward, unwieldly, eaten through with sea worm, and her engines — taken from the tug *Uncle Ben* — wouldn't move her. Even the presence of the pugnacious Lieutenant Billy Glassell as her executive officer and commander during a short span of 1863-1864 failed to bring her into combat.

Anchored in the Cape Fear or moored to a wharf near Wilmington, she went through a succession of commanders beginning with Lt. Glassell at her launching. In March of 1864, Glassell was relegated to the post of executive officer when Commander William T. Muse assumed command. Muse died on April 8, 1864. Glassell had been sent to Charleston for torpedo service and command devolved on Lt. Patrick McCarrick, Glassell's old executive officer. It then went to Lt. J. Pembroke Jones. Commander William

L. Maury, after a successful cruise in the commerce raider *Georgia*, assumed command in mid-summer with Jones his first lieutenant.

In September, 1864, while at anchor in the Cape Fear River, a section of the *North Carolina's* worm-eaten wood gave way, and she sprung a leak and sank.

7

The Mobile Squadron

After the Tredegar Iron Works in Richmond, the most productive naval ordnance works in the Confederacy was at Selma, Alabama. Miles above Mobile on the winding Alabama River, the little town on the bluffs had been, in 1861, the sight of a brand new iron foundry opened by Colin McRae. As the war grew, demanding all the material resources of the entire South, the navy commandeered the foundry, enlarged it, retooled, and sent Catsby Jones — who had commanded the *Virginia* for a day — over from Charlotte ordnance works to take command. Brooke rifles were cast there — eventually in calibers as large as 10-inch — from iron mined at Brierfield, Alabama. General Dabney H. Maury, commenting in later years on the Mobile campaign, was moved to say of the Brierfield iron: "It must be the best gunmetal in the world." He spoke of the great number of Brooke guns turned out at Selma — from 6.4-inch on up — and remarked with wonder that he had never seen a Selma-cast gun even so much as strained by repeated firing of heavy charges.[1]

204

A small navy yard had grown up at Selma, crowning the bluffs near the gun foundry. In mid-1863, three ironclads were in the course of construction there. Franklin Buchanan, flag officer of the Mobile squadron, was at Selma to personally superintend the construction of the *Tennessee*, building on one of the bluffs. Designed to draw around 14 feet of water, she was 209 feet in length and 48 feet abeam. A 25 inch thickness of oak and yellow pine planking created the foundation for a casemate 79 feet in length, 29 feet wide at the roof, and 8 feet high, its sides inclined at an angle of 45°.

Her armor plates were rolled at Atlanta to a thickness of 2 inches, a width of 7 inches. Three layers of these went down on the front of her casemate, while her broadsides and after-shield were protected by two layers of 2-inch plate and one layer of 1-inch plate. The armor continued at it 45° slope for 2 feet below the water line, forming a knuckle as protection against ramming, then reversed its angle to join the hull 7 feet farther down.[2]

The twin rams *Huntsville* and *Tuscaloosa* were under construction on the bluffs along with the *Tennessee*, building on the same plan, but boasting a length of only 150 feet, approximately the size of the North Carolina rams. They were to be armored with 4 inches of Atlanta iron rolled out in 2" x 10" plates, and would each carry a Brooke 6-inch rifle and four 32-pounders. Commander Charles H. McBlair, who had so infuriated Issac Brown with his lack of interest in the *Arkansas*, was on hand to superintend their construction, arriving at Selma after commanding, briefly, the gunboat *Morgan* at Mobile. He was, apparently, still quite as lackadaisical as Brown had found him, for work dragged on the two small rams while the *Tennessee's* construction went ahead with creditable haste. The construction of another ironclad, a side-wheeler, was begun on the Selma bluffs in 1864. She was so badly damaged in launching as to render her completely ineffective, and was never finished.[3]

Four other ironclads were in the process of construction in the state of Alabama — the *Nashville* at Montgomery, and two small unnamed craft and a four-gun steam sloop building under contract on the Tombigbee River. The *Nashville* may have been the ironclad provided for by an act of the Alabama State Legislature in 1861. She was larger than the *Tennessee* — 271 feet in length (she is occasionally quoted as being 250 feet in length, the length of her keel), and 63 feet abeam, 95 feet 5 inches over her side-mounted paddle wheels. Her casemate was 142 feet in length, inclined in to a 40-foot width at its top. She drew 10 feet 9 inches of water with a 13-foot depth of hold. Her side-wheels — an unusual feature on a Confederate ironclad — were each driven by a separate engine, each with a cylinder 30 inches in diameter with a 9-foot piston stroke. Steam was provided by seven 40-inch double flued boilers. Both boilers and engines were kept in good working order throughout the war, and her speed was adequate. Her armament consisted of three 7-inch Brooke rifles and one 24-pounder howitzer, pivoted to fire straight on or in broadside, similar to the ordnance layout of the *Missouri*. Her bottom was not coppered and, at war's end, the Federals found her to be hog-braced athwartships, indicating an inherent weakness in her hull. She could never have stood the full weight of her armor, and it is doubtful that she could have lived in a heavy sea.[4]

The Mobile squadron already boasted one ironmailed "ram," the C.S.S. *Baltic*. She was a common river steamer of 624 tons, purchased from the state of Georgia, where she had been used as a towboat. Armored with 2½ inches of iron, she was armed with one 42-pounder, two 32-pounders, and two 12-pounder howitzers. Her two engines, "of the usual Western river type," were kept in good repair. They carried cylinders of 22-inch bore with a 7-foot stroke. Steam was supplied through four old and leaky boilers, 24 feet by 3 feet. Her quarters consisted of a small room on deck for her commanding officer, a large room below for the officers' berth and mess, and bunks below for petty officers. Crew's quarters were on deck.[5] She was commanded, from 1861 through 1863, by Commander James D. Johnston. Johnston was relieved in 1863 by Lieutenant Julian M. Spencer, who was, in turn, relieved in February, 1864, by Lieutenant Charles C. Simms. Federal reports quote the *Baltic's* speed at an optimistic five knots.

Admiral Buchanan, in a letter to Commander Jones at the gun foundry, asked him to relay to Captain Eben Farrand the information that all work on the *Nashville* had come to a complete standstill for want of materials and money. The story was too painfully familiar. Eight ironclads — including the decrepit towboat *Baltic* — were in at least intermediate stages of construction in Alabama waters. At Mobile, the blockade in early 1864 consisted of no more than nine wooden vessels,[6] with the closest monitors tied up watching the ironclads building at Savannah. Could the ironclad *Tennessee, Nashville, Huntsville,* and *Tuscaloosa,* and the three Tombigbee rams be completed, armed, provisioned, and manned, they could have — without question —crushed the blockade at Mobile, opening the port to world trade. They could, perhaps, have swept the Gulf of Federal warships for a time, opening the great stretch of Confederate coastline from the tip of Florida up to and across Alabama, Mississippi, Louisiana (threatening New Orleans — opening an opportunity for its recapture) all the way to the tip of Texas. But the dream dissolved into the sad reality of opportunities missed, not for want of daring and industrious leaders — the Alabama naval high command of Buchanan, Farrand, Jones, Johnston, and Simms had proven their worth in service to the United States and, in the four years past, had done doubly so to the Confederacy — but for want of finished materials not available when needed, for provisions and ordnance rotting and rusting in Texas or interior North Carolina instead of being put to use in Mobile or Savannah, for skilled labor that had never existed and for sailors packing muskets in Tennessee instead of training naval guns down the Alabama River. Selfishness, ignorance, narrowmindedness, and interservice rivalry were perhaps not so much to blame for the Confederate Navy's plight as has so often been stated. Even the War Department's directive allowing only blue-water sailors released from the army to serve in the navy was not as petty as it may have seemed. The need for men to shoot rifles at the blue hosts of Grant and Thomas was just as great as it was for gunners and engineers to man iron boats attempting to break open the grip that strangled a sea port. When a service or commodity was needed by both the army and navy at the same time, it cannot be denied that the navy invariably lost out to its senior service, but little of the blame can be laid to pride, jealousy, and short-sightedness. The all-embracing problem confronting the navy was the same as that confronting the entire Confederacy: too much to do and too little of everything — time, money, supplies, people —with which to do it. Time and again—at New Orleans, at Memphis, at Charleston and Savannah, on the Yazoo and the Roanoke and at Wilmington and again at Mobile — a potentially superior Confederate fleet was crushed because an initially inferior fleet was able to draw on and put to use the men, services, and supplies that, for the Confederacy, simply did not exist.

On February 20, Flag Officer Buchanan came up from Mobile for a three-hour visit and inspection. On a short trip downriver the *Tennessee* grounded twice.[7]

She was pierced for six guns, with ten ports. Her armament was to consist of Brooke rifles, four 6-inch guns to give her a two-gun broadside and two 7-inch rifles to mount, pivoted, at bow and stern. The pivot guns would fire on each quarter also, as had the guns of the *Virginia*. The 7-inch guns were cast under Commander Jones' supervision at Selma, but the 6-inch guns were brought in from Atlanta. Her engines were pulled from the steamer *Alonzo Child** on the Yazoo, then transported overland to the Tombigbee, then floated down to Selma.[8] Once again, they would propel her, but were incapable of moving such a great weight of wood and iron at any great speed. Completed, she had cost an estimated $883,880.[9]

Buchanan mentioned to Comm. Jones that he would like Charles Simms for the *Tennessee's* commander. Simms, on the gunboat *Morgan*, went instead to the *Baltic*, replacing Spencer and, in March, Commander James D. Johnston received command of the new ironclad. Other officers on the *Tennessee's* final rolls were:

Lts.—Wm. L. Bradford, A. D. Wharton, E. J. McDermett; Masters—J. R. Milroy, Henri W. Perrin; Master's Mates— W. A. Forrest, Wm. Beebe, R. M. Carter; Engineers—George D. Linning, J. C. O'Connell, John Hayes, Oscar Benson, Wm. B. Patterson; Paymaster's Clerk—J. H. Cohen; Boatswain—John McCredie; Gunner—H. L. Smith.

Lieutenant William Bradford had served aboard the gun-

---

* In May of 1863 the Federal ironclad *Baron de Kalb* found the *Alonzo Child* at Snyder's Bluff on the Yazoo. She was "much knocked to pieces," lying on the bottom across the river as an obstruction.

boats *Jackson* and *Ivy* at New Orleans and the *Selma* at Mobile. He was brave enough, and would be captured twice within a year. McDermett had seen action with the *Louisiana* at New Orleans, and aboard the captured *Harriet Lane* in Texas. He had been assigned to the *Huntsville* while she was building, transferred to the ram *W. H. Webb* on the Red River, then come back to Alabama for service on the *Tennessee*. A prisoner with his ship, he would escape his captors in New Orleans, and die during the last weeks of the war in a minor engagement at Lake Maurepas. Arthur Dickson Wharton, an Alabamian by birth, had already — at the time of his appointment to the *Tennessee* — written an excellent record in the Confederate Naval Service. Imprisoned at the war's outbreak for refusing to take the oath of allegiance to the United States, he was released in February, 1862, commissioned in the Confederate Navy, and had served with distinction on the *Arkansas* in her brilliant cruise through the combined Union fleets above Vicksburg, then aboard the *Harriet Lane*, and had briefly commanded the *W. H. Webb*. He would be imprisoned his third and final time early in 1865, captured while engaged in guerilla activities near Loudon, Tennessee, after brief service aboard the ironclad *Richmond*, James River Squadron. The naval officers at the Mobile station were a well-seasoned, courageous lot. One could have expected much to be accomplished there.

David Farragut had arrived off Mobile and had immediately begun preparations to force a fight. It was men of this type — the Farraguts, the Grants, the Shermans — that had the knack for marshalling the power, men, and resources that were the North's strength, and striking heavy and decisive blows before the harassed Confederacy could prepare to defend. He began shelling the outlying forts immediately, softening up the outer defenses and gathering a fleet preparatory to a thrust at the city. He had heard of the *Tennessee* and, on March 1, imagined he saw her. In a dispatch to Secretary Welles he wrote:

In my last dispatch I informed you that the ram *Tennessee* in Mobile Bay had not yet crossed Dog River Bar; but today to our great surprise she appeared in full view in the bay opposite Grant's Pass, where I was at the time, having been at work all day yesterday shelling Fort Powell. This morning at 7:00 A.M. we perceived three gunboats and two ironclads lying near the fort; about one hour afterwards the *Tennessee* made her appearance, coming down the bay. The wind freshened and she came to anchor.[10]

The only ironclad at Mobile at the time was the thin-skinned and decrepit *Baltic*. The *Tennessee* was still at Selma, afloat and operable, but with her guns and provisions still ashore and no more than a skeleton crew aboard.

The draft of the *Tennessee* presented a problem. Without her guns, ammunition, provisions, and fuel aboard she drew 13 feet of water. There were only 9 feet of water over Dog River Bog, just above Mobile. Naval constructor Sidney Porter came up with a solution to the problem, suggesting that the *Tennessee* be floated across between several "camels." These were barge-type floats, weighted to ride low in the water, lashed securely to the ship's sides, then relieved of their weight to float high, bouying the ship several feet. Construction of the camels was begun immediately at Selma and they were almost all completed when a fire destroyed the entire lot. More were built and, on May 18 the *Tennessee*, riding high in the water, floated effortlessly over Dog River Bar. Her coal, ordnance, and provisions followed on two steamers for transfer to the ironclad.

The ram's first action was to run aground. She was pulled off, towed up the Mobile River, then down the Spanish River, a distance of 30 miles, and anchored in the lower bay.[11]

On May 22, at 10:00 A.M., Buchanan boarded the *Tennessee*. He raised his pennant, inspected the crew aft, and made a short speech. The *Tennessee* was now flagship of the Mobile squadron and Franklin Buchanan, hawk-nosed, blue-eyed, and sprightly at sixty-five, had a real ironclad in his squadron for the first time since the *Virginia's* first historic day in Hampton Roads.

During the last of May the twin ships *Tuscaloosa* and *Huntsville*, both incomplete, were shepherded over the Dog River Bar and brought down to Mobile to be finished. By June 4 the *Nashville* had joined them. Advancing Union armies soon threatened the three Tombigbee ironclads.[12] The two small rams were launched and floated downriver to swell even more Mobile's fleet of unfinished ironclads; the sloop was burned. Only the *Tennessee* and *Baltic* were finished, and the *Baltic* was hardly fit for combat. Simms, in a letter to Catsby Jones, left a picture of her condition: "Between you and me, the *Baltic* is as rotten as punk, and is about as fit to go into action as a mud scow." He added a warning, concerning his wife: "Don't say anything of this to Bet, however, as it would probably make her uneasy."

The *Baltic* was soon employed in placing obstructions in the bay. Farragut's fleet was gathering strength, and the Confederates were looking to shoring up their defenses, fearful of another defeat at the hands of the conqueror of New Orleans. From Fort Gaines, situated on an island on the eastern side of the bay, a double line of piles stretched westward, reaching for Fort Morgan on the west bank. They failed to reach the width of the bay's entrance, however, and the *Baltic* laid about 180 floating torpedoes in three lines, leaving a gap about 100 yards wide for use by blockade runners. The lack of a full crew hindered the old towboat in even this, the only task she was physically capable of.

Aware of the *Baltic's* worthlessness as a fighting ship, naval constructor Porter suggested that the old Georgia scow be stripped of her armor and the iron used to begin armoring the *Nashville*. Buchanan and his staff thought it a fine idea and the tired little *Baltic* was soon to be denuded of all her precious armor.[13]

Commander Johnston quickly found a fault in the *Tennessee's* construction — a weakness that was to be her undoing. Her steering chains, instead of running through the hull under her armored afterdeck, had been run out through her aft casemate shield and along the top of her deck, exposed to fire.[14] General Dabney H. Maury stated that the chains were run through a groove in the deck, overlaid — as an afterthought — with a sheet of 1-inch armor that would, in the battle, become jammed down on the chains by an 11-inch shot.[15]

The *Tennessee* was nearly destroyed before she could be brought into action. One morning several of the crew noticed a floating object in the water nearby and called the officer of the deck. First opinion voiced was that it was a devilfish and its brood. Spyglasses, however, revealed a torpedo — one of those laid by the *Baltic* — that had broken its mooring and had come drifting up the bay with the tide. The marine guard was called out; they commenced firing and sank the "infernal machine" only 20 feet from the *Tennessee's* side.[16]

Throughout the summer, Farragut watched for Buchanan and the *Tennessee* to come out. In mid-July he wrote

Admiral Theodorus Bailey: "Now is the time: the sea is as calm as possible and everything propitious for his ironclads to attack us . . ."[17] But Buchanan remained behind his mines and obstructions, waiting for Farragut to come in.

The Union fleet grew. By July 5 it numbered 17 vessels, and Farragut was now calling for monitors. General Grant had planned the capture of Mobile as a combined land-sea operation. His intentions were to bring General Nathaniel P. Banks' army out of New Orleans and send it against Mobile, at the same time striking up the bay with Farragut's fleet. But Banks, instead of turning east for Mobile, had headed up the Red River in an attempt to amass a fortune in captured cotton. Near Sabine Crossroads, General Edmund Kirby Smith's ragged Confederates had fallen on the cotton thieves, putting them to flight and posing such a heavy threat to the area that Banks' successor, Canby (who had ended the Confederate occupation of New Mexico by ably disposing of Henry Hopkins Sibley's army at Glorieta Pass), found himself so hard-pressed that he could send only a few thousand men. On July 8 Canby himself, in company with General Granger, came aboard the *Hartford* to confer with the Admiral.[18]

On July 21 Lt. Charles Simms was relieved of the command of the now wrecked *Baltic* to take command of the still incomplete *Nashville*.

On July 12 Farragut issued preliminary battle orders. His directive stated that the wooden ships would be lashed in pairs — gunboat and sloop to a couple — as they had at New Orleans, so one could be pulled through by her consort if disabled. Firing would be at will, as fast as guns could be brought to bear, using shells with 5-to10-second fuses.

The Union commanders, veterans all, made good use of various tricks learned at New Orleans. The *Richmond* armored herself with over 3,000 sand bags. Other ships used almost as many. Chains were hung alongside to protect boilers and engines, and coal was shifted in the bunkers to lay up against the walls for additional protection. Boat howitzers were mounted in the tops: they had been found quite effective in clearing the decks of gunboats.

Farragut clamored for monitors. By late July he had been promised four, but they were slow in arriving. The admiral complained to Secretary Welles:

It appears that it takes us twice as long to build an ironclad as anyone else . . . While the Rebels are bending their whole energies to the war, our people appear to be expecting the war to close by default, and if they do not awake to a sense of their danger soon it will be so.

To his son, Farragut wrote: "One thing appears to be certain, that I can get none of the ironclads. They want them all for Washington."[19]

But the monitors straggled in. On August 3, Percy Drayton, commanding Farragut's flagship, wrote to Pensacola: "If you can get the *Tecumseh* out tomorrow, do so; otherwise I am pretty certain that the admiral won't wait for her."[20] The next day the *Tecumseh*, last of the promised monitors, arrived off Mobile. Union sailors were up late that night, preparing for battle. Canby's troops had arrived, landing — on August 3 — behind Fort Gaines under the protection of a bombardment by the gunboat flotilla.

Dawn had to struggle to announce its arrival on August 5, 1864. The sky was cloudy and overcast. Conditions seemed to favor the Federals: they could ride into the bay with the help of the flood tide, and the wind would blow the smoke away from them, into the faces of the gunners at Fort Morgan.

Outside Mobile Bay, the Federal forces prepared. Wooden ships formed in a long line, lashed in pairs. Off to their right, also in line, bobbed the four monitors: small, dark, and vicious.

Inside the bay, preparations were being made to receive the invaders. At Forts Morgan and Gaines gray-clad gun crews stood by, their big guns cast loose and readied for action. The *Tennessee*, along with the wooden gunboats *Selma*, *Morgan*, and *Gaines*, rode at anchor on the north side of Fort Morgan. The Confederates, with a fairly good ironclad and three armed river boats, were to be pitted against 14 heavy gunboats and sloops of war and four monitors, all mounting the newest guns of heavy caliber. As word reached Mobile that the Federals were forming up to enter the bay, Major General Danby Maury sent word to have the *Huntsville* and *Tuscaloosa* (both still unfinished) sent down outside the obstructions to meet the Yanks. They never arrived.

As the Federal fleet got underway, the *Tennessee* and her consorts moved westward. From this position, their port broadsides would rake the Federals as they came on. Posting the *Tennessee* nearest the channel to meet the lead monitor, *Tecumseh*, Buchanan addressed his men:

Now men, the enemy is coming, and I want you to do your duty; and you shall not have it to say when you leave this vessel that you were not near enough to the enemy, for I shall meet them, and then you can fight them alongside of their own ships; and if I fall, lay me on the side and go on with the fight until you sink yourselves, but do not surrender.

The *Tecumseh's* big guns had been provided with flathead projectiles and 60-pound powder charges, supposed to pierce the *Tennessee's* armor without difficulty.

At 6:22 A.M. the monitor *Tecumseh* opened the ball, throwing a shell at Fort Morgan. It burst high in the air, directly over the big brick structure. At 7:06, the fort thundered its reply. A Union ship unleashed a salvo and the fort returned with a few individual shots. A surgeon aboard the *Lackawanna* described it:

It is a curious sight to catch a single shot from so heavy a piece of ordnance. First you see the puff of white smoke upon the distant ramparts, and then you see the shot coming, looking exactly as if some gigantic hand had thrown in play a ball toward you. By the time it is half way, you get the boom of the report, and then the howl of the missile, which apparently grows so rapidly in size that every green hand on board who can see it is certain that it will hit him between the eyes. Then, as it goes past with a shriek like a thousand devils, the inclination to do reverence is so strong that it is almost impossible to resist it.[21]

Fort Morgan's firing became heavier and the Federal warships roared in answer, coming one by one into the fray. The Confederate squadron reserved its fire and waited, watching the Union fleet advance. Then, as the Federals neared the line of torpedoes, the *Tennessee* got underway and moved away from the channel to the opposite end of the torpedo line. The monitor *Tecumseh* cut sharply and headed straight toward the *Tennessee* on a course that took her directly across the mine field. She pushed purposefully ahead, her bow parting the water evenly, closing the gap between herself and the armored ram. The two ironclads were about 100 yards apart when a huge geyser of water erupted alongside the monitor and the dull rumble of an exploding torpedo cut through the roar of Federal and Confederate guns. Within seconds the monitor's bow was underwater and her stern was high in the air, her still-revolving screw exposed. She went down quickly, taking almost all her crew with her.

The suddenness of the *Tecumseh's* destruction stunned everyone. Firing ceased and a stillness settled over the harbor as everyone turned to stare at the frothing, bubbling waters on which, a moment before, had steamed an invincible monitor. Then the gunners at Fort Morgan set up a cheer and the firing resumed.

The three little Rebel gunboats opened fire as the Federals closed the distance. Their guns were doing some mean execution on the wooden ships, but their heaviest shot failed to do more than dent the armor of the remaining monitors.

The commander of the *Brooklyn*, whose ship had been crowded off her course by the *Tecumseh's* maneuverings, soon sighted the menacing black shapes of torpedoes in the water before him. He stopped, bringing the entire Federal line to a confused halt. Gunners at Fort Morgan and on the gunboats quickly ranged in on that mass of ships. Farragut, seeing the danger of being stopped under the Confederate guns, pushed ahead of the *Brooklyn* and moved across the torpedo line. The Yanks plainly heard several primers pop as mine triggers brushed the *Hartford's* bottom, but no torpedoes exploded: the water had corroded their firing mechanisms.

The *Tennessee* sat, waiting quietly, as the Union armada pushed unharmed through the torpedo lines on the path cut by the *Hartford*. Farragut's flagship emerged from the field, steaming placidly across the *Tennessee's* bow at a range of 200 yards. A. D. Wharton brushed aside the bow gun's commander, intent on putting a fatal shot into the hated *Hartford* with his own hand. He depressed the piece to send a 7-inch shell through the *Hartford's* water line, then depressed it again, just to make sure. As the *Hartford* moved into its sights the long black rifle spoke, sending the projectile screaming. It struck the water just short of the *Hartford's* side and ricocheted, punching a hole in the flagship just above the water line.[22] How Wharton must have despaired at seeing the big Federal steam past undisturbed with a large hole in her side, scant inches high of being fatal!

With the dreaded torpdoes behind them, the Federals pressed on. Fort Morgan had holed each ship repeatedly, but sand bags and chain armor had kept all from being disabled, save one. The *Onieda*, as she passed the fort, caught a shell in her forward pivot-gun carriage, had her wheel-ropes shot away, then took a disabling shot in her starboard boiler. She was towed across the torpedo lines by her consort, *Galena*.[23] By 8:20, the entire Union fleet was in the harbor, leaving Fort Morgan completely out of the fight.

The *Hartford* somehow got about a mile ahead of the fleet, and the three Confederate gunboats swooped down on her. They took up positions 700 to 1,000 yards in front of her and opened an accurate fire with their stern guns, strewing her deck with dead and wounded. The *Tennessee* came up as if to ram but, when within 100 yards, sheared off and made for the advancing fleet.[24]

As the ironclad closed for combat she demonstrated that she possessed two defects characteristic of her class — low speed and a bad helm. She tried to ram, in succession, the *Brooklyn, Richmond,* and *Lackawanna*. All three sheared off quickly and the Confederates had to be content with offering each a broadside.[25] Return shots from the Federals were harmless, either shattering on impact or ricocheting from the *Tennessee's* thick hide.

Observing the *Tennessee's* immunity to shot, the Federals turned to attempts to beat her at her own game. The *Monongahela*, fitted with a ram just below her cut-water, suddenly turned and attempted to run the Confederate down. The force of the blow twisted the Federal's ram and crushed in her bow, but failed to dent the *Tennessee*. The *Monongahela's* consort, *Kennebec*, received the Rebel's retaliation: the ironclad rasped along her quarter and, as she slid past, unleased a shell that lodged in the Federal's berth deck, knocking over an officer and four men.[26]

The *Tennessee* straightened her course and slipped down the Federal line. She unleashed two shots at the *Ossippe*, then swung under the *Oneida's* stern, firing two broadsides. Her shots dismounted two guns, shot away most of the craft's lower rigging, and took off Union Commander Mulaney's arm.[27] The *Tennessee* then broke off the action and steamed over to rest up under the guns of Fort Morgan.

Farragut, under the impression that the *Tennessee* was through for the day, resolved to wait for dark, then send his monitors in to finish the ironclad. Union decks were swabbed, dead and wounded carried below, and the gun crews were at breakfast when the cry of alarm went up: the *Tennessee* was coming out. Guns were cast loose and crews stood ready, breakfast forgotten. "I did not think Old Buck was such a fool," muttered Farragut.[28]

The *Tennessee* was indeed underway, moving with all the speed she could muster toward the *Hartford*. Union ships turned to meet the Rebel, bows-on; and guns began to speak as the massed Federal armada began to move. The *Monongahela* pushed out in advance and picked up speed. Pivot guns in Federal bows roared, their shot finding, but failing to penetrate, the *Tennessee's* casemate.

The *Monongahela* made first contact. She rammed the Rebel in the side and received two shells in her berth deck for her efforts. The Yank rounded-to and heaved a tremendous broadside into the *Tennessee's* mailed side. The shot and shell had no effect on the iron giant.[29]

The fleet was now upon the *Tennessee*. They closed in and encircled, gathering close to hammer from every side. The ironclad replied with every gun, and a smoke cloud billowed out around her, spreading to encompass the Confederate and her antagonists alike. Muzzle flashes stabbed through the smoke, sending Confederate shell crashing through oak sides and United States shot ringing against iron armor. An army lieutenant with the Confederate battallion on Dauphin Island observed with awe: "The bay for a mile around is boiling with the ricochet of the shot and shell."[30]

The *Lackawanna* soon ceased bombarding, built up a head of steam, and thrashed in at full speed to ram. She struck the *Tennessee* such a hard lick that the ironclad swung around and listed briefly to port. Several small leaks were started in the hull and a chance shot jammed a port shutter. Greater damage was done to the *Lackawanna*, which had struck the ironclad's sharp knuckle, smashing in her bow.

In drawing off, the *Lackawanna* fouled the *Hartford*. Both the *Tennessee's* broadside guns were brought to bear on the Union flagship, striving to disengage herself, and eager hands snapped primer lanyards. One gun misfired. The other sent a shell crashing into the *Hartford's* berth deck, where it exploded, peppering the area with iron splinters.[31]

The monitor *Chickasaw*, heretofore unengaged, began creeping up on the *Tennessee's* port side. A. D. Wharton spotted her and called for everyone to stand clear of the port wall. A moment later a 440-pound solid shot struck the iron side with tremendous force. Smoke filtered into the casemate from somewhere and, when it cleared, daylight could be seen through a wall that had previously been 30 inches of solid wood and iron. Netting, hung on the inside of the walls before battle, was full of wood and iron splinters.[32] The *Chickasaw* steamed slowly to the rear and took up a position on the *Tennessee's* stern. From there she could fire at her leisure, impervious to the solid shot thrown back from the *Tennessee's* 7-inch stern rifle. "That damned ironclad is hanging on to us like a dog," snarled the *Tennessee's* pilot. "Fight him! Sink him if you can!"[33] The *Chickasaw*, in answer, sent another of her steelpoint shot winging off the *Tennessee's* quarter. The *Monongahela*, *Hartford*, and *Lackawanna* continued ramming, and the entire fleet poured tons of shot down on the lone Confederate. Farragut said: "She was at this time sore beset."

The *Tennessee's* rate of fire dropped. Both her afterquarter ports were jammed shut, the bow gun's port cover and the cover of the No. 1 gun on the port side were damaged.[34] Two of her broadside port covers had been shot away. The smokestack, already riddled, toppled overboard and coal smoke and gas began seeping into an already unbearably hot casemate.

Then disaster struck — the *Tennessee's* exposed steering chains were shot away. The relieving tackle was quickly manned and was just as quickly shot through. She no longer had control of her movements.

Buchanan descended from the pilot house to take personal command of the battery. A mechanic was called to back the pin out of the jammed after-port shutter to allow the stern rifle to resume firing. He succeeded, allowing the battered shutter to fall free, and a shell entered the open port, exploding on the gun deck and killing him instantly. Buchanan caught a fragment in the leg and was carried below to be placed under the care of fleet surgeon D. B.

Conrad. Commander Johnson assumed command of the *Tennessee*.

The *Tennessee's* situation was desperate. The *Chickasaw* was still off her stern, jolting her with ponderous 11- and 15-inch shots on her hull and casemate; the wooden fleet was clustered close, pounding and ramming, the monitors *Winnebago* and *Manhattan* were belatedly coming into position to engage, and the *Tennessee*, out of control, could work no more than half her guns. Johnston consulted Buchanan and was told: "Do the best you can, Johnston, and when all is done, surrender."[35] The *Tennessee* had already done her best. Further fighting could only end with the ship and her crew at the bottom of the bay. The time had come for surrender.

Since the flag staff had been shot away, the colors had flown from a boat hook stuffed up through the roof grating. This was lowered into the ship, but Federal fire failed to slacken. To halt the fire before another shell came through an open port, Johnston tied a white flag to a boat hook and dashed out onto the fireswept roof, where he stood amid flying shot and shell, waving the banner of defeat until firing ceased. The *Ossipee*, bearing down to ram as Johnston appeared with the white flag, reversed her engines and butted the *Tennessee* harmlessly. Commander William E. Le Roy, captain of the *Ossipee* and a lifelong friend of Johnston's, called over: "Hello, Johnston, how are you? Le Roy — don't you know me? I'll send a boat alongside for you."[36] As Johnston stepped aboard the gunboat he was heard to growl: "If it hadn't been for that damned black hulk under our stern we would have beaten you." Le Roy's good spirits were not dampened, however. He handed the Confederate a glass of ice water, then said: "But I've something better for you down below." He led Johnston to his cabin, where he produced a bottle of sherry and a pitcher of ice water. Boarding the *Hartford* later, Johnston was met by Farragut with: "I'm sorry to meet you under such circumstances."

"You're not half as sorry as I am," snapped Johnston. Percy Drayton, moved by the glory of the *Tennessee's* futile and desperate attack, paid tribute to the *Tennessee* and her gallant crew: "You have one consolation, Johnston. No one can say that you have not nobly defended the honor of the Confederate flag today."[37]

Union casualties for the battle totaled 180 killed, 170 wounded. One ship, the monitor *Tecumseh*, was lost to a mine.[38] The Confederate Navy lost the iron-clad *Tennessee* and the gunboats *Selma* and *Gaines* — three-fourths their active Mobile Bay squadron — and suffered 12 killed and 19 wounded.[39]

Although the *Tennessee* had been captured and the United States blockading fleet was inside the bay, the city of Mobile was still to be taken. Forts Morgan and Powell and the chain of earthworks ringing the city were still in Confederate hands and the unfinished ironclads down from Selma, Montgomery, and the Tombigbee posed a potential threat. The Federal army paused to draw in supplies and reinforcements preparatory to continuing the campaign, and the citizens and soldiery of Mobile prepared themselves for a siege. The Federals hastily repaired the *Tennessee* and pressed her into service against Fort Morgan.[40]

On November 26, 1864, Lt. Charles Simms was relieved of his command of the *Nashville* and received orders to report to the naval works at Selma. Lieutenant John W. Bennet was ordered down from command of the battery at Choctaw Point to receive command of the *Nashville*. She was armored, by this time, with three layers of 2-inch plate on the front of her casemate and pilot house — the first

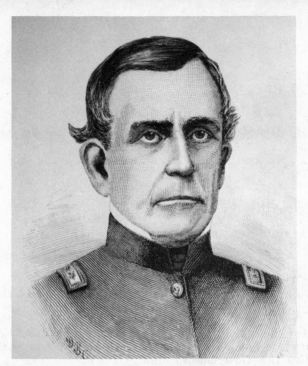

Captain Duncan N. Ingraham, C.S.N. (*History of the Confederate States Navy*, Rogers and Sherwood, New York)

Lieutenant James H. Rochelle, C.S.N. (*History of the Confederate States Navy*, Rogers and Sherwood, New York)

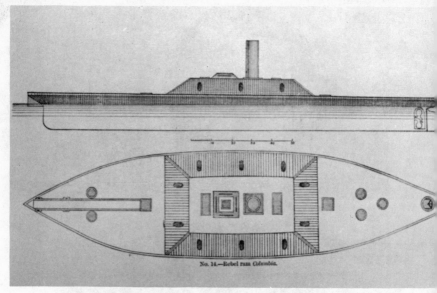

Side view and deck plan of the *C.S.S. Columbia*. (*Official Records of the Union and Confederate Navies in the War of the Rebellion*, U. S. Government Printing Office)

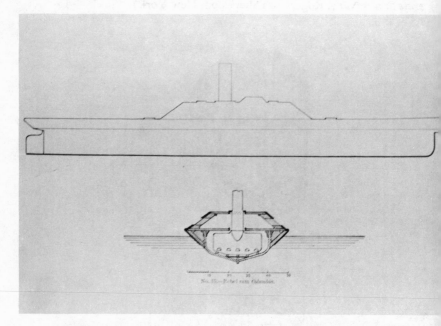

Outline drawing and longitudinal cutaway of the *Columbia*. (*Official Records of the Union and Confederate Navies in the War of the Rebellion*, U. S. Government Printing Office)

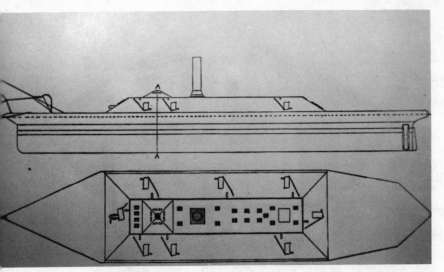

Side view and deck plan of the *Atlanta*. (*Official Records of the Union and Confederate Navies in the War of the Rebellion*, U. S. Government Printing Office)

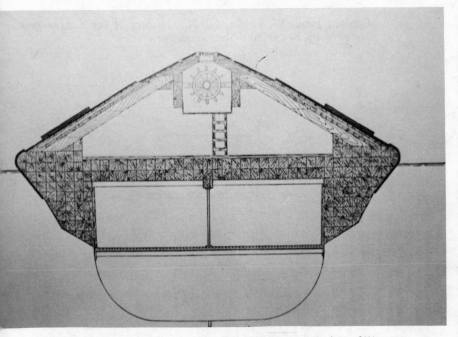

Longitudinal cutaway of the *Atlanta*. Note timber filling around the *Fingal's* hull. (*Official Records of the Union and Confederate Navies in the War of the Rebellion*, U. S. Government Printing Office)

Captain James W. Cooke, C.S.N. (*History of the Confederate States Navy*, Rogers and Sherwood, New York)

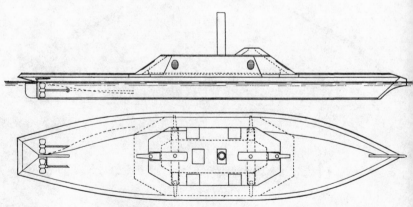

Side view and detailed deck plan of the *Albemarle*.

The *C.S.S. Albemarle.* (*Official Records of the Union and Confederate Navies in the War of the Rebellion,* U. S. Government Printing Office)

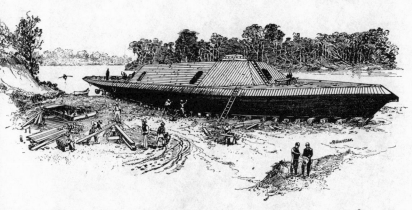

The *Albermarle* under construction at Edwards Ferry. (*Battles and Leaders of the Civil War,* Thomas Yoseloff, New York)

The *Sassacus* ramming the *Albermarle*. (*Battles and Leaders of the Civil War*, Thomas Yoseloff, New York)

The *Albermarle* sinking *the Southfield*. (*Battles and Leaders of the Civil War*, Thomas Yoseloff, New York)

Commander John N. Maffitt, C.S.N. A native of Ireland, Maffitt made his name as commander of the cruiser *Florida*, and the blockade runners *Lilian* and *Owl*. (*History of the Confederate States Navy*, Rogers and Sherwood, New York)

The *Albemarle* at Norfolk. (*Miller's Photographic History*)

The destruction of the *Albermarle*. (*Battles and Leaders of the Civil War,* Thomas Yoseloff, New York)

Commander James D. Johnston, C.S.N. (*Battles and Leaders of the Civil War,* Thomas Yoseloff, New York)

Admiral Franklin Buchanan, C.S.N. (*History of the Confederate States Navy,* Rogers and Sherwood, New York)

The *C.S.S. Tennessee.* (*Official Records of the Union and Confederate Navies in the War of the Rebellion,* U. S. Government Printing Office)

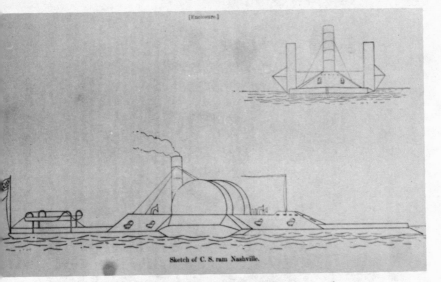

[Enclosure.]

Sketch of C. S. ram Nashville.

Reproductions of David Farragut's line drawings of an unfinished Confederate ironclad: the *Nashville*. (*Official Records of the Union and Confederate Navies in the War of the Rebellion*, U. S. Government Printing Office)

The *C.S.S. Richmond*. (*Official Records of the Union and Confederate Navies in the War of the Rebellion*, U. S. Government Printing Office)

Admiral Raphael Semmes, C.S.N. (*History of the Confederate States Navy,* Rogers and Sherwood, New York)

The *C.S.S. Stonewall.* (*Miller's Photographic History*)

Commander John M. Kell, C.S.N. (*Miller's Photographic History*)

Bulloch's Birkenhead rams (left foreground and center back), guarded by the H.M.S. *Majestic* (center). (*Secret Service of the Confederate States in Europe*, Thomas Yoseloff, New York)

Commander James D. Bulloch, C.S.N. (*Secret Service of the Confederate States in Europe,* Thomas Yoseloff, New York)

A detailed study of the *Stonewall's* bow. (*Miller's Photographic History*)

A detailed study of the *Stonewall's* bow. The two men at the bottom of the picture give an idea of the size of the ship. (*Miller's Photographic History.*)

layer put down horizontally, the top two laid vertically —
and one layer of 2-inch plate laid vertically on the back of
the casemate. Her sides were unarmored.[41]

On the morning of March 27, 1865, the *Nashville* first
entered into the defense of Mobile, weighing anchor to
steam down toward Spanish Fort, a main bulwark of Confederate defense on the Blakely River. Coming to anchor
near the fort, Bennet held a hurried conference aboard ship
with Dabney H. Maury and St. John Liddell. The Federals,
they told him, had been attacking in force, pressing the thin
Confederate line severely. The *Nashville* and her gunboat
consorts were asked to act in conjunction with the army,
using their heavy guns loaded with grape, canister, or shell
to help break up enemy concentrations and halt attacks.[42]

When the conference closed, Bennet moored his ironclad
between batteries Tracy and Huger to await developments.
Action was not long in coming. Firing broke out in the
vicinity of Spanish Fort as Federal attacks began, then
spread all along the line. At 1:00 P.M. Lieutenant Bennet
received a dispatch from Maury, asking that the gunboat
Morgan be sent down across the obstructions near Battery
Huger to commence shelling the enemy's right. The *Morgan*, however, was not on the scene at the time, and the
Nashville, due to her great draft, could not get across the
obstructions. At 2:00 P.M. a second message arrived, desperately calling for the *Morgan* to steam down and take
some of the pressure off General Gibson's left. With the
little gunboat still absent, Bennet fumed and fretted: something had to be done to relieve Gibson. Finally, the lieutenant sent a pilot down the river to take soundings on the
off-chance that the *Nashville* — even with her immense
draft — might be able to get over the obstructions and
down the river where she was needed. The pilot soon re-

turned, reporting that there was just enough depth and width of water over a line of submerged pilings for the *Nashville* to squeeze through. The *Nashville* got underway immediately. She glided with surprising ease over the obstructions, steamed down the river with no difficulty, then ran hard and fast aground at the junction of the Apalachee and Blakely Rivers. She would be of no use to the army that day . . . or the next. It was the 29th before she was finally floated free.[43]

On March 30, the *Nashville* again came to anchor between batteries Tracy and Huger, bringing her guns to bear on a group of Federal soldiers digging and occupying entrenchments in front of Spanish Fort. General Liddell came aboard to direct firing and the *Nashville's* battery soon opened on the Federals. At a range of about 3,200 yards, her gunnery was excellent. Shells knocked over scores of skirmishers and sharpshooters, and twice stampeded Yankee work parties engaged in digging approaches toward the Confederate work. The ironclad kept firing all day, finally ceasing as night fell.

The hard-pressed garrison of Spanish Fort had suffered heavy casualties during the late Union attacks. On the night of the 30th the *Nashville's* small boats were pressed into service to remove the wounded. The ironclad fired occasionally during the night, just enough to keep the Federals from getting any sleep.

The next morning the Confederates discovered a masked battery on the shore of Minette Bay. A message was quickly gotten off to General Liddell, warning him of the new danger. Liddell requested that the *Nashville* steam down and shell the battery, and the ironclad made ready to move to a more favorable position. She was too slow, however. The Yanks spotted the big ironclad so placidly reposing on the river and opened fire, quickly getting the range. Eight shots hit the *Nashville* before she could get out of the Federals' range. One of these disabled the after-gun carriage. No other damage was done.[44] The ironclad anchored a little above battery Tracy in a position that afforded her protection from the Union battery. Again that night her small boats were employed in taking a gory cargo of wounded from Spanish Fort.

On April 1, the *Nashville* steamed back to Mobile. She spent that day and the next having her shattered gun carriage and a leaking boiler repaired, then she returned to the Blakely River. The big ironclad had no sooner arrived than General Liddell had an officer aboard, pointing out various positions he wanted shelled. A signal station was established downriver to report the effects of the firing and, at 1:00 P.M., the *Nashville* opened up. All during the day the station flashed in reports of the damage the ironclad's screaming shells were doing, while the cheers of the Southern soldiers in the trenches announced the more spectacular hits. At 5:00 P.M. the *Nashville* ceased firing, beginning again at nightfall with shots at intervals of one hour. The ironclad held her position all the next day, occasionally shelling spots pointed out by General Liddell.

In the early morning hours of the fifth of April the ironclad took up a position at a point between the Raft and the Upper Tensas (or Tensaw) Rivers. From there she again disturbed the sleep of Federal troops with occasional firing.

The *Nashville* continued her harassment of the Federals throughout the next day, directing a slow fire at Union pickets and sharpshooters. Bennet had requisitioned more shells, but they hadn't arrived, and ammunition was low. Toward nightfall the lieutenant received a communication from General Liddell, asking him to anchor the *Nashville* alongside General Gibson's left and send several of her small boats as pickets to protect the telegraph line to Spanish Fort. Bennet had anticipated this last request and the boats, manned by armed sailors, were already at their stations. The *Nashville* arrived off Gibson's left at 11:45 P.M., near her old anchorage off Battery Tracy.

At daylight on April 7 the *Nashville* got underway and steamed upriver to replenish her magazines. Near sunset, while the ammunition was still being loaded, her two largest boats left her and headed for Spanish Fort and service with General Liddell. The ironclad got underway soon afterward and returned to her anchorage off Tracy. A picket boat was set out for Minette Bay and one of the launches returned from her patrol off Spanish Fort around midnight, concluding the night's activities.[45]

At dawn of April 8, the *Nashville* was underway, steaming first to the Blakely River, then to the junction of the Raft and the Upper Tensas, where she was joined by the *Morgan* and *Huntsville*.

At 7:00 A.M. the Union Army launched an attack on Gibson's garrison in Spanish Fort. The three ships lay quiet for an hour, then opened a galling fire on the Federal right. They were busily involved in this when surprised by the fire of a Federal battery — 30-pounder Parrotts of the 1st Indiana — shooting from about 1,600 yards and masked by trees. The *Nashville* shifted her fire from the Federal attack to the masked battery. She could only fire at the Yankees' smoke, the guns being completely hidden. The defectiveness of the shells she had so recently received soon became apparent: many of them were crushed by the force of the propelling charge, leaving the guns' muzzles in pieces and scattering like grape or canister, falling at a distance of from 50 to 500 yards. Many of the shells didn't take the gun's rifle motion. To correct this, heavier powder charges were used. They nearly tore the gun carriages apart

and blew the bushing out of the after gun's vent. The ironclad threw seventy 7-inch shells at the battery, using all of
her 12-pound powder charges and doing the Federals no
serious damage. The Union battery concentrated most of
its fire on the unarmored *Morgan*. The little gunboat caught
seven 30-pound shells and was forced to retire. The *Nashville* eventually followed, although she had not been hit.
Only the *Huntsville* remained in the open, bravely slugging
it out with the battery.

At 7:00 P.M. the *Nashville* anchored in the middle of
the Blakely River, moving at General Liddell's request to
her old anchorage close to Battery Tracy.

General Dabney Maury had ordered General Gibson not
to hold Spanish Fort to the point of endangering its garrison with capture.[47] With Federal siege lines drawing ever
close and the garrison worn out, that point seemed danger-
ously near. Accordingly, Gibson decided to evacuate, calling on Bennet to send every available boat to help carry off
his men. Bennet complied and the *Nashville* moved into the
middle of the river — between batteries Tracy and Huger
— where she could draw any Federal fire to herself and
away from the men moving out of Spanish Fort. Federal
artillery, spotting the ironclad, threw a few shells at her.
The *Nashville* failed to reply — Confederate troops were
between the ironclad and the Union battery and would be
endangered by crushed shells.

On the morning of April 9, with the evacuation of Spanish Fort completed, the *Nashville* moved to the mouth of
the Tensas River to take on more ammunition. It was Palm
Sunday. While the *Nashville* lay quietly in the river under
the warm Mobile sun taking in shot, shell, and cartridges,
far to the northeast a broken-hearted Robert E. Lee was
surrendering the skeletal remains of the Army of Northern
Virginia. The Confederacy was dying.

A little after 5:00 P.M. Liddell sent a message to Lieutenant Bennet, requesting that the *Nashville* drop down to a specific point on the Blakely to shell Federal troops. The currents were unknown there, however, and there was no holding ground. And the *Nashville*, from that position, would likely spray Confederate troops with fragments of crushed shell. For these reasons, Liddell's request was not complied with and the *Nashville* did not move.

Slowly but surely, the Confederates were driven back. Spanish Fort had been lost. Other fortifications were evacuated or taken by assault, and the blue ring of Federals coiled tighter about Mobile. On April 12, the blow fell . . . Mobile surrendered. The *Huntsville* and *Tuscaloosa* steamed into the main channel of the Spanish River and anchored. The crews of the two ironclads, along with most of their supplies, were transferred to the *Nashville* and a few other steamers, and the two little rams were scuttled.[48] The *Nashville*, *Morgan*, and a few blockade runners headed up the Tombigbee River. The steamer *Southern Republic* took on as many supplies as she could from the navy yard and followed, leaving the yard in flames behind her.

On the Tombigbee the little Confederate naval force paused to make a stand. The blockade runners were armed and converted to gunboats, though Union shot and shell would easily pierce their thin hulls in an engagement.

A Federal fleet soon appeared to seal off the mouth of the Tombigbee, keeping a close watch on the *Nashville* and her consorts throughout the month of April. Finally tiring of the watching game, Acting Rear Admiral H. K. Thatcher planned an attack for May 3. Several days before the designated attack date, however, Thatcher received a communication from Captain Eben Farrand, commanding the Tombigbee flotilla, suggesting a peace talk and possible surrender.[49] Thatcher was immediately on the move and, that night, met Farrand at Citronelle. When the conference concluded, Farrand and Thatcher had drawn up a set of surrender terms. The Confederates were to surrender at Nanna Hubba Bluff on May 10.

Captain Farrand appointed Lieutenant Julian Meyers — late of the *Huntsville*, now commanding the *Southern Republic* — to represent him at the surrender. Thatcher chose as his representative Fleet Captain E. Simpson. Meyers set out on the 6th: Simpson arrived at the Bluff on the 9th. He brought with him the ironclads *Cincinnati*, *Chickasaw*, and *Nyanza*. The Confederate sailors received approximately the same terms as had Lee's men. The terms read as follows:

First. The officers and men to be paroled until duly exchanged or otherwise released from the obligations of their parole by the authority of the Government of the United States. Duplicate rolls of all officers and men surrendered to be made, one copy to be delivered to the officer appointed by Acting Rear-Admiral H. K. Thatcher, an the other retained by the officer appointed by Commodore E. Farrand; officers giving their individual parole and commanders of vessels signing a like parole for the men of their respective commands.

Second. All vessels of war, their guns and equipment, all small arms and ammunition and stores on board the said vessels to be delivered over to the officers appointed for that purpose by Acting Rear-Admiral H. K. Thatcher. Duplicate inventories of the property surrendered to be prepared, one to be retained by the officer delivering and the other by the officer receiving it for our own information.

Third. The officers and men paroled under this agreement will be allowed to return to their homes with the assurance that they will not be disturbed by the authorities of the United States so long as they continue to observe the conditions of their paroles and the laws in force where they reside, except that persons residents of Northern States will not be allowed to return without special permission.

Fourth. The surrender of property will not include the side arms or private baggage of officers.

Fifth. The time and place of surrender will be fixed by us, respectively, and will be carried out by officers appointed by us.

Sixth. After the surrender, transportation and subsistence to be furnished by Acting Rear-Admiral H. K. Thatcher for officers and men to the nearest practicable point of their respective residences.[50]

The U. S. Navy, in their capture of the *Nashville* and her consorts, took 112 officers, 285 men, and 24 marines.

8

The James River Again

On March 17, 1862, Colonel Blanton Duncan of the Treasury Department had published in the Richmond Dispatch an appeal for funds to aid in the construction of a second ironclad — patterned after the *Virginia* — at Norfolk. He asked for donations from patriotic men who could give "from $500. to $5,000. and not miss it," and started the ball rolling with a $2,000 contribution of his own. The first response to his appeal came from Charles M. Wallace, who contributed $1,000. Milton J. Jarnagin next telegraphed a $500 contribution from Athens, Tennessee, and fire-eating Edmund Ruffin donated $500. Edmund, Jr., outdid his father with a contribution of $1,000.[1]

To aid in the fund raising, a "Ladies Defense Association" was formed. The ladies of Richmond held fairs, plays, and similar entertainments, and solicited the donation of jewelry to raise needed money. Going further, they marched on Richmond tobacco factories, persuading owners to break up machinery and donate the iron for use as armor.

The navy's ordnance office received a contribution of 1,623 lbs. of church bells, to be cast into cannon for the ironclad, donated by the Methodist, Presbyterian, Baptist, and Episcopal churches of Marietta, Georgia.[2]

Acting naval constructor William A. Graves superintended the ironclad's construction, under the direction of Commander Eben Farrand. She was 160 feet in length, 41 feet abeam, and drew 12½ feet of water. Her casemate frame — oak and pine — was 18 inches in thickness, to be covered with a 4-inch layer of iron plating. Her armor was to continue at its inclined angle down past the water line, reversing to form a knuckle that extended 4 feet from the hull. A 2-inch plating of armor covered the underside of the knuckle. She would mount four 7-inch Brooke rifles, cast at Richmond.

Work progressed rapidly and, by April, construction was in its advanced stages. In early May, however, the Federals began closing in around Norfolk. George McClellan had brought his Army of the Potomac down to the vicinity of Fort Monroe and Newport News with the intention of making his thrust at Richmond up the banks of the James; and John Magruder's 12,000 Confederates had withdrawn before the pressure of McClellan's forces, leaving Norfolk indefensible. On May 6, the ironclad was launched, christened the C.S.S. *Richmond*. That night she was taken in tow by the *Patrick Henry*. The little *Jamestown* took a barge laden with the ram's ordnance stores, and the ships and barge moved quietly up the James River, stealing silently past batteries of heavy Federal guns. At Curles Neck the ironclad and her barge were turned over to Lieutenant William Sharp of the *Patrick Henry*. The *Patrick Henry* and *Jamestown* returned to Norfolk while the *Richmond* continued to the city whose name she had taken. She was completed in July.

Federal prisoners being exchanged from Richmond caught glimpses of the new ironclad. Their reports so exaggerated her size that the North christened her "*Merrimack* No. 2." Robert B. Pegram first commanded her, with B. P. Loyall the ram's 1st lieutenant. In 1864 Pegram left to take command of the newly launched *Virginia* II, handing the *Richmond* over to William A. Webb, exchanged in October, 1864 after his capture in the *Atlanta*. By the time the ironclad entered action in early 1865, she was under John McIntosh Kell, late of the raider *Alabama*, sunk off Cherbourg, France.

On July 30, 1862, the *Richmond* steamed down the James to Drewry's Bluff. The Federal ironclads *Monitor* and *Galena*, stationed downriver from Confederate Fort Darling, sighted the *Richmond* and hurried off to inform Flag Officer Charles Wilkes that the ironclad had come down. Wilkes sat in a sort of lethargy for some time, finally stirring to steam slowly up the river with his flagship, the two ironclads, and six gunboats. By the time he arrived below Drewry's Bluff, the *Richmond* had retired.

Throughout the remainder of 1862 and 1863 the *Richmond* made only occasional appearances. She was too vulnerable to single-handedly attack the Union blockading fleet with its growing ironclad strength, so she remained above the obstructions, a part — along with the bluff batteries and Hunter Davidson's occasional floating torpedoes — of the James River defensive system.

Even though she failed to make any dangerous demonstrations, the *Richmond* was regarded by the North as a major threat to the safety of the lower James, and elaborate plans were offered (mostly by civilians) to destroy her. One such plan involved lashing two fast gunboats together with a fork of springy timber projecting from their bows. They were to make a dash at the *Richmond*, run the fork onto her bow or stern, and push her ashore while the rest of the fleet came up to close in and pounded her to pieces with heavy guns. The operation was never attempted.

By mid-1864 two other ironclads, the *Virginia* II and *Fredricksburg*, were on the scene. Both had been built at Rocketts, the Richmond naval yard. The *Fredricksburg* was armored with 4 inches of iron and drew 11 feet of water. She carried four 6-inch rifles. The *Virginia* II, somewhat stronger, was protected by a 6-inch iron plating and mounted two 8-inch and two 6-inch rifles. All three rams mounted their bow and stern chasers on pivots, allowing them to be fired in broadside.

Also building at Richmond during this period, Mallory reported two ironclad sloops and a double-ender — propellers and rudders at each end for easier navigation in narrow inland waterways — mounting one gun pivoted and tracked in a short casemate. None of these would ever reach completion.[3]

By 1864 the Federals had amassed a rather formidable fleet to blockade the James River. There were wooden gunboats and sloops beyond counting, plus the monitors *Saugus*, *Tecumseh*, *Canonicus*, and *Onondaga*. All the monitors mounted 11- and 15-inch guns — ten of them — against the Confederate squadron's ten 6-inch and two 8-inch guns.

In the spring of 1864 Commander John K. Mitchell, flag officer of the James River Squadron, erected a masked battery of naval guns on a hill near Howlett's House, a landmark on the James River. The battery — known as Battery Dantzler — was in a position to fire across a point of land and strike enemy vessels at a curve in the river. Mitchell's aim was to draw the cautious Federal monitors up the river and into combat with his ironclad and shore batteries.

About 10:30 on the morning of June 21, the trees and

brush masking Battery Dantzler were felled and the battery opened fire on the *Tecumseh, Canonicus,* and *Saugus*. The monitors *Canonicus* and *Saugus* replied immediately while the *Tecumseh* lay silent, unable to see her target through the trees.[4] At 12:15 the *Virginia* and *Fredericksburg* arrived. They dropped light anchors and sent out kedges to shore to spring and steady themselves as necessary. The *Fredricksburg* and her tender — *Nansemond* — anchored near the ferry and the *Virginia* near Dutch Gap "so as to command as much as possible of the lower part of Trent's Reach and Varina Reach." The *Richmond* was to have accompanied them, but a wheel rope had parted, fouling her propeller, and she had been towed off to Chaffin's Bluff to have it cleared. On the way down a piston had fouled and quit aboard the *Virginia*, accounting for the delay in the ironclads' arrival. The flagship's cylinder assembly had been dismantled, and a chisel had been found inside.[5]

At 12:30, the two ironclads opened fire. Commander T. A. M. Craven's *Tecumseh* had, by this time, joined in the general firing, shooting at Dantzler's smoke. At 1:30, Craven ceased fire to give the crew dinner, resuming fire at 2:00. A 10-inch Brooke bolt from Dantzler struck the *Saugus'* deck, glancing to her turret. Several of the deck's 1½-inch armor plates were cracked, a plank was splintered, and a beam started. A 3½-inch crack was started in a plate on the inside of the turret's 10-inch thick layer of armor, and 44 bolts were "more or less affected by this shot." One of the ironclads' 7-inch bolts struck the *Canonicus'* deck, fracturing two plates. Its rifling studs left clear marks as the shot plowed a furrow 7½ inches wide and 25 inches long in the deck. Another shot perforated her smokestack, leaving a hole 8½ inches in diameter. Only one shell broke near the *Tecumseh*, ineffectually peppering her deck.[6]

In all, damage was negligible. The monitors sustained

four hits, suffering a half-dozen broken armor plates and one punctured smoke stack. Neither Battery Dantzler nor the two ironclads were struck by return fire. The engagement somewhat awakened the Union navy to the small upsurge of Confederate activity in the area. Admiral Samuel Phelps Lee, pressed to send monitors to David Farragut at Mobile, telegraphed Secretary Welles that: "Instead of withdrawing the *Tecumseh,* it is necessary to largely increase the ironclad force here . . . . The enemy seems determined to control this stretch of the river."[7]

The Howlett's House battery continued to make a nuisance of itself throughout the summer. In August, General Benjamin F. Butler ordered a canal dug for the purpose of getting ships behind it to eliminate it. The battery constantly shelled the work parties engaged in digging the ditch, inflicting fifteen to twenty casualties per day.

At 5:00 A.M. on August 13, the *Virginia* and *Fredricksburg* moved into position and opened fire on an early work party.[8] The *Richmond* and several gunboats moved down to Cox's Reach and opened in conjunction with the batteries at Signal Hill and Howlett's House. The Union gunboats *Delaware* and *Mackinaw* and the monitor *Saugus,* downriver, remained at anchor and opened a return fire, directed by a lookout in the *Mackinaw's* masthead. Their fire was ineffective: they struck the *Virginia* twice, the *Fredricksburg* once, inflicting no damage.

On September 19, the Federals took Confederate Fort Harrison near the James, giving them an opportunity to build a masked battery near the Boulware House. These guns remained undetected until October 22, when they opened fire on the three ironclads and the gunboats *Hampton* and *Drewry,* lying nearby. The fragile gunboats beat a hasty retreat, but the ironclads weren't to be chased. The *Virginia* got underway and steamed to within 500 yards of the Federal guns, signaling the *Richmond* and *Fredricks-burg* to follow. From this range they opened a galling fire. The Federals, informed that the *Fredricksburg* was the weakest of the trio, concentrated their fire on her. One shell exploded directly over the roof grating, wounding six men. Other than that, they did no damage except to shoot off a few rivet heads. Confederate return fire was vicious. At times Union firing dwindled to almost nothing as bursting 6-, 7- and 8-inch shells, grape, and canister drove Union gunners to seek shelter.[9] Finally, after some time under Federal guns, the ironclads moved away and anchored near the obstructions below Drewry's Bluff, hoping the firing would attract a few monitors or gunboats. The Federal Navy failed to appear, however, and the ironclads remained at the obstructions, making them their station throughout autumn.

On December 7, the three Confederates dropped down below the obstructions and engaged in a shelling match with Union Fort Brady. It didn't last long, beginning just before sunset and ending at dark. The *Richmond* caught the only Union shell that found its mark, a rifled shot that glanced away, doing no damage.

The year 1865 dawned dim indeed for the Confederacy. Lee's magnificent Army of Northern Virginia had dwindled to a mere skeleton of its former self. In the West, Hood was out, his army shattered at Nashville. Sherman was relentlessly pressing Hardee's legion, and had made Lincoln a Christmas present of Savannah. A Southern victory was needed, and needed soon, or the entire Confederacy, split into fragments and overrun by Union armies, would surely die. And only the Army of Northern Virginia, as ragged and hungry and ill-equipped as the legions of Johnston or Taylor or Kirby Smith, but under the magnificent spiritual and physical leadership of Robert E. Lee, seemed capable of striking one last decisive blow. To pit them against the numerous and well-equipped hosts of Grant in a standup, man-to-man battle, however, could result in nothing but their total annihilation. A diversion was needed, some sort of mild disaster to be laid upon the Army of the Potomac to help even up the odds. And an excellent disaster, it was thought, would be the disbursing of the Union blockading fleet on the James and the destruction of the mountains of supplies at the Union Army's City Point supply depot. If the James River Squadron could accomplish this it could, perhaps, promote a panic in Washington and along the Atlantic seaboard comparable to that engendered by the old *Virginia* in her heyday. Perhaps the destruction of the Federal army's supplies in the midst of a bleak winter would demoralize it. Perhaps the hoped-for panic in Washington would force Lincoln to draw off troops from Grant's army and ironclads from the Charleston and Wilmington blockades to defend the capital and the seaboard. Perhaps, finally, the navy would be able to serve as the key to an operation — possibly the beginning of a new campaign — of the utmost importance.

Of the four monitors that had been stationed on the James, only the double-turreted *Onondaga* (along with the captured Confederate *Atlanta*) remained. The rest had been dispatched to Wilmington, North Carolina to take part in the reduction of Fort Fisher. Mitchell hoped to surprise the monitor and sink or capture her before she could bring her rifles into play. But a flood tide — to give the big *Virginia* adequate water in which to maneuver — would be needed to offer any hope of success in the venture.

On January 22, the awaited flood came. The day was unseasonably warm and the ice and snow melted, running out of fields and woods, filling the river. Soon after nightfall Lt. "Savez" Read, now commanding Battery Wood, along with Master's Mate J. W. Billups and two other men from the battery, made a reconnaissance of the obstructions placed by the Federals to fence the squadron in. At one point they found a gap 80 feet wide, with 14 feet of water under it, closed only by a spar anchored to lie across it. Read reported back to Mitchell and was dispatched to inform the army that the time for the attack had come. He went first to the headquarters of General Pickett, who sent him to see Lee at Petersburg. Lee questioned him closely about the obstructions and the gap, then sent him to Mallory back in Richmond to receive orders to launch the attack. Mallory wrote out the necessary orders and Read was back on the James the next day.[10]

Preparations for the strike consisted of lashing the ships into small groups for the run down. The gunboat *Nansemond* and the torpedo boats *Scorpion* and *Torpedo* were lashed alongside the *Virginia*. The *Richmond* had the gunboat *Beaufort* and the torpedo boat *Drewry* lashed alongside while the *Fredricksburg* carried along the *Hampton* and *Hornet*. At 6:30 P.M. of January 23, the squadron got underway. They drifted slowly downriver, all lights covered, all noise muffled. Two hours of silent running brought them just above the Dutch Gap Canal, where the *Torpedo* grounded, her lashings pulling apart. The *Nansemond* was cut adrift and sent to pull her off, and both boats returned a half hour later to be lashed alongside once more. Meanwhile, the squadron had anchored and Mitchell had boarded the *Scorpion* to inspect the obstructions. A few quick blows with a cold chisel set the floating spar adrift and the *Scorpion* glided through, taking soundings. She was at this when a Union sentry discovered her — and the fleet — and fired a shot. His alarm set off a flurry of musketry, and the fire was quickly taken up by field artillery wheeled into position to fire down on the fleet. The *Scorpion* steamed slowly through all this, unmindful of flying shot, until soundings were finished. She then returned to the ironclads. Mitchell boarded the *Fredricksburg* and took her through the gap, followed by the *Scorpion*. He then returned on the torpedo boat and found that the falling tide had left the *Richmond* and *Virginia* aground. The gunboats strained to pull them off, but without success. Union fire, meanwhile, became hotter. Nearby Confederate batteries replied and the firing grew in volume, continuing for several hours before finally dying away. About 4:00 the next morning Mitchell sent Lt. Read down to bring the *Fredricksburg* back. The element of surprise was gone, and the attack had collapsed.

Daybreak revealed that the squadron had gone aground directly under the guns of Union Fort Pearson. The fort opened fire at daylight, wrecking the *Drewry* and the torpedo launch *Wasp*. The rest of the wooden ships scooted in under the bluff, safe from Federal fire while a hail of shot, shell, and musketry hammered on the ironclads.

The *Onondaga* now arrived on the scene, attracted by the firing. Calmly, quietly, she maneuvered through the cut in the obstructions and dropped anchor broadside-on to the *Virginia*. The Confederates loaded with solid shot, opened their ports to run the pieces out and were greeted by a hail of musketry. The ports were quickly closed. The *Onondaga* swung her turrets to bear on the stranded *Virginia* and, from point-blank range, opened a slow fire. Lieutenant Dunnington's official report gives an excellent account of the beating administered to the *Virginia* by the *Onondaga* and Fort Pearson.

At 7:30 A.M. received a shot on starboard side forward that started timbers on berth deck. Repaired same as soon as possible.

At 8:15 A.M. pendant for starboard bow port was shot away. Repaired it, and triced up port again.

At 8:35 A.M. a heavy shell struck iron grating over gun deck, breaking it in and crushing timbers. Shored up timers.

At 9:A.M. received a shot on starboard pipe that loosened it.

At 9:15 A.M. smoke came from shield deck. Water was thrown on and hose turned on it, which stopped the smoke.

At 9:35 A.M. the smokestack was hit by a shell. During all this time it had been frequently struck by fragments of shell and was completely riddled. Most of the stays were also carried away.

At 9:40 A.M. a heavy shot struck the ship, jarring her from stem to stern.

At 9:45 A.M. smokestack struck by another shot, and one struck forward that shook the vessel.

At 10 A.M. a heavy shot struck the knuckle forward the starboard side that broke the iron.

At 10:10 A.M. smokestack struck twice.

At 10:15 A.M. struck by two shots, one hitting just over the starboard bow port, the other over starboard broadside port.

At 10:17 A.M. smokestack, hurricane deck, and knuckle forward on starboard side all hit.

At 10:20 A.M. a shell struck and exploded in forward bow port, wounding one man.

At 10:30 A.M. a small shell struck starboard bow port, glanced inboard, struck starboard compressor of bow gun and exploded, wounding Lt. Mason, and 7 men slightly, filled gun deck with smoke. This shell passed entirely through the starboard side of gun carriage before exploding.

At 10:32 A.M. ship was found afloat, weighed the kedge; at 10:35 A.M. got underway, swinging ship. A heavy shell struck forward, glancing over shield and bursting near smokestack.

At 10:40 A.M. fragments of shell struck smokestack, two shells bursting over shield deck.

At 10:55 A.M. shell struck forward.

At 11:15 A.M. struck by a heavy projectile on port quarter,

which broke the iron and crushed in the woodwork, bent stanchions inboard.

At 11:20 A.M. headed upstream.

At 11:30 A.M. a heavy shot struck on after part of shield between after center and port ports, breaking the iron and crushing the woodwork completely in, making a large hole there. One man was killed and 2 wounded by the concussion and splinters. Steamed up the river under heavy fire of the batteries and one monitor.

At 11:38 A.M. fired a 5-second shell from the after gun at the turreted monitor.

At 12:15 P.M. came to anchor at Battery Dantzler, with starboard anchor.

The *Richmond*, which had floated free at 11:10, had the bars of her starboard ventilator shot away, along with her smokestack stays. Her stack was riddled. The *Fredricksburg* caught one 200-pound projectile in her fantail. It shot away an anchor and started a small leak.[11]

In the waters below Battery Dantzler, council was called aboard the *Virginia*. Lieutenant Read urged an immediate attack. He suggested that the ironclads and gunboats stand off and throw a volume of fire at the *Onondaga* while the little torpedo boats get in close to sink her. Other officers were divided in their opinions. After some discussion, however, it was decided to attack on Lt. Read's plan at 9:00 P.M.

At nine o'clock the squadron dropped downriver, the *Virginia* and *Scorpion* leading. As they approached the Point of Rocks, a half-mile above Trent's Reach bar, the river's dark suddenly turned to glaring brightness — the Federals had turned on a calcium light. Shot and shell began whistling as the Federals opened fire. The *Virginia's* pilot, directing the squadron from the top of the flagship's casemate, jumped down to the safety of the pilot house. Once there, he declared it impossible to see through the narrow viewing slits, and he refused to return to the exposed spar deck. Mitchell, in despair, gave the order to withdraw.[12] In a few hours, the squadron was anchored under Chapin's Bluff.

The Federal blockading squadron, alarmed by this sudden foray, hurriedly strengthened the obstructions and placed two more monitors on guard.

On February 18, Raphael Semmes, newly appointed to the rank of rear admiral for his exploits in the *Alabama,* received the flag over the James River Squadron. He found his new command in sad condition. All the ships were undermanned, their crews being depleted to supply gunners for batteries Wood, Semmes, and Brooke. Recruits from the army had been brought aboard to fill some of the vacancies and — on half-rations, poorly clad, and with no confidence in the ships — their discipline and morale was generally poor. Semmes instituted a reconstruction program, forming the sailors into infantry platoons to drill ashore, tightening discipline aboard ship, and shifting men and commanders throughout the squadron.

The fall of Charleston and the blockade-running port of Wilmington cured the James River Squadron's short-handedness. The loss of the two great naval stations released over 300 seasoned naval officers and seamen, all of whom reported to Richmond. It also released scores of ships from blockade and assault duty, and groups of monitors and fast gunboats began drifting into the James River area, raising fears — in Confederate higher circles — of a water-borne invasion of Richmond. Semmes, however, assured Mallory and the President's cabinet that an assault by way of the James could not succeed. Confederate obstructions — logs, sunken ships, rafts, spars, and precussion and electrical torpedoes — blocked the river. Batteries of great guns all along the river — guardians of the capital for four long years — were now fully crewed by sailors expert in the use of heavy guns against enemy vessels. The James River Squadron — ironclads, gunboats, and torpedo boats — stood as a second line of defense between the Federals and their goal. But the fears of an invasion attempt were groundless — there was no offensive action for the river batteries and the James River Squadron. Semmes visited Richmond weekly, and was weekly told there were no orders other than to defend the James.[13]

Eight vessels, fully crewed, now comprised the James River Squadron. Their commanders were:

Virginia—Lt. John W. Dunnington
Fredricksburg—Comm. Wm. T. Glassell*
Richmond—Lt. Hamilton H. Dalton**
Hampton—Lt. Joseph D. Wilson
Nansemond—Lt. Walter R. Butt
Roanoke—Lt. Wm. W. Pollock
Torpedo—Lt. Wm. W. Roberts
Beaufort—Lt. Joseph Gardner

On April 2, Grant broke Lee's Petersburg line. The Con-

---

* Commander Glassell, Comm. Thomas R. Rootes, and Lt. F. E. Shepperd are all listed by the naval register as commanding the *Fredricksburg* throughout 1864–1865. Rootes appears to have assumed command in 1864 and alternated with Shepperd until late February, 1865, when Glassell arrived from the fallen Charleston station to assume final command. Shepperd had apparently gone from a brief stay aboard the *Richmond* to the flagship *Virginia*, handed command of that ship to Dunnington and returned to the *Richmond*, where he held the post of command at the time of the attempted attack on the Federal blockading squadron on January 22. He had also filled in briefly as commanding officer aboard the *Hampton*.

** In the closing days of the war Lieutenant Dalton was detached and ordered to Mobile, but he failed to reach that station before Farrand's surrender at Nanna Hubba Bluff.

federates evacuated, retreating toward Amelia Court House. Richmond was no longer tenable. Near four o'clock on that sunny, calm afternoon Admiral Semmes was at dinner in his cabin aboard the *Virginia* when a messenger entered and handed him a dispatch:

Rear Admiral Raphael Semmes,
    Commanding James River Squadron
    Sir:—General Lee advises the Government to withdraw from this city, and the officers will leave this evening, accordingly. I presume that General Lee has advised you of this, and of his movements, and made suggestions as to the disposition to be made of your squadron. He withdraws upon lines toward Danville this night; and unless otherwise directed by General Lee, upon you is devolved the duty of destroying your ships this night, and with all the forces under your command joining General Lee. Confer with him, if practicable, before destroying them. Let your people be rationed, as far as possible, for the march, and armed and equipped for duty in the field.
Very respectfully,
        your obedient servant,
                    S. R. Mallory, Secretary of the Navy[14]

Semmes was somewhat taken aback: during a visit to Lee in Petersburg before assuming command of the James River Squadron, Semmes had heard the general admit that the Confederacy was lost, but the admiral had been given no inkling that Petersburg was about to fall. He quickly called in his commanders, however, informing them of the situation and stressing the need to keep the news secret. After a brief conference, his gunboat captains returned to their boats to begin preparations for scuttling the ships.

The news appeared to have been well kept from lower level officers and city officials, for boats bearing exchanged prisoners were still cruising past the *Virginia,* carrying Federals to a point a few miles below the squadron's anchorage, and bringing back freed Confederates. Semmes watched them from the spar deck of his flagship.

As those boats would pass us, coming up the river, filled to overflowing with our poor fellows just released from Yankee prisons, looking wan and hollow-eyed, the prisoners would break into the most enthusiastic cheering as they passed my flag. It seemed to welcome them home. They little dreamed, that it would be struck that night, forever, and the fleet blown into the air; that their own fetters had been knocked off in vain, and that they were to pass, henceforth, under the rule of the hated Yankees. I was sick at heart as I listened to those cheers, and reflected upon the morrow.

Semmes sent an officer ashore to the Fort Darling (Drewry's Bluff) signal station to communicate with General Lee, but the man soon returned, unable to establish contact. Mallory's orders were clear, however: the ships were to be destroyed, the men formed into a naval foot brigade and marched to Danville to join the falling Army of Northern Virginia.

The work of stripping the vessels started at night-fall. The ironclads began landing their crews, each of which was to be armed, provisioned, and formed as part of the brigade. It was Semmes' intention to take the squadron to Drewry's Bluff, quietly scuttle the ironclads there, send the men aboard the gunboats, and land them at Manchester — opposite Richmond — where the gunboats would be scuttled. A few hours after sunset, however, the city of Richmond went up in flames, making secrecy unnecessary.

It took until nearly three o'clock on the morning of the 3rd to get the men armed and provisioned. They were then loaded aboard the gunboats to await the firing of the iron-clads before casting off for Manchester for the first leg of a

march that would eventually end in surrender at Greens-
boro, North Carolina. Aboard the ironclads, barrels of
powder were opened and spread about the decks. The
woodwork was put to the torch and the destruction parties
escaped to the little gunboats to steam for Manchester.
They had not gone far when the first of the ironclads — the
Virginia — blew up.[15] She threw her shells high into the
air, the explosives trailing tails of fire, the fuses —cut to different lengths — setting them off at different altitudes. The
Richmond and *Fredricksburg* soon exploded, creating spec-
tacles after the example set by their flagship.

Later in the day Federal troops entered Richmond. At
Rocketts they found the partially completed ironclad *Texas*.
She was excellently constructed, probably the best ironclad — except for the *Mississippi* — the Confederates had
ever attempted to put afloat. She was a twin-screw, twin-
engined vessel, 215 feet in length, 48½ feet abeam, and
designed to draw 13 feet of water. A furnace 7 feet in
length with a grate surface area of 96.8 square feet heated
two boilers, each 22 feet in length. An inspecting Union
officer appraised her as "One of the best and most valuable
hulls built by the Rebels."[16]

9

The European Ironclads

On May 17, 1861, Lieutenant James H. North, C.S.N., received orders to proceed to Savannah, Georgia, from which port he was to depart for London, England. Secretary Mallory informed him that:

The Confederate States requires a few ships . . . that can receive without material injury the fire of the heaviest frigates and liners at short distance and whose guns, though few in number, with shell or hot shot, will enable them to destroy the wooden navy of our enemy.

North was to purchase such a ship — an ironclad of the *Glorie* class — from the French Imperial Navy. Should France, for some reason, decline to sell any of their new ironclads, North was to get permission — in either England or France — to contract for ironclads to be constructed for the Confederate Navy. Mallory advised him to "acquaint yourself . . . with all the advances made in building iron-armored ships. The *Warrior,* now being built upon the Thames, must have your attention."[1]

Thus began the great dream — a dream to endure until Dixie's death — of launching from Europe a powerful armored attack to break the strangle-hold of the Union blockade and reopen the Southern coast to an unstifled flow of the war materials needed to keep the armies of the South in the field and the Confederate nation alive. The Confederate Navy could — Mallory hoped — through the efforts of naval officers like North, Commander James D. Bulloch, and European Flag Officer Samuel Barron, Sr., build and equip in the friendly countries of England and France a small squadron of rams carrying six or eight heavy guns and plated with the highest grade of European armor, capable of withstanding the fire of the heavy guns of the Union Navy.

On August 16, in his first dispatch from abroad, North voiced the opinion that he would be unable to either buy or build an ironclad for the South, "as both France and England are anxious to get all the ironclad ships they can."[2] By mid-September he appears to have made some worthwhile contacts, however, as he wrote Mallory, in code: "Can do anything in the way of building if I only had the money."[3]

On January 14, 1862, Mallory asked Comm. Bulloch to attempt to secure "iron or steel clad ships" of eight to ten guns and 2,000 tons burden in England. "The evident changes of feeling and opinion in England in relation to our country," he said, "induces me to believe that we may now contract for the construction and delivery of such a vessel." To circumvent Great Britain's newly announced foreign enlistment act, the Secretary suggested that "The vessel might be contracted for in the name of a Brazilian, Sardinian, or Spanish house and delivered to us at a neutral port, where her armament might be placed on board." He

sent drawings and specifications of an armored ram proposed
by John L. Porter and William P. Williamson, commenting
that:

The model which I have shows very clean, sharp, and beautiful lines of a 2,300-ton ship; but the principal novelty is in the
manner of mounting the guns, which are placed amidships in
an iron casemate, the two after and forward guns in which are so
pivoted as to fire in broadside or fore and aft. Besides these,
two heavy guns are pivoted near the ends. The decks are clean
and all accommodations are below them. The hull is ironed and
is low in the water, and by the device of the single casemate
much iron is dispensed with.[4]

In mid-March, 1862, North — now in London after an
extended Paris visit — wrote Richmond, again lamenting
the lack of cash on hand. He reported offers to build gunboats plated with 2¼ to 2½ inches of armor, and screw
corvettes of 1,800 to 2,000 tons, armored with 4½ inches
of iron on 9 inches of teak backing. "If only I had the
money . . ." he said, "These people here will do nothing
without they know you have money ready to plank down,
and that is what I have tried to impress upon you in all my
letters."[5] On March 25, the necessary funds came through.
Mallory had, on March 20, submitted to Secretary of the
Treasury Christopher G. Memminger an appropriation for
$2,000,000 to build ironclads in Europe. Five days later it
was approved.[6]

On April 10, President Davis submitted to T. R. Bab-
cock of the House of Representatives a proposal sent to
Secretary Mallory by George Saunders. The gentleman
proposed to build, at his expense, six ironclads to act in the
capacity of blockade runner and commerce raider. The
government was to underwrite their cost in return for space
in their bottoms to carry cotton on the government account

out through the blockade. G. A. Trenholm, of Frazer, Trenholm, & Co., quickly punctured the scheme, pointing out the impossibilities of the venture.

The iron covering of such a vessel is, I think, nearly equal to the weight she is capable of carrying in freight. Some ballast must be used to prevent her from being top-heavy, and when to this is added six heavy guns, ammunition, provisions for a large crew, coal for 20 or 30 days, I do not think it would be possible for her to take any freight.

To make war and take prizes she would have to sail under the national flag, either as a national ship or a privateer, and as such she would not be permitted (matters remaining as they are) to enter a foreign port even for coal, far less to take in cargo, and sail out of such port to levy war.[7]

Trenholm's arguments were lost on Congress, however. On April 16, it gave its consent for Saunders' six private ironclads to be built abroad.

In early April Lt. North opened negotiations with James and George Thompson of the Clyde Bank Foundry and Shipyard, Glasgow, for an ironclad of 3,000 tons.[8] Plans and specifications were drawn by May 9, and early modifications immediately increased her beam over the original specifications to keep the shallow draft North had specified. Her coal bunkers were arranged to carry 400 tons of water ballast when her coal was gone "so that the great weight of armor plating aloft might not prove troublesome in sailing."[9] Specifications called for a length of 270 feet, a beam of 50 feet, a 14-foot draft, and power by horizontal direct-acting engines of 500 collective horsepower. She was to have cylinders of 75 inches diameter, a 13-foot piston stroke with one packing ring with steel springs per piston, and double ported slide valves. She would carry one air pump per engine, with one bilge injection cock per pump, and two feed and bilge pumps. Her fire grate surface would come to 350 square feet, with 9,500 square feet of boiler heating surface, and blow-off cocks both under and above water. Her funnel was to be telescoping like those of the Union monitors, and her boilers would be coated with felt and lagged with lead or wood where practicable. Her boiler bottoms were to be double-riveted, and the whole stand well braced "so as to stand a water pressure of 50 pounds per square inch." Her bunkers would carry 1,000 tons of coal, and she would move by way of a single three-blade propeller. Her armament was to be housed in two round monitor-like turrets mounted on deck. The contract was signed on May 21, 1862.[10] It stipulated completion by June 1, 1863, delivered at Glasgow for £182,000. Payment was to be in ten installments, each with a notice from Thompson ten days before due, with a grace period of two months on each payment before termination of contract.[11] Alterations and fittings over and above the original plans included extra plating on the stem, armoring of the forward peak bulkhead, widened gun ports (with waterproof port covers inside, shotproof covers outside), the bottom cemented inside, and an armored lookout shack on deck aft. These extras raised the base price by £13,225.[12]

George Thompson suggested to North that the ironclad's ram bow be moulded in a plowshare shape, projecting 6 feet below the water line and 6 feet beyond the stem to strike an armored adversary under its heavy armor. When questioned on the danger of losing such a projecting bow, Thompson replied that:

Even granting that the prow was carried away, which, from the exceedingly strong construction, I think scarcely possible, the fore part of your ship would still remain perfectly sound, with exception of a few rivet holes, the rivets of which may be torn out; but the strong bulkhead forward would confine any water flowing in by these holes to the fore peak of the vessel.[13]

On July 21, James Bulloch signed a contract with the Lairds' shipyard, Birkenhead, for two ironclads. They, like North's ship, were to be turreted rather than casemated, so that "the sides would be relieved of much strain and the heavy weights be thrown near the center . . ." Of 1,800 tons burden, the rams were to be around 220 feet in length, 42 feet abeam, and, with crew and stores for three months aboard, would draw 15 feet. Ten knots was to be achieved from 350 hp. engines. Armor was to be to a thickness of 4½ inches on 12 inches of teak backing amidships, tapering to 2 inches on a 6-inch backing at the ends, reaching 3½ feet below the waterline. Their ends were divided in watertight compartments, and two parallel bulkheads running fore and aft about 16 feet to each side of the center line and riveted to the athwartships bulkheads formed a boxlike section amidships. The spaces between these bulkheads and the sides were divided into small watertight compartments so that, if the armor was penetrated, only the compartments in the immediate area of the breach would fill, "and it is calculated that filling the whole of them on one side would only list the ship a few inches." Each ship was to mount three fixed turrets armored with 5½ inches of iron on 12-inch teak backing. Turret decks were to be smooth iron for the guns to run on,

the whole shored up by a series of stanchions resting upon the keelsons and frames of the floor. The decks will rise gradually from the sides to the center and be plated with iron five-eighths of an inch thick at the waterways, increasing to three-fourths at the base of the turrets, and there will be an open watercourse all around the upper deck . . . It is known that five-eighths iron plates will break up shells and hollow shot (Admiral Halstead, R.N., on iron-cased ships), and as no verticle fire can be thrown from one ship upon another it is thought that this deck covering will be sufficient.

Bulwarks abreast of the turrets were to drop to allow fire, and Lairds suggested an ingenious method of port coverage: the port shutters were to slide in grooves over the ports. Steam would actuate a rod and piston at the turret base to push the covers up over the port and, to open the port, an exhaust valve bled off the steam to let the cover fall clear by its own weight.

Bulloch proposed bark-rigging, with iron lower masts "supported by three large shrouds on each side." Upper masts were to be of wood, fitted so that in action or in steaming into the wind they could be lowered into the lower masts, "the upper topsail rolling up as the yard is lowered, after the manner known as 'Cunningham's Patent.' " The bowsprit was to be hinged to turn inboard when the ship was to be used to ram. A false bottom, about 2½ feet above the hull, was to serve as an engine and boiler platform, and the space below was to be flooded to keep the ship down when her fuel was consumed. Bulloch had wanted revolving turrets after Captain Cowper Coles' patent, but the admiralty had bought the patent, and had not yet decided whether or not to release it for private use. Cost was set at £93,750 each complete, less battery and magazine fittings.[14] Mallory asked Bulloch to name the pair *North Carolina* and *Mississippi*.[15]

In mid-August Lt. North suddenly discovered that his contract stipulated a three-blade propeller, precluding its being raised to reduce drag while under sail. He called the Thompsons' attention to it, but they seemed little inclined to make the change. On August 30 and September 2, to insure its getting through, North sent identical dispatches asking for funds. His outstanding contracts on behalf of the Navy Department called for $2,000,000 to $2,500,000, and not one-quarter of that was on hand. He reported his ironclad almost half in frame, and work had already begun on her machinery.[16] On September 19, he wrote again for money, complaining that he had no word since May 2, and reporting his ship's frame nearly all up and the bigger pieces of her machinery completed. He was watching Royal Navy gunnery experiments daily, and, with the rapid advancements being made in the field of ordnance, stated that he would wait until the last minute before deciding on a battery. By this time one of Bulloch's ships was half in frame, and the other had her keel laid. Mallory, meanwhile, was laying plans for the three, commanded by Bulloch, North, and Lt. George Terry Sinclair, Sr., to strike New Orleans, lead the liberation of that city, and reopen the Mississippi River.[17]

By late September three installments on North's ram and two each on Bulloch's *North Carolina* and *Mississippi* had been paid, a total of $725,000. All that remained to be paid was $1,375,000, but there was only $695,000 left in the Navy Department's European account in the London office of Fraser, Trenholm, & Co.

Bad weather set in around mid-October and work fell off, though both Lairds and Thompsons erected sheds over the ships to protect the workers and keep construction going. The weather broke in mid-November, however, and Thompson informed North that they expected to have his ship's light interior plating half laid down by the new year.

On October 23, North was promoted to the rank of commander, to rank from May 6, 1862.

Bulloch now began looking for batteries. He wrote the Manchester Ordnance & Rifle Co. and received the following specifications for Whitworth guns:

size	bore	weight	charge	cost
32-pounder	4.4 in.	32 hundredweight	5¼ pounds	£400
70-pounder	5.5 in.	75 hundredweight	12 pounds	£700

Projectiles for the pieces would run at costs of:

	solid	hollow	flat-front (armor-piercing)
32-pounder	£30 per hundred	£35 per hundred	£4 each
70-pounder	£60 per hundred	£65 per hundred	£5 each

Bulloch thought the Whitworth too complicated for work in the cramped turrets, but concluded that he might mount one on deck, under a small shield in the forecastle. North, however, thought the gun ideal, writing Mallory that he proposed to arm his ship with them. "The Whitworth shell thus far," he said, "is the only shell that has penetrated the *Warrior* target; the effect is described by some of the English officers as 'terrific.'" Besides, officers looked on the more popular Armstrong gun as dangerous, and the men were afraid of it.

By late 1862 the ominous rumblings were issuing from British parliament. On December 2, Bulloch wrote Mallory that:

I begin to fear that the Government will interfere with any attempt to get them [the iron-clads] out. The United States ministry is pressing hard to induce the authorities to interfere, and the number of real and pretended agents of the Government over here has unfortunately given great publicity to the proceedings.

The Royal Navy at this time agreed to release Captain Coles' revolving turret design to the public, and Bulloch incorporated it into the plans for his ships. The number of turrets was cut from three per ship to two for better positioning and easier arrangement of the bulkheads below. Armament was to be four 9-inch Armstrong guns (weighing 11 tons each), firing 240-pound projectiles, two per turret, mounted parallel, 5 feet from center to center. A 70-pounder Whitworth was to be mounted at each end, unprotected but for a bulwark.

North's ironclad was to be iron throughout. Her frame was of iron beams rather than timber, her bottom of 15/16 and 11/16 inch iron plate rather than planking. Her armor and teak backing were to be bolted to a shell of ½ inch plating.

By late December half of her backing was down, and North was predicting the laying of her teak toward the end of January. He asked Mallory to suggest a name, and requested that most of her officers — six lieutenants, a paymaster, a surgeon and one or two assistants, a master, an engineer, and eight or ten midshipmen — be sent as soon as possible. He specifically requested James Thurston, at the time serving on the Savannah station aboard the *Atlanta*, to captain her marine contingent, and asked in particular for Midshipman Henry S. Cooke of Virginia, who had seen action on the *Arkansas* and with the James River Squadron, and Palmer Saunders,* then aboard the *Chicora* in Charleston.

United States Minister Charles Francis Adams had, by this time, constructed in Great Britain a well-knit, far-reaching, and effective espionage system to stifle, as well as possible, the flow of arms and munitions going to the Confederacy, and divert and delay the ships of war being built for the South. Said Bulloch on November 26, 1863:

The extent to which the system of bribery and of spying has and continues to be practiced by agents of the United States in

---

* Ordered to the C.S. Naval Academy (aboard the *Patrick Henry*) in 1864, Saunders, as a reward for excellent grades, was allowed to take part in a boat attack in conjunction with Pickett's campaign against New Bern, N.C. He was killed in the capture of the U.S.S. *Underwriter*, February 2, 1864.

Europe is scarcely credible. The servants of gentlemen supposed to have Southern sympathies are tampered with, confidential clerks and even messengers from telegraphic offices are bribed to betray their trust, and I have lately been informed that the English and French post offices, hitherto considered immaculate, are now scarcely safe methods of communication.[18]

With spies increasingly active at the yards of both Lairds and Thompsons, and parliament — presented with increasing stacks of evidence on the intended destination of all three ships — talking more and more of detaining the ironclads, both North and Bulloch kept construction going on all three ships on the hope that, somehow, they could still be gotten to sea. North ordered from the Manchester Ordnance & Rifle Co. four 70-pounder Whitworths with slide carriages, 240 flat-front steel shells for armor piercing, 400 common shells, 1,000 friction tubes, 750 lubricating wads, and 150 sabots. His downpayment of £710, 18s, one-third the purchase price, completely exhausted Confederate naval funds on hand in Europe.

North's hopes for the beginning of teak-laying by the last of January declined as that month passed with little progress on the ship. On February 12, George Thompson assured the lieutenant that the under-plating would be finished by the 23rd of that month, but it was March 3 before that portion of construction was finally finished. Thompson informed him of it on that day and took the opportunity to ask for payment of the next installment.[19]

North asked Bulloch about a fighting turret for the ship commander. Bulloch advised a sentry box affair of 5½-inch iron, to be placed on deck directly over the wheel to be used in combat. North passed the idea on to Thompson.[20]

With chances of getting the three ships out of Great Britain in Confederate hands growing slimmer, North began looking to recoup the money already sunk into the ship. In a Paris conference with Flag Officer Barron, ministers Mason and Slidell, and General McRae, he decided to contact James Galbraith of Scotland to discuss the sale of the ship to another country, either as a blind to get her out of England and return her to the Confederates, or as a legitimate sale to save the money already invested.[21] Mallory, in a communiqué to Slidell on the subject, proposed that the ships be sent to Louis Arman of Bordeaux, France, to be finished, loaded with supplies for the French army in Mexico, cleared for Vera Cruz, then sold back to the Confederacy at Terceira "or elsewhere." Said the Secretary: "Our early possession of these ships in a condition for service is an object of such paramount importance to our country that no effort, no sacrifice, must be spared to accomplish it."[22]

Despite Emperor Napoleon III's 1861 proclamation forbidding any French citizen to take part in or aid in any manner the building, arming, or equipping of a vessel of war for either the United States or the Confederacy, John Slidell, in 1862, began receiving intimations that French shipbuilders might be allowed to build, without interference, ships for the Confederate Government. He reported to the Secretary of State that he'd gotten from a source close to the Emperor the promise that such warships might be built and "the vessels when completed would be permitted to leave the French ports upon any plausible plea the builders might state."[23] With the two Laird rams and North's ironclad under construction, Bulloch found the Navy Department too far over its head in contracts in England to open new ones in France, but Slidell persisted, begging Bulloch to come to Paris and open negotiations with French shipyards rather than "depending upon the wavering policy of the British Ministry . . ." Mallory, at the moment, was urging the construction of more commerce raiders like the rampaging

Florida and *Alabama* and, with the United States down about John Bull's ears concerning the commerce being lost to the two English-built cruisers, it appeared that getting several more of the raiders constructed in and to sea from England was going to be exceedingly difficult. French shipyard agents began visiting the commander in London and, in March, with a portion of an up-coming, multi-million dollar European loan promised for his purposes, Bulloch went to Paris to treat with Louis Arman. The ship builder assured Bulloch that he had the ear of the Minister of State — M. Rouher — and even of Napoleon himself, and had been assured by Rouher that Napoleon would allow him to build, arm, and equip warships for the Confederacy and deliver them at sea under a French flag.[24] With these assurances in hand, Bulloch, on March 30, wrote Mallory that he was on the verge of contracting for four 12-gun corvettes — he had no more money for ironclads — in France, and planned to return to Paris the next day "to complete specifications and set the work in progress."

As to the Laird ironclads, Bulloch told the Secretary that they were "nearly ready. Still doubtful if they can be got out, but officers should be sent without delay."[25] Mallory already had officers on the way; they had left for Nassau around the 13th.[26]

By April 3, North's ironclad's teak-backing was half down, her gun and berth decks nearly laid.[27] With pressure from Great Britain on the Thompsons growing as the result of the *Alabama's* successful cruise, North questioned Slidell about transferring her to a French or other Continental house. Slidell suggested that, if she wasn't far enough advanced to be launched in six or eight weeks, it would be better to transfer several other vessels to discern the true situation in France and, if they were completed and let go, then transfer the ironclad.[28] In a May 6 dispatch to Mallory, Comm. North stated that:

The minister of foreign affairs is a strong Northern sympathizer, and the Yankee minister is said to have a wonderful influence over him. For the first time I begin to fear that our vessels stand in much danger of being seized by this Government.

He had added an 8-inch shell gun to the four Whitworths for his ram, then added two 150-pounder Armstrongs to that, borrowing money from friends to pay for them. He was fascinated by the Armstrong 300-pounder, stating that "it could destroy anything the enemy have at present." The ironclad's teak-backing, he said, was almost all laid.[29]

On May 6 Mallory wrote Bulloch, informing him of the £2,000,000 South European Act for the construction of wood and iron naval vessels in Europe, and appointing Bulloch superintendent over all construction there. He stressed again that the ironclads must be heavy enough to stand up to 15-inch guns, light enough to navigate the Mississippi River, and seaworthy enough to stand the ocean voyage.

In your contracts you will provide for the delivery of the vessels to us at a place or places to be designated by you, and you will regard the amount appropriated, £2,000,000, as the only fund for building, equipping, manning, providing, and furnishing the vessels for one year's service.[30]

On May 14, Commander G. Terry Sinclair (he had been promoted the day before) told North that it had been decided to send Bulloch's ships to France for completion, and that Lts. R. R. Carter and William C. Whittle, Jr., had arrived to serve aboard them.

On June 6, North wrote the Manchester works, calling their attention to the fact that the guns, mounted as planned, could not be sufficiently elevated, and that they had neglected to include compressor screws to regulate recoil — of the most importance in the confines of a turret. He asked that these faults be corrected, and that the guns be pivoted by radial bars rather than with original flap-type pivot.[31] The noose of English law was drawing tighter about the ship, however, and, on June 13, L. Q. C. Lamar, Mason, and Slidell wrote North that:

The seizure of the *Alexandra*, the information lodged against the *Phantom* and *Southerner*, the effort to stop the *Lord Clyde*, and the organized system of espionage everywhere contenanced and encouraged in England disclose a determination on the part of the British Government to construe and enforce its 'foreign enlistment act' in a manner not only injurious to the interests of the Confederate States, but so as to prohibit any further operations in their behalf within her Majesty's dominions.

They suggested that North sell the ship immediately to save the money invested. The commander, however, retained the hope of getting his command to sea, and, after unsuccessfully atempting to sell the vessel to Russia, pushed on with construction, voicing his hopes that some sort of an understanding could be reached with the British Government.[32]

Bulloch, deep in a massive construction program in both England and France, decided to forego the command of one of his ironclads, and informed Mallory of such by dispatch. Said Bulloch:

No officer would be justified in placing his personal preferences in opposition to the wishes of his departmental chief, and I accept the sphere of duty you have thought proper to assign me with the full determination to give my best energies to the work.

Mallory, anxious to keep Bulloch at the work at which he had proved so capable, expressed his satisfaction and directed the Commander to remain in Europe "to attend to other contracts."[33]

Louis Arman, meanwhile, had introduced Bulloch and Slidell to Bravay & Co. of Paris who would, it was hoped, be able to purchase Bulloch's ironclads "for a nominal sum," have them finished to Bulloch's specifications, and, once clear of England, resell them to the Confederacy. With spies numerous, and bribes in high places opening the most confidential files and correspondence, Bulloch found himself compelled to disassociate himself completely with the ships, leaving all further details of construction to an overseer from Bravay's. He also found it necessary, as the constructors would be called as principal witnesses in any government hearing, to "prevent them [Lairds] from suspecting that there was any collusion between the nominal purchasers and myself." So he wrote Lairds, stating that government interference seemed likely to keep them from completing the ironclads for him and, as he was unwilling to run the risk of seizure, they were to sell the ships and release him from the contract. Bravays were on hand to buy, ostensibly for the Pasha of Egypt.[34]

Bulloch's fears of hounding by spies and the use of bought secrets by the government proved justified. On October 20, Lairds, under intense pressure from the government, asked M. A. Bravay to make an open declaration of ownership of the ironclads. Bravay compiled and was soon called on by Captain Hoare, RN, who questioned him closely about the ships, the purchase, and their intended sale. Hoare concluded with an offer on behalf of the Royal

Navy to purchase the ironclads, which Bravay declined. Evidently unconvinced by Bravay's answers, the government first directed Lairds to refrain from making trial runs on either ship without notification and consent of customs officials, and finally, not to move either ship at all without a marine guard aboard. The ships were seized in mid-October, taken by customs officers, and placed under guard of a gunboat and the H.M.S. *Majestic*. Contingents of marines from the frigate were placed aboard.[35] The British Government declared that Emperor Napoleon III would have to make claim on the ships for French citizens to move them from a British port, and the Emperor told both Bravay and Slidell that he couldn't do it. Said Bulloch:

> There was a good deal said about the personal sympathy of the Emperor for the South and his earnest desire that by some means or other we might get our ships out, but he could not help us, so the sympathy and the hope were but sheer mockery, when we had been bouyed up with the expectation of something more.[36]

Slidell, Barron, and Mason all confided to Bulloch that they could see no possible hope of getting the ironclads out. Accordingly, Bulloch, on Febraury 7, 1864, sent Bravay a contract cancelling all former engagements between them, and giving them the right to dispose of the vessels in any way they could with the stipulation that:

> No offer for their purchase will be accepted unless made in writing, either by a regularly commissioned officer or one of the European Governments, or the ambassador of that Government, this precaution being deemed necessary to prevent the possibility of a purchase by agents of the United States.

Bravay & Co. signed on February 10 and the rams were, eventually, sold to the Royal Navy.[37]

On June 30, 1863, Bulloch received by way of Lt. George Shryrock Secretary Mallory's May 6 dispatch informing him of the South European Act.[38] Louis Arman had, on Bulloch's visit to contract for the corvettes, shown the commander drawings he had made up of ironclads suitable "for service on the Southern coast." Bulloch had suggested corrections to decrease the draft and Arman had promised to incorporate them if Bulloch ever wished the ships built.[39] Bulloch returned to Paris in early June to confer with Arman on the subject of the ironclads and, on July 28, 1863, informed Mallory that he had contracted in France for two ironclads, at a price of $400,000 each, "well suited in size and draft of water for service in our shoal rivers and harbors.[40] They were to be 171 feet 10 inches in length, 32 feet 8 inches abeam, and were to draw (with 220 tons of coal, battery, and all stores aboard) 14 feet 4 inches. They were to be propelled by four engines of 300 collective horsepower turning twin screws, and their after-hulls were to be divided into twin sternposts for quicker turning and better stability. Armor, backed by teak, was to be 4¾ inches amidships tapering to 3½ inches at the ends, in single plates for more resisting power. Their armament was to be a 300-pounder Armstrong gun housed in the bow turret, and a pair of French 6-inch naval guns mounted in the turret aft on deck. All fittings were to be of top quality, conforming in demensions and material to French Imperial Navy specifications, and they were to have a guaranteed speed of 12 knots in smooth seas.[41] The commander told Mallory that if North sold his ship, he'd have enough money to contract for two more.[42]

Mallory had suggested, several times, buying surplus ironclads from the French Navy: North had been sent over specifically for this purpose. But after receiving this suggestion again on May 26, 1863 in a coded dispatch from Mallory, Bulloch closed the case for secondhand ironclads by writing the Secretary that:

The transaction would necessarily be managed through intermediaries, who, from the very nature of the negotiations, would be forced to sacrifice principle by prevaricating, and then all sorts of objectionable means would have to be used, even bribery, and after we would only get cast-off vessels.[43]

On July 29, M. Voruz of Nantes submitted to the Minister of Marine a request for permission to cast at his gun foundries forty-eight 30-pounder rifles for the four corvettes being constructed by Louis Arman. The guns were to be built on the Blakely pattern — cast iron banded in steel — and he was to provide 200 cylindro-conical shot per gun. The Minister, on August 1, granted his permission.

North's ironclad, by this time, had 25 of her cumbersome iron plates fitted. By September 25 Thompsons reported the ship to be one-third armored, and North had resigned himself to seeing her completed no earlier than December.[44]

By November 16 Arman's ironclads' deck beams were across and the first layers of teak were going down. Bulloch considered them three-fifths finished and predicted their completion by contract time unless delays arose in armoring. The plating was being rolled by Messrs. Petin, Godet & Co. at Rive de Gier, and the plates had to be sent by a circuitous route.

The 300-pounder weighed 12 tons. There were to be no side ports — just the single port directly forward — as the twin sternposts would allow pivoting and pointing of the entire ship as quickly as the gun could be moved by training tackles in the turret. Bullock theorized that the turret would be stronger for having only one port cut into it, and that there would be less opportunity for entry by an enemy shell. The French 6-inch guns had been discarded in favor of

70-pounder Armstrongs which could be trained aft or pivoted to fire to broadside and forward as far as within 25° of the line of the keel.[45]

By late November Bulloch was beginning to feel apprehensive about the French-built ships. The corvettes seemed safe, but the Federal spy network had shifted from England to France, and the ironclads had for some time been drawing the Federal's undivided attention. Northern newspapers had all the details, were reporting the rams' probably destination, and were confidently announcing that U.S. Minister William L. Dayton had received assurances from French Minister of Marine Chasseloup Laubat that the ironclads would not be allowed to sail.[46]

One of the Federal spies about which Bullock was so apprehensive was Commander C.R.P. Rodgers, U.S.N. In civilian dress he had strolled Arman's shipyard, inspecting both the *Sphinx*, just launched, and her sister ship, unnamed and still on the stocks. He reported to his superiors that:

The ram of the *Sphinx* is of great length—about 35 feet—and is a prolongation of her keel. It is hollow, heavily plated, and its end consists of a ponderous forging of excellent workmanship. It is intended to pierce the side of an armored adversary beneath his plating. Its hollowness will give it bouyancy, and it rises with a gradual curve, until it is lost in the forward turret which forms the bow of the ship, above water, a movable bowspirit being rigged out from the turret's top.

Despite Bulloch's theories on single ports and greater turret strength, and double sternposts and quicker turning, Rodgers reported that the forward turret had been cut with three ports, one ahead and the other two on either side.

The after turret is about 30 feet from the stern, and is much like the forward one, but has two ports on each side, and a door both forward and aft.

The *Sphinx* has two screws and, as it were, two stems, for abaft the mainmast are two keels and two separate sternposts, with a wide space between. There is a rudder on each sternpost, but I could not learn the arrangement for steering. The double screw will give great facility in turning, and the double stern will increase the stability. This double stern is not perceptible above the water, and would not be suspected.

Rodgers estimated that the armor of these ships would be unable to effectively withstand the fire of the Union 15-inch guns, but erred in voicing his suspicions — built on the size of the gun port pivot plates — that they were not to carry heavy armament.[47]

In mid-February Emperor Napoleon proved the Northern newspapers correct, announcing to Arman, through his ministers of marine and foreign affairs, that the ironclads could not be permitted to sail for the Confederacy and that the corvettes must not be armed in France. Arman proposed the sale of the vessels to a Danish banker "as if for his own Government, and that there should be a private agreement providing for a redelivery to us at some point beyond the jurisdiction of France." But, in the light of his experiences with the Birkenhead runs, Bulloch told Mallory that:

This would simply be substituting France for England, Denmark for France, and the Danish banker for Messrs. Bravay, and if the two most powerful maritime nations in the world have not been able to resist the importunities of the United States, it would be simply absurd to hope for success through the medium of Denmark, a weak nation at best, and just now struggling almost hopelessly for her very existence.[48]

Arman then proposed to sell both ships to Sweden, one ship then to be sold to Denmark to throw the Federals off the track, and the other, if possible, to be returned by Sweden to Bulloch and the Confederates. With Sweden as yet to draw any activity from the South or any notice from the North, and with the first ram legitimately sold as a decoy, the commander agreed to try it.[49] Arman then requested and was granted an audience with Napoleon III and, when he divulged his plan, was threatened with immediate imprisonment and ordered to sell both ships at once in an open and legitimate deal. One ram — the *Sphinx* — went to Denmark and two corvettes were sold to Peru, while the other ram and the remaining corvettes went to Prussia.

North's ironclad, by this time, was gone. With little hope of getting her out of Great Britain, Mallory, on February 24, 1864, reluctantly consented to her sale. She was bought by Denmark.

Arman, conscientious and faithful to his business associates, informed Bulloch that he still hoped to recover for the South the Denmark-bought ram, and suggested that the Confederate Navy keep in as close touch with the ship as possible. Afraid his continued presence at Bordeaux would excite further suspicion and put the ironclad completely beyond their reach for all time, Bulloch sent his aide, Captain Eugene Tessier, C.S.A., to keep watch on the vessel. Tessier soon reported the Danish representative, in the interests of hurrying completion, making alterations — principally in the securing of the armor — of which Tessier didn't approve. There was nothing to be done, however: completion of the vessel was now completely in the hands of the Danish Navy.

The Danish naval officer's efforts to hurry the ironclad's completion were in vain — by the time she was finished the Danish-Prussian war was over. With the Danish Minister of Marine quite outspoken about his disinclination to accept the ship with no more need of it, Arman promised almost positively to deliver the ship back to Bulloch. On December 16, Bulloch entered into a lengthy and detailed agreement with Arman's agent, Henri A. de Riviere, "an irresponsible soldier of fortune," which read, in part:

The *Sphinx* has been sold under certain conditions to the Government of Denmark, and while en route to Denmark she was taken into a Swedish port, was nominally sold to a Swedish gentleman, Mr. N———, and then proceeded, under the Swedish flag to Copenhagen, where she now lies in charge of Mr. Puggard, a banker of that city. The Government of Denmark being no longer pressed by the demands of war, does not seem anxious to confirm the bargain of sale, and some defect or failure in the conditions on the part of the seller presents a favorable opportunity for annulling it in a manner which it is thought will not excite suspicion . . . Under the above circumstances Mr. de Riviere proposes to manage the further negotiations with the Danish Government in such a way as to cause its agents to reject the *Sphinx*, under the plea that her performances do not come up to the stipulations of the contract, and he then proposes to close the transaction in the ordinary business way, and to bring the *Sphinx* from Copenhagen as if to return her to Mr. Arman, which orders, with the view of allaying all suspicion, are to be made known to the Danish minister of marine, and to the French minister or consul at Copenhagen . . .

For the above-mentioned services, truly and faithfully rendered, Mr. de Riviere will receive from J. D. Bulloch the sum of 375,000 francs, which sum it is understood shall include all commissions and all contingent expenses incurred by Mr. de Riviere, and which sum shall be paid . . . as soon as he returns from the rendezvous with a letter from the Confederate States officer appointed to command the *Sphinx* stating that he is in possession of her.

An additional 80,000 francs would be necessary for banker Rudolph Puggard, as the commission he was to have received for selling the *Sphinx* to the Danish Navy.[50]

M. de Riviere had already, at the time of the signing of the above agreement, managed to give sufficient cause to the Danes for rejecting the ship. During her trial run he had secretly opened a bilge cock, causing her to partially flood, lose speed, and react sluggishly to her helm.[51] Bulloch later disclaimed all knowledge of this, declaring it an unethical and ungentlemanly trick, worthy of the scoundrel Yankees. It was a successful ruse, however, Denmark positively refusing to take delivery.

Bulloch devised a simple system of coded telegraphic communication with de Riviere, with set questions and answers.

Riviere to Bulloch

Bulloch
A. Mabbs, 17 Saville Row, London, W.

Translation	Code
We are ready to sail.	What are Schleswig shares?
I am off for Niewe Diep today.	Thank you for the shares.
Will leave for Niewe Diep tomorrow morning.	I have filled your order for coffee in Amsterdam.
Detained at Niewe Diep. Wait for instructions.	No coffee on the market.
Difficulty is removed. I sail tomorrow.	Coffee is bought.

Bulloch to Riviere

A. de Riviere
Rudolph Puggard, Copenhagen
Goll & Co., Amsterdam

My preparations are progressing favorably.	Do you want any Schleswig shares?
Go to Niewe Diep.	I have bought 1,000 shares.
I can not be ready for —— days.	Buy if no change in the market for —— days.
Will be ready in —— days.	Buy for delivery in —— days.[52]

A bitter winter crossing appeared in the offing for the first cruise of an iron-clad across the ocean. Said Bulloch:

If there had been no interference with the work, and no prohibition of their delivery to the Confederate States, both rams would have been in our possession, outside of the river Gironde, in the early part of June, 1864, and we would have had mild summer weather to drop them safely over to their working ground, with the Azores, Nassau and Havana for coaling stations.[53]

Tessier was sent to Copenhagen, arriving a few days after the ram. He got aboard for an inspection before she was repainted and put in trim for delivery, and reported to Bulloch that the ship, after her winter cruise north, "exhibited no signs of strain." He said:

The sheer of the ship was true, and the putty or cement filling between the edges of the plates was not even cracked. On deck I tried the butts of the deck-planks, the water-way seams, the butts and scarfs of the water-ways, covering boards and rails, and found them in perfect order. The *Sphinx* certainly did then show no signs of weakness.

Tessier managed to obtain a copy of the French captain's official report of the Bordeaux-to-Copenhagen voyage, but it was little more than an amplification of the log, giving her speed and comments on her performance. From Bordeaux to Cherborg she had averaged 10½ knots, and from Cherborg to Beachy Head, in moderate weather with a head wind, 10 knots. The report concluded with statements that her screws worked satisfactorily, and that she steered and behaved well in heavy weather, "especially during heavy squalls on the 5th and 6th of November, when sailing vessels were scudding under very short canvas."[54]

Chosen to command the new ironclad was Captain Thomas Jefferson Page, "an old and experienced officer," said Bulloch, "bred in the United States Navy . . . ." Commanding batteries at Glochester Point on the York River and Chaffins Bluff on the James until mid-1863, Page had been sent to replace Bulloch as commander of one of the Birkenhead rams.

In orders to Page dated December 17, 1864, Flag Officer Barron suggested that a likely job for the ironclad would be the raising of the blockade of Wilmington, as this had been particularly stressed by Mallory in instructions to the flag officer. He informed Page that the U.S.S. *Minnesota* occasionally cruised off Wilmington, but that the blockade was generally maintained by a fleet of light, fast cruisers "not specially calculated for war purposes." Perhaps remembering the Charleston incident, Barron admonished the Captain that:

The dispersion of the blockading fleet and the raising of the blockade must both be so unquestionable and clear that human ingenuity will find difficulty in inventing a valid denial of the fact, as upon the flimsiest foundation the enemy will dispute it.

He offered a few optional targets. "The interception of the California steamers offer a tempting service . . . A dash at the New England ports and commerce might be made very destructive, and would be a heavy blow in the right place." And, "a few days' cruising on the banks may inflict severe injury on the fisheries of the United States." In commerce raiding, he warned against bonding vessels unless as a last resort, and cautioned against destroying United States commerce being carried in foreign-registered bottoms.

During this war Federal owners of ships and cargoes have adopted the practice of placing them under British protection, which may at times cause you embarrassment; but you will be careful to observe the strictest regard for the rights of neutrals, and not to lose any opportunity in cultivating friendly relations with their naval and merchant services and of placing the character of the struggle in which we are engaged in its proper light.

He gave Page authority to make acting appointments at sea to fill vacancies in his staff of officers.[55]

Page was sent off to Copenhagen along with Tessier "to pick up such personal acquaintances with the ship as possible, to supervise the local expenditure, and to take passage in her for the rendezvous." Bulloch sent Lt. R. R. Carter to Niewe Diep to arrange for coaling there. He would join her when she touched at that port, taking the post of executive officer.[56]

With no funds available for the purchase of a tender, Bulloch contacted W. G. Crenshaw, late of Lee's army and sent by the Confederate Government to organize the British side of the government blockade-running effort, to borrow a ship to coal and supply the ironclad. Crenshaw offered the *City of Richmond* under Hunter Davidson, loaded with commissary stores and railway supplies and set to run into Wilmington on the January moon.[57] Officers for the ram — to be renamed, at Bulloch's request, the *Stonewall* — were being selected from among those of the late cruiser *Florida*. They were now stationed aboard the *Rappahannock* at Calais.[58] The *Stonewall's* officers were:

Captain, T. J. Page; Lts., R. R. Carter, Geo. S. Shryock, Geo. A. Borchert, E. G. Read, Samuel Barron, Jr.; Surgeon, B. W. Green; Assist surgeon, J. W. Herty; Paymaster, R. W. Curtis; Chief engineer, W. P. Brooks; Assist engineers, W. H. Jackson, J. C. Closh; Master, W. W. Wilkinson; Boatswain, J. M. Dukehart; Gunner, J. B. King; Sgt. of Marines, J. M. Prior.

On January 4, Bulloch telegraphed his Copenhagen contact: "Sail as soon as you can." The reply on the 5th stated that the ram would leave the next day, and telegrams throughout the next few days informed him of her progress.
January 7: "Ship is off."
January 8: "Ship has been gone one day, and I have heard of no interruption."
Later in the day: "Ship stopped; heavy gale and snowstorm at Elsinore."[59]
A silence of several days ensued, while the *Stonewall* waited out the storm.

On the night of January 9 Bulloch sent Lt. Samuel Barron, Jr. to Calais to take charge of all the *Florida's* officers and crew assigned to the *Stonewall* and bring them over to England. Lt. Borchert was to take charge of the contingent of the *Rappahannock's* crew so assigned, and bring them across at the same time, while Lts. George Shryock and Edmund Gaines Read were to report to Bulloch in person.

Bulloch wrote Davidson aboard the *City of Richmond* that:

. . . the U.S.S. *Niagara* is at Dover, waiting, I fear, to intercept your ship. I offer no suggestion on this point, because you will know how to give her the slip when you get to sea far better than I can point out the method to you from land.[60]

Lts. Shryock and Read arrived at Bulloch's at 6:30 A.M., January 11, and the three talked for an hour, Shryock receiving verbal instructions and dispatches. Bulloch directed him to place himself in charge of the *Stonewall's* crew aboard the *City of Richmond*, and:

When you reach the appointed rendezvous and meet the *Stonewall,* you will report with your command to Captain T. J.

Page, and take all further instructions from him . . . I wish you to instruct the paymaster to make out a correct list of the entire command, officers and men, and send it to me by the pilot, or by Mr. Early, under cover of M. P. Robertson, Esq., Rumford Court, Liverpool . . .[61]

The officers and men from the *Rappahannock* had arrived at Gravesend that morning and were shepherded aboard the *City of Richmond* by Lt. W. F. Carter. Davidson put to sea that afternoon, without sighting the *Niagara*, "but was forced to seek shelter under Cherbourg breakwater from a heavy gale . . ." He remained there, riding out the storm, until the 18th, arriving at the rendezvous at Quiberon

. . . where we found a snug anchorage on the 20th, and laid quietly, permitting no communication with the shore until the morning of the 24th at 10 o'clock, when the *Stonewall* hove in sight, to the rapturous delight of all who were in the secret . . .[62]

Of the *Stonewall*, Davidson said: "She was in a horribly filthy condition, and required more labor to clean her than to receive and get things in order afterwards." The weather was wet and the seas heavy, making coaling operations difficult.

Early on the morning of January 28, the *Stonewall* and *City of Richmond* upped anchor, making for San Miguel. On the 29th, Davidson recalled,

. . . Old Neptune thought it proper to pay his respects to the first ironclad expedition across his waters, and so he commenced. It blew a storm at times, with as heavy a seas as I have ever seen in any part of the world. The *Stonewall*, which we kept close to night and day, would often ship immense seas, they seeming at times to cover her from knighthead to taffrail;

but yet she never seemed to be injuriously affected by them, and would keep her heading very steady.

At about noon of the 30th, with the weather clearing, the following exchange of signals took place.
Richmond: "How do you do?"
Stonewall: "All right."
Richmond: "Shall I go on?"
Stonewall: "Am very short of coal, and must make port — Ferrol."
Richmond: "Shall I follow?"
Stonewall: "Suit your convenience about following."

With that the *City of Richmond* set her course for Bermuda, keeping the *Stonewall* in sight until well into the afternoon.[63] That night the storm came up again. The pounding of the seas had shaken the *Stonewall* considerably, and numerous small leaks had sprung up, both where caulking had been knocked loose, and where there was none and should have been. A large leak had been started, but could not be immediately located. Her speed now was 8½ knots, dropping to 5 or 4 when running against a moderate head sea — well below the 10½ knots recorded on her trip to Copenhagen. At that time, however, the engines had been under the supervision of an engineer from Messrs. Mazelin, where they had been built. It was hoped that, when the Confederate engineers became familiar with them, her speed would increase back toward its guaranteed 12 knots.[64]

She ported at Ferrol, where full port facilities were granted, and Page was invited to remain as long as he liked. A dry hulk was put at his disposal, into which were unloaded the ironclad's stores and provisions, for the purpose of finding the large leak. The United States Minister to Spain, H. J. Perry, was immediately at work, however, telling Spanish authorities that the ironclad was stolen and a pirate. She had not been legitimately sold, he said, and France had several warships after her.[65] His actions were most effective, as evidenced by Page's communication to Bulloch of February 7:

> To-day there came off an officer to inform us that in consequence of the protest of the American Minister the permission to repair damaged had been suspended, and I must restore the things in the hulk to the ship.

The main leak, however, caused by the defective construction of a rudder casing, had been found and was being plugged, and the insides of the turrets were being caulked.[66] In addition to the leaks and a lack of adequate living space, Page found the port shutters hard to handle and, in his opinion, of insufficient strength, and noted that no combings had been provided around the hatches and magazine scuttles to keep the water out.[67] With repairs and alterations promising to take several weeks, Page wandered off to Paris for a conference — the necessity of which is questionable — with Bulloch and Barron. He spent six weeks.[68]

Bulloch, meanwhile, had diverted the blockade runner *Louisa Ann Fanny* to take Chief Engineer Pearson, late of the cruiser *Georgia*, to the *Stonewall*. He opened a credit account for the *Stonewall* in Page's name with Messrs. Perez & Co. of Ferrol and, at the captain's request, opened another for $5,000 with Frederick Huth & Co., London.[96] Bermuda was set as the ironclad's final supply base. Major Walker, C.S.A., would make arrangements for final coaling outside the harbor, an additional 14 of the old *Florida's* crewmen and a final load of ordnance stores would be taken aboard, and the *Stonewall* would strike Port Royal, Sherman's supply base.[70]

During the first week in February the steam sloops *Niagara* and *Sacramento* made port at Coruna, nine miles distant from Ferrol, to keep track of the *Stonewall*. The *Niagara*, one of the fastest ships in the U.S. Navy, mounted ten 150-pounder Parrott rifles. The *Sacramento*, somewhat slower, carried two 11-inch guns, two 9-inch shell guns, and a 60-pounder rifle.

The Federals soon moved across the bay to Ferrol, anchoring near the *Stonewall*. The ironclad raised steam and a barge put out from the navy yard. As it pulled alongside, a Spanish naval officer asked Lt. Carter, in command during Page's absence, if he intended to attack the Northerners. Carter replied that he had no intention of attacking, but intended to defend himself against a repetition of the Bahia affair, in which the C.S.S. *Florida* had been attacked and captured by the U.S.S. *Wachusett* in the neutral Brazilian port. "This is not Brazil," said the Spaniard. "The Admiral requests that you will let your fires go out, and warns against any attempt to break the peace." Carter ignored them, keeping the steam up and the chain unshackled, "so as to get the ram pointed fair, in case the *Niagara* moved our way."[71]

On March 21, the *Stonewall*, all repairs completed, stood out to engage. The *Niagara* and *Sacramento* kept to their anchorages, eyeing the Rebel warily. The ironclad stood off and on before Ferrol harbor for some time, but the seas were rough and the Yankees apparently weren't going to fight, so she returned inside. On the 23rd Page took the *Stonewall* back out to again attempt to provoke a fight. Again they remained at their anchorages — probably to the relief of Page, for the sea was still rough — and again the *Stonewall* returned inside without a battle. The next day the ironclad ventured out in company of the Spanish steam frigate *Conception*, come along to guard against any breach of Spanish neutrality. The *Stonewall*, with upper yards sent down and cleared for action, steamed all day outside the bay, but was still unable to provoke a fight. Commander Thomas T. Craven of the *Niagara*, in a letter to Minister Perry at Madrid, said:

With feelings that no one can appreciate, I was obliged to undergo the deep humiliation of knowing that she was there, steaming back and forth, flaunting her flags, and waiting for me to go out to the attack. I dared not do it. The condition of the sea was such that it would have been perfect madness for me to go out. We could not possibly have inflicted the slightest injury upon her, and should have exposed ourselves to almost instant destruction—a one-sided combat which I do not consider myself called upon to engage in.

As the ironclad had left her boats behind, Craven assumed that she would return to Ferrol. Page had fully intended to do so, but was barred from returning by Spanish authorities. . . . Mr. Perry had the pressure on. Craven reported to Welles that ". . . on Saturday (the 24th) morning she was reported as being still outside and lying under a point of land to the northward of Ferrol. In the afternoon, however, I learned that she was last seen early in the morning steaming rapidly westward . . ." The Federals hurriedly paid their coal bills and followed, their progress being "considerably retarded by the inability of the *Sacramento* to keep up . . ."

On March 27, the *Niagara* and *Sacramento* made port at Lisbon, Portugal. The *Stonewall* had arrived 31 hours before. A Portuguese officer boarded the *Niagara* and stated that the *Stonewall* had just finished coaling and had orders to depart immediately. The Federals, he said, were to remain at anchor for 24 hours after the ironclad had sailed.

The *Stonewall* did not depart immediately, however. It

was after 6:00 P.M., the tide was going out, and the ironclad's pilot informed Page that it was too late to get out of
the harbor until the next tide.[72] It was 11 A.M., March 28,
1865, before the *Stonewall* steamed out of Lisbon. Across
the Atlantic, President Lincoln was meeting with Generals
Grant and Sherman at City Point, Va., to discuss the peace
terms they would offer the dying South.

Easily outdistancing the *Niagara* and *Sacramento* at sea,
Page made port at Santa Cruz, on the island of Teneriffe,
coaled, and stood down for a rapid cruise in the northeast
trades.[73] On April 25, he hauled up for Bermuda to recoal
and prepare to strike Port Royal, but as he "encountered
north-west winds and heavy swell immediately after leaving
the trade winds," he reset his course for Nassau. He touched
there on May 6, and proceeded to Havana.

On May 17, Captain C. S. Boggs of the U.S.S. *Connecticut* in Havana wrote Page:

Dear Sir:
   Relying upon our former acquaintance, I beg leave to offer
to your notice the following considerations:
   In view of the great and decided change that has taken place
in the position of your Government—that all the armed forces in
opposition to the Government of the United States east of the
Mississippi formerly held by the Confederates are now in the
possession of the U.S. Government; that the President of the
Confederate Government and his Cabinet are now fugitives, the
Confederate Government virtually at an end—I need not suggest to you what would be your position should you, as commander of the *Stonewall*, undertake any further hostilities
against the Government of the United States or its commercial
marine.
   By all these considerations I beg of you to reflect whether it
will not be better for you to surrender the Confederate steamer
Stonewall to me, with the officers and all the crew that may be
with her at time of surrender, upon the same terms granted to

Generals Lee, Johnston, and others who have heretofore surrendered.

Page replied:

Sir:

Your communication of this date addressed to me has been received. I beg leave to decline acceding to your suggestions and proposals.[74]

But Boggs was right. The whole of the Confederacy east of the Mississippi had collapsed. Only Texas and parts of Arkansas, blind and leaderless, remained unoccupied. The account opened for the *Stonewall* at Ferrol had gone dry — there was no money to pay the crew — and Major Charles J. Helm at Havana was powerless to help. Page surrendered the ship to the Captain-General of Cuba in return for enough money to pay off the crew.

Thomas Craven of the *Niagara* received a court-martial. He was charged with "Failing to do his utmost to overtake and capture or destroy a vessel which it was his duty to encounter," and found guilty. The naval board, afraid to set a precedent that would hinder or infringe an officer's right to appraise a situation and act to his best judgment, sentenced him to two years suspension of duty with leave pay. Said Gideon Welles: "Such punishment as this no officer could obtain from the Department as a favor."[75] He released Craven from arrest and returned him to duty.

Captain Page returned to his native Virginia, where he took up farming. He eventually went into the practice of law.

The *Stonewall* was turned over to the United States Government. She went to the Washington navy yard, then to Norfolk, then was sold to the Government of Japan. She was eventually lost in a storm off Zanzibar.

Notes

CHAPTER 1
THE JAMES RIVER SQUADRON

[1]Particulars of the destruction of Gosport Navy Yard are from the *Official Records of the Union and Confederate Navies in the War of the Rebellion* (hereafter *ORN*), Ser. II, Vol. 2, p. 109.

[2]From *Battles and Leaders of the Civil War* (hereafter *B&L*), Vol. I, p. 712.

[3]The conditions of the ships burned by the evacuating Union Navy are described in *ORN*, Ser. II, Vol. 2, p. 110.

[4]Mallory's view, as expressed to Mr. H. M. Conrad, chairman of the House Committee on Naval Affairs, are found in *ORN*, Ser. II, Vol. 3, p. 69.

[5]*Ibid.*, pp. 66, 70.

[6]Gideon Welles words on the subject of ironclads are from *B&L*, Vol. I, p. 616.

[7]Forrest's telegram is from *ORN*, Ser. I, Vol. 5, p. 801.

[8]The discovery of the cartridges in the *Merrimack's* powder tanks is from V. C. Jones' *The Civil War at Sea* (hereafter Jones), Vol. I, p. 97.

[9]The similarity of the designs submitted by Brooke and Porter created a controversy that raged for years over who was actually responsible for the design of the *Virginia*. Porter's design is outlined in *ORN*, Ser. II, Vol. 2, p. 174, however, and it is evident that it was Brooke's pattern that was finally accepted.

[10]From W. C. White & Ruth White, *Tin Can on a Shingle* (hereafter White), p. 15.

[11]From *ORN*, Ser. II, Vol. 2, p. 175.

[12]*Ibid.*, p. 78.

[13]Brooke's armor experiments may be found in J. Thomas Scharf's *History of the Confederate States Navy* (hereafter Scharf), pp. 147–48.

[14]Details of the *Virginia's* casemate dimensions and construction may be found in *B&L*, Vol. I, pp. 693–94.

[15]From White, p. 17.

[16]Lt. Wood's tales of his adventures with the *Virginia* may be found in *B&L*, Vol. I, p. 695.

[17]The list of the *Virginia's* officers is from *B&L*, Vol. I, p. 695.

[18]Franklin Buchanan's story is told — in brief — in White, p. 53.

[19]*ORN*, Series I, Vol. 6, p. 777.

[20]Van Brunt's bold words are from Jones, Vol. I, p. 399.

[21]James M. Morgan, *Recollections of a Rebel Reefer*, p. 86 (hereafter Morgan).

[22]*ORN*, Ser. I, Vol. 6, p. 778.

[23]Buchanan's communication to Comm. Tucker may be found in Jones, Vol. I, p. 406.

[24]Lt. William Harwell Parker in *Confederate Military History*, Vol. 12, p. 36.

[25]The conversation between Buchanan and Ramsey is reported in White, p. 65.

[26]Buchanan's speech is reported in Scharf, p. 154.

[27]White, p. 66.

[28]The *Zouave's* part in the battle of March 8 is reported in *B&L*, Vol. I, p. 715.

[29]Jones, Vol. I, p. 415.

[30]*Ibid.*, p. 415.

[31]Ramsey's words are from Jones, Vol. I, pp. 415–17.

[32]Lt. Woods' oft-quoted description is from *B&L*, Vol. I, p. 698.

[34]*Ibid.*, p. 701.

[35]*Ibid.*, p. 698.

[36]This description is from Jones, Vol. I, p. 421.

[37]*ORN*, Ser. I, Vol. 7, p. 4

[38]This Rebel soldier's wry wit is displayed in Shelby Foote's *The Civil War: A Narrative*, Vol. I, p. 258.

[39]White, p. 9.

[40]*Ibid.*, p. 9.

[41]*Ibid.*, p. 90.

[42]*B&L*, Vol. I, p. 723.

[43]*ORN*, Series I, Vol. 7, p. 14. Carpenter's report.

[44]Jones, Vol. I, p. 435.

[45]Eggleston's comment is from *B&L*, Vol. I, p. 723.

[46]*Ibid.*, p. 723.

[47]Scharf, p. 170.

[43]Lt. Wood's account of his Richmond trip may be found in *B&L*, Vol. I, pp. 703–05.

[49]Jones, Vol. II, p. 6.

[50]*Ibid.*, p. 9.

[51]*ORN*, Ser. II, Vol. 2, p. 267.

[52]Details of the *Virginia's* modifications are listed in *B&L*, Vol. I, p. 706.

[53]*Ibid.*, p. 707.

[54]The firing of a gun to windward — the sailor's traditional gesture of contempt and disdain — is recounted in *B&L*, Vol. I., p. 709.

[55]Morgan, p. 79.
[56]Scharf, p. 223.

CHAPTER 2
THE LOSS OF NEW ORLEANS

[1]*ORN*, Series II, Vol. 2, p. 63.

[2]Jones, Vol. I, p. 241.

[3]From Charles L. Dufour's *The Night the War Was Lost*, p. 71 (hereafter Dufour).

[4]A thumbnail history of the *Enoch Train* is given in William Morrison Robinson, Jr's. *The Confederate Privateers*, p. 154 (hereafter Robinson).

[5]The *Enoch Train's* dimensions may be found in Dufour, p. 71.

[6]Robinson, p. 156.

[7]Dufour, pp. 72–73.

[8]Robinson, p. 156.

[9]Dufour, p. 71.

[10]The Tifts' communications with Mallory may be found in *ORN*, Series II, Vol. 1, p. 571.

[11]Dufour, p. 100.

[12]Jones, Vol. II, p. 76.

[13]The Tifts' itenerary and their first problems were revealed in letters to Mallory found in *ORN*, Series II, Vol. 1, pp. 532, 571–72.

[14]*ORN*, Series II, Vol. 1, p. 757.

[15]The particulars of Murray's contract may be found in Dufour, p. 103.

[16]*Ibid.*, p. 61.

[17]Morgan, p. 55.

[18]*ORN*, Series I, Vol. 16, p. 699.

[19]Dufour, p. 76.

[20]Morgan, p. 56.

[21]Dufour, p. 78.

[22]Jones, Vol. I, pp. 243–44.

[23]Dufour, p. 78.

[24]*Ibid.*, p. 78.

[25]*Ibid.*, p. 79.

[26]*Ibid.*, p. 79.

[27]*Ibid.*, p. 79.

[28]*Ibid.*, p. 80.

[29]*Ibid.*, p. 81.

[30]Robinson, p. 163.

[31]Dufour, pp. 81–82.

[32]The reasons behind Handy's abandoning ship are set forth in Dufour, p. 82.

[33]The Federal's description of Handy's report is from Jones, Vol. I, p. 245.

[34]Dufour, p. 82.

[35]Battle damage is reported in Jones, Vol. I, p. 247.

[36]Hollins' dispatch may be found in *ORN*, Series I, Vol. 16, p. 728.

[37]Dufour, p. 83.

[38]Robinson, p. 161.

[39]*ORN*, Series II, Vol. 1, p. 517.

[40]James M. Merrill in *The Journal of Southern History*, Vol. XXVIII, No. 1, p. 87.

[41]From testimony given in C. S. Senate's investigation of the Confederate Navy Department, recorded in *ORN*, Series II, Vol. 1, p. 573–74.

[42]*Ibid.*, pp. 574, 608.

[43]*Ibid.*, pp. 573–75.

[44]*Ibid.*, pp. 573–74.

[45]*Ibid.*, pp. 532–33, 575.

[46]*Ibid.*, pp. 756, 771.

[47]*Ibid.*, pp. 755–56.

[48]*Ibid.*, pp. 580, 584.

[49]*Ibid.*, p. 577.

[50]*ORN*, Series II, Vol. 2, p. 122.

[51]*ORN*, Series II, Vol. 1, p. 753.

[52]*ORN*, Series I, Vol. 22, p. 738.

[53]*Ibid.*, p. 822.

[54]Jones, Vol. II, pp. 71–72.

[55]Dufour, pp. 66, 90.

[56]Welles' orders may be found in *ORN*, Series 1, Vol. 18, p. 8.

[58]*Ibid.*, p. 176.

[59]The story of the acquisitions of the *Mississippi's* armor may be found in testimony in the Navy Department investigation, *ORN*, Series II, Vol. 1, pp. 534, 763, 772.

[60]Mallory's telegrams may be found in *ORN*, Series II, Vol. 1, pp. 597, 604–05.

[61]*Ibid.*, pp. 535, 774–75.

[62]*Ibid.*, pp. 604–05.

[63]Correspondence from Comm. Sinclair concerning the *Mississippi* may be found in *ORN*, Series I, Vol. 18, p. 353.

[64]The launch controversy is recorded in *ORN*, Series II, Vol. 1, pp. 595–96.

[65]*Ibid.*, p. 694.

[66]This telegraphic exchange is recorded in *ORN*, Series I, Vol. 18, p. 323.

[67]*Ibid.*, p. 290.

[68]Wilkinson's meeting with De Camp may be found in Robert Carse's *Blockade*, p. 10.

[69]Charges by Duncan, Higgins, and Duncan's son that Mitchell was solely responsible for the fall of New Orleans by his refusal to cooperate continued to be hurled for years after the war. Correspondence between Duncan and Mitchell is reproduced in *B&L*, Vol. II, p. 101.

[70]*Ibid.*, p. 101.

[71]*Ibid.*, p. 101.

[72]*Ibid.*, p. 101.

[73]Mitchell's problems with Stevenson are related in *ORN*, Series I, Vol. 16, p. 328.

[74]Jones, Vol. II, p. 94.

[75]Jones, Vol. II, pp. 90–92.

[76]*B&L*, Vol. II, p. 101.

[77]Dufour, pp. 255–56.

[78]*ORN*, Series I, Vol. 18, p. 329.

[79]Dufour, pp. 255–56.

[80]*B&L*, Vol. II, p. 101.

[81]Dufour, p. 257.

[82]*B&L*, Vol. II, p. 442.

[83]*Ibid.*, p. 101.

[84]*ORN*, Series I, Vol. 18, p. 294.

[85]*Ibid.*, p. 225.

[86]*B&L*, Vol. II, p. 102.

[87]*Ibid.*, p. 100.

[88]*ORN*, Series I, Vol. 18, p. 294.

[89]*B&L*, Vol. II, p. 100.

[90]Dufour, p. 102.

[91]*Ibid.*, p. 274.

[92]*ORN*, Series I, Vol. 18, p. 206.

[93]Jones, Vol. II, p. 107.

[94]*B&L*, Vol. II, p. 65.

[95]*Ibid.*, p. 48.

[96]Jones, Vol. II, p. 103.

[97]*B&L*, Vol. II, p. 90.

[98]Jones, Vol. II, p. 105.

[99]*B&L*, Vol. II, p. 91.

[100]Reports of Commander Craven and the *Brooklyn's* carpenter, *ORN*, Series I, Vol. 18, pp. 182, 336.

[102]*B&L*, Vol. II, p. 69.

[103]Jones, Vol. II, p. 113.

[104]Dufour, p. 295.

[105]*ORN*, Series I, Vol. 18, p. 351, Series II, Vol. 1, pp. 492, 535, 761, 763, 770.

[106]Dufour, p. 297.

[107]*ORN*, Series I, Vol. 18, p. 352.

[108]*ORN*, Series II, Vol. 1, p. 492.

[109]Dufour, p. 318.

[110]Dufour, p. 318.

[111]*Ibid.*, p. 323.

[112]*B&L*, Vol. II, p. 102.

[113]Scharf, p. 298.

[114]*ORN*, Series I, Vol. 18, p. 439.

[115]*Ibid.*, p. 300.

CHAPTER 3

ON AND OFF THE MISSISSIPPI

[1]Scharf, p. 303.

[2]*ORN*, Series II, Vol. 2, p. 154.

[3]*ORN*, Series I, Vol. 22, p. 827.

[4]Fletcher Pratt, *Civil War on Western Waters*, p. 57 (hereafter Pratt).

[5]*Ibid.*, p. 230.

[6]*Ibid.*, p. 237.

[7]Jones, Vol. II, p. 163.

[8]*Ibid.*, p. 163.

[9]Scharf, p. 303.

[10]*ORN*, Series II, Vol. 1, p. 268.

[11]*ORN*, Series I, Vol. 18, p. 647.

[12]*B&L*, Vol. III, p. 572.

[13]Lt. George Gift in *Southern Historical Society Papers* (hereafter *SHSP*), Vol. 12, p. 51.

[14]Issac Brown's story of the ironclad and her adventures may be found in *B&L*, Vol. III, p. 572.

[15]Brown's views on the *Arkansas* and river strategy are

revealed by Lt. Charles W. Read in *SHSP*, Vol. 1, pp. 356–57.

[16]*Ibid.*, p. 352.

[17]*Ibid.*, p. 352.

[18]The story of the *Arkansas'* wet powder and Farragut's unconcern for the ironclad are from Scharf, p. 310.

[19]*ORN,* Series I, Vol. 18, p. 675.

[20]*B&L*, Vol. III, p. 574.

[21]Scharf, p. 330.

[22]*Ibid.*, p. 314.

[23]*Ibid.*, p. 314.

[24]*Ibid.*, p. 314.

[25]*B&L*, Vol. III, p. 575.

[26]Scharf, p. 315.

[27]*B&L*, Vol. III, p. 555.

[28]Jones, Vol. II, p. 196.

[29]*Ibid.*, p. 197.

[30]*B&L*, Vol. III, p. 575.

[31]Scharf, p. 319.

[32]*B&L*, Vol. III, p. 576.

[33]Jones, Vol. II, p. 200.

[34]*B&L*, Vol. III, p. 557.

[35]*ORN*, Series I, Vol. 19, p. 133.

[36]Scharf, p. 315.

[37]*B&L*, Vol. III, p. 577.

[38]*ORN*, Series I, Vol. 19, p. 7.

[39]*ORN*, Series I, Vol. 23, p. 236.

[40]Jones, Vol. II, p. 203.

[41]*ORN*, Series I, Vol. 19, p. 8.

[42]*ORN*, Series I, Vol. 19, p. 8.

[43]Jones, Vol. II, p. 206.

[44]*ORN*, Series I, Vol. 19, p. 8.

[45]*Ibid.*, pp. 10, 12.

[46]*B&L*, Vol. III, p. 577.

[47]*ORN*, Series I, Vol. 19, p. 10.
[48]*B&L*, Vol. III, p. 577.
[49]Scharf, p. 331.
[50]*Ibid.*, p. 331.
[51]*B&L*, Vol. III, p. 579.
[52]*SHSP*, Vol. 12, p. 208.
[53]Jones, Vol. II, p. 222.
[54]*ORN*, Series I, Vol. 19, p. 136.
[53]*ORN*, Series I, Vol. 25, p. 9.
[56]Robert MacBride in *Civil War Ironclads*, p. 135. (Hereafter MacBride.)
[57]Pratt, p. 133, 138.
[58]*Ibid.*, p. 136.
[59]MacBride, p. 135.
[60]*ORN*, Series I, Vol. 19, p. 335.
[61]*Ibid.*, p. 328.
[62]Jones, Vol. II, p. 372.
[63]*ORN*, Series I, Vol. 25, p. 162.
[64]*ORN*, Series I, Vol. 26, p. 163.
[65]*Ibid.*, pp. 547, 550.
[66]*Ibid.*, pp. 540–41, 547.
[67]*Ibid.*, p. 550.
[68]*Ibid.*, p. 537.
[69]*Ibid.*, p. 546.
[70]*Ibid.*, p. 545.
[71]*Ibid.*, p. 104.

CHAPTER 4
THE CHARLESTON SQUADRON

[1]Scharf, p. 670.
[2]Wm. Still, *The Journal of Southern History*, No. 3, 1961, p. 336.
[3]Scharf, p. 671.

[4]*Confederate Miliary History,* Vol. 12, p. 69.

[5]Jones, Vol. II, p. 360.

[6]*Ibid.,* p. 336.

[7]*Ibid.,* p. 367.

[8]*Ibid.,* p. 368.

[9]*ORN,* Series I, Vol. 14, p. 110.

[10]*Ibid.,* pp. 738-39.

[11]*ORN,* Series I, Vol. 15, p. 344.

[12]Scharf, p. 672.

[13]*ORN,* Series II, Vol. 1, p. 251.

[14]*ORN,* Series II, Vol. 2 pp. 752–53.

[15]*ORN,* Series II, Vol. 1, p. 251.

[16]*ORN,* Series I, Vol. 16, pp. 372–73.

CHAPTER 5

THE SAVANNAH SQUADRON AND THE *Muskogee*

[1]Estimates on the exact number of each list of items run in by the *Fingal* vary. This cargo list is from *ORN,* Series I, Vol. 12, p. 227.

[2]The *Fingal's* early misadventures are detailed in Philip Van Doren Stern's *The Confederate Navy,* p. 36.

[3]From Charles Girard, *A Visit to the Confederate States of America in 1863,* p. 60.

[4]*ORN,* Series II, Vol. 1, p. 208.

[5]Scharf, p. 641.

[6]Commander Webb's official report of the action may be found in *ORN,* Series I, Vol. 14, p. 290.

[7]Webb's surrender address is from Scharf, p. 644.

[8]*ORN,* Series I, Vol. 14, pp. 724–26.

[9]*ORN,* Series I, Vol. 14, p. 766.

[10]*ORN,* Series I, Vol. 13, p. 776.

[11]*ORN,* Series II, Vol. 2, p. 752.

[12]Scharf, p. 651.

[13]*Ibid.*, p. 651.
[14]*ORN*, Series II, Vol. 2, pp. 532, 638, 752.
[15]Scharf, p. 622.

CHAPTER 6
NORTH CAROLINA WATERS

[1]The Smith family saga is recounted in Jones, Vol. III, pp. 69–70.
[2]*Ibid.*, p. 68.
[3]MacBride, p. 94.
[4]*Ibid.*, p. 94.
[5]*ORN*, Series I, Vol. 2 p. 827.
[6]Jones, Vol. III, p. 70.
[7]*Ibid.*, pp. 69–70.
[8]*Ibid.*, p. 156.
[9]*Ibid.*, pp. 62–63.
[10]*ORN*, Series I, Vol. 9, p. 656.
[11]Jones, Vol. III, p. 154.
[12]Commander Cooke's official report and other correspondence pertaining to the engagement is to be found in *ORN*, Series I, Vol. 9, p. 657.
[13]Jones, Vol. III, p. 155.
[14]*ORN*, Series I, Vol. 9, p. 657.
[15]*Ibid.*, p. 657.
[16]Scharf, p. 407.
[17]Jones, Vol. III, p. 159.
[18]*B&L*, Vol. IV, p. 628.
[19]Jones, Vol. III, p. 160.
[20]*Ibid.*, p. 162.
[21]*Ibid.*, p. 161.
[22]*Ibid.*, p. 161.
[23]*B&L*, Vol. IV, p. 628.
[24]Jones, Vol. III, p. 287.

[25]*Ibid.,* p. 285.
[26]Scharf, p. 413.
[27]Jones, Vol. III, pp. 287–88.
[28]*Ibid.,* p. 291.
[29]*Ibid.,* p. 294.
[30]*B&L,* Vol. IV, p. 642.
[31]*ORN,* Series II, Vol. 2, p. 751.
[32]*ORN,* Series I, Vol. 9, p. 801.
[33]MacBride, p. 95.
[34]*ORN,* Series II, Vol. 2, p. 523.
[35]*Ibid.,* p. 751.
[36]*ORN,* Series I, Vol. 10, p. 19.
[37]Jones, Vol. III, p. 201.
[38]*ORN,* Series II, Vol. 2, pp. 74–75.

CHAPTER 7

THE MOBILE SQUADRON

[1]Gen. Dabney H. Maury in *SHSP,* Vol. 5, p. 4.
[2]*B&L,* Vol. IV, p. 401.
[3]*ORN,* Series II, Vol. 2, p. 746.
[4]Survey report by Rear-Admiral H. K. Thatcher, U.S.N., in *ORN,* Series I, Vol. 22, pp. 225–26.
[5]*Ibid.,* p. 226.
[6]Jones, Vol. III, p. 232.
[7]*ORN,* Series I, Vol. 21, p. 934. Extract from the log of the *Tennessee.*
[8]*SHSP,* Vol. 5, p. 44.
[9]James M. Merrill in *The Rebel Shore* (hereafter Merrill), p. 181.
[10]Jones, Vol. III, p. 235.
[11]*SHSP,* Vol. 5, p. 44.
[12]*ORN,* Series I, Vol. 21, p. 361.
[13]*Ibid.,* p. 886.

[14]Jones, Vol. III, p. 256.

[15]*SHSP,* Vol. 5, p. 44.

[16]Merrill, p. 182.

[17]Jones, Vol. III, p. 241.

[18]*Ibid.,* p. 240.

[19]*Ibid,* p. 238.

[20]*Ibid.,* p. 244.

[21]*Ibid.,* p. 248.

[22]Scharf, p. 562.

[23]*B&L,* Vol. IV, p. 394.

[24]*Ibid.,* p. 391.

[25]*Ibid.,* p. 393.

[26]*Ibid.,* p. 394.

[27]Scharf, p. 564.

[28]Merrill, p. 193.

[29]*B&L,* Vol. IV, p. 395.

[30]Jones, Vol. III, p. 254.

[31]*ORN,* Series I, Vol. 21, p. 426.

[32]Scharf, p. 568.

[33]Merrill, p. 195.

[34]Jones, Vol. III, p. 256.

[35]Scharf, p. 570.

[36]Jones, Vol. III, p. 257.

[37]*Ibid.,* pp. 257–58.

[38]*ORN,* Series I, Vol. 21, p. 406.

[39]*Ibid.,* p. 578.

[40]Jones, Vol. III, p. 261.

[41]*ORN,* Series I, Vol. 22, p. 225.

[42]*ORN,* Series I, Vol. 22, p. 99. From Bennet's official report.

[43]*Ibid.,* p. 99.

[44]*Ibid.,* p. 100.

[45]*Ibid.,* p. 100.

[46]C. C. Andrews, *History of the Campaign of Mobile*, p. 187.

[47]*SHSP*, Vol. IV, p. 220.

[48]*ORN*, Series I, Vol. 22, p. 95.

[49]*Ibid.*, pp. 176–77.

[50]*Ibid.*, p. 178.

CHAPTER 8
THE JAMES RIVER AGAIN

[1]Scharf, p. 725.

[2]*Ibid.*, p. 725.

[3]*ORN*, Series II, Vol. 2, p. 532.

[4]*ORN*, Series I, Vol. 10, p. 179.

[5]*Ibid.*, p. 186.

[6]*Ibid.*, pp. 181–82.

[7]*Ibid.*, pp. 176–77.

[8]Scharf, p. 725.

[9]*Ibid.*, pp. 739–40.

[10]*Ibid.*, p. 737–40.

[11]*ORN*, Series I, Vol. 11, pp. 675-77.

[12]Scharf, p. 742.

[13]Raphael Semmes, *Memoirs of Service Afloat*, pp. 803, 805.

[14]*Ibid.*, p. 809.

[15]*Ibid.*, pp. 811–12.

[16]*ORN*, Series I, Vol. 22, p. 269.

CHAPTER 9
THE EUROPEAN IRONCLADS

[1]*ORN*, Series II, Vol. 2, pp. 70–71.

[2]*Ibid.*, p. 87.

[3]*Ibid.*, p. 88.

[4]*Ibid.*, p. 131.

[5]*Ibid.*, p. 167.

[6]*Ibid.*, p. 173.

[7]*Ibid.*, pp. 181, 226.

[8]*Ibid.*, p. 185.

[9]*Ibid.*, pp. 191–192.

[10]*Ibid.*, p. 197.

[11]*Ibid.*, p. 199.

[12]*Ibid.*, pp. 200–204.

[13]*Ibid.*, pp. 218–19.

[14]*Ibid.*, pp. 222–26.

[15]*Ibid.*, p. 286. The names were never again to appear in any official correspondence.

[16]*Ibid.*, pp. 254, 258.

[17]*Ibid.*, pp. 268, 271. Lt. Sinclair had briefly held command of the ironclad *Atlanta,* before being transferred to Europe. His son, George Terry, Jr., a midshipman, was captured aboard the raider *Florida* in Bahia Bay, and was held in Fort Warren until February 1, 1865.

[18]*Ibid.*, p. 526.

[19]*Ibid.*, pp. 360, 370.

[20]*Ibid.*, p. 362, 364.

[21]*Ibid.*, p. 326.

[22]*Ibid.*, p. 396.

[23]James D. Bulloch, *Secret Service of the Confederate States in Euorpe,* p. 23. (Hereafter Bulloch.)

[24]*Ibid.*, p. 24.

[25]*ORN*, Series II, Vol. 2, p. 397.

[26]*Ibid.*, p. 369.

[27]*Ibid.*, p. 398.

[28]*Ibid.*, pp. 413–14.

[29]*Ibid.*, p. 415.

[30]*Ibid.*, p. 416.

[31]*Ibid.*, p. 434.

[32]*Ibid.*, pp. 439, 443.

[33]*Ibid.*, p. 444.

[34]*Ibid.*, pp. 444–446.

[35]*Ibid.*, p. 508.

[36]*Ibid.*, p. 585.

[37]*Ibid.*, p. 585.

[38]Bulloch, p. 32.

[39]*Ibid.*, p. 32.

[40]*ORN*, Series II, Vol. 2, p. 471.

[41]Bulloch, p. 33.

[02]*ORN*, Series II, Vol. 2, p. 471.

[43]Bulloch, p. 37.

[44]*ORN*, Series II, Vol. 2, pp. 474, 490.

[45]*Ibid.*, p. 525.

[46]Bulloch, p. 38.

[47]*ORN*, Series I, Vol. 3, 207–08.

[48]*ORN*, Series II, Vol. 2, p. 588.

[49]Bulloch, p. 46.

[50]*ORN*, Series I, Vol. 3, pp. 722–24.

[51]Bulloch, p. 443.

[52]*ORN*, Series I, Vol. 3, p. 724.

[53]Bulloch, p. 76.

[54]Bulloch, pp. 79-80.

[55]*ORN*, Series I, Vol. 3, pp. 719–20.

[56]Bulloch, p. 82.

[57]*Ibid.*, pp. 84–85.

[58]*Ibid.*, p. 87.

[59]*Ibid.*, p. 88.

[60]*ORN*, Series I, Vol. 3, p. 727.

[61]Bulloch, p. 90.

[62]*Ibid.*, pp. 93-94.

[63]*ORN*, Series I, Vol. 3, p. 733.

[64]Bulloch, p. 80.

[65]*ORN*, Series I, Vol. 3, p. 734.

[66]Bulloch, pp. 96-98.
[67]*ORN*, Series I, Vol. 3, p. 738.
[68]Bulloch, p. 444.
[69]*ORN*, Series I, Vol. 3, p. 738.
[70]*Ibid.*, p. 738.
[71]Bulloch, p. 98.
[72]*ORN*, Series I, Vol. 3, p. 745.
[73]Bulloch, pp. 100–01.
[74]*ORN*, Series I, Vol. 3, pp. 520–21.
[75]*Ibid.*, p. 461.

Bibliograpy

Andrews, C. C. *History of the Campaign of Mobile,* D. Van Nostrand, New York, 1867.

Bulloch, James D. *Secret Service of the Confederate States in Europe,* Thomas Yoseloff, New York, 1959. 2 Vols.

Carse, Robert. *Blockade,* Holt, Rinehart & Winston, New York, 1958.

Dufour, Charles L. *The Night the War Was Lost,* Doubleday & Co., New York, 1960.

Foote, Shelby. *The Civil War: A Narrative,* Random House, New York, 1963. 3 Vols.

Girard, Charles. *A Visit to the Confederate States of America in 1863: Memoir Addressed to His Majesty Napoleon III,* Confederate Publishing Co., Tuscaloosa, Ala., 1962.

Jones, Virgil C. *The Civil War at Sea,* Holt, Rinehart & Winston, New York, 1960. 3 Vols.

MacBride, Robert. *Civil War Ironclads,* Chilton Books, New York, 1962.

Merrill, James M. *The Rebel Shore,* Little, Brown & Co., Boston, Mass., 1957.

Miller, Francis, Editor. *The Photographic History of the Civil War,* Thomas Yoseloff, New York, 1957.

Morgan, James M. *Recollections of a Rebel Reeefer*, Houghton Mifflin Co., Boston, Mass., 1917.

Pratt, Fletcher. *Civil War on Western Waters,* Holt, Rinehart & Winston, New York, 1956.

Robinson, Wm. Morrison, Jr. *The Confederate Privateers,* Yale University Press, New Haven, Conn., 1928.

Semmes, Raphael. *Memoirs of Service Afloat,* Baltimore Publishing Co., Baltimore, Md., 1887.

Scharf, J. Thomas. *History of the Confederate States Navy,* Rogers & Sherwood, New York, 1886.

Stern, Philip Van Doren. *The Confederate Navy,* Doubleday & Co., Garden City, N. Y., 1962.

White, W. C. and Ruth. *Tin Can on a Shingle,* E. P. Dutton & Co., New York, 1957.

Battles & Leaders of the Civil War, Thomas Yoseloff, New York, 1959. 4 Vols.

Confederate Military History, Confederate Publishing Co., Atlanta, 1899. 12 Vols.

Journal of Southern History.

Official Records of the Union and Confederate Navies in the War of the Rebellion, U. S. Government Printing Office, Washington, D. C., 1894-1922. 30 Vols.

Southern Historical Society Papers, Richmond, 1876-1944. 46 Vols.

Index

305